KIDS

♥ LOVE

Pennsylvania

I0522074

An Organized Family Travel Guide to Exploring Kid-Friendly Pennsylvania

600 Fun Stops & Unique Spots

Michele Darrall Zavatsky

Dedicated to the Families of Pennsylvania

In a Hundred Years...It will not matter, The size of my bank account...The kind of house that I lived in, the kind of car that I drove...But what will matter is...That the world may be different Because I was important in the life of a child.

- author unknown

For the latest major updates corresponding to the pages in this book visit our website:

www.KidsLoveTravel.com

- **_REMEMBER_**: *Museum exhibits change frequently. Check the site's website before you visit to note any changes. Also, HOURS and ADMISSIONS are subject to change at the owner's discretion. If you are tight on time or money, check the attraction's website or call before you visit.*

- **_EDUCATORS_**: *There are suggestions for finding FREE lessons plans embedded in many listings as helpful notes for educators.*

KIDS ♥ PENNSYLVANIA ™ Kids Love Publications, LLC

TABLE OF CONTENTS

General Information..Preface
(Here's where you'll find "How to Use This Book", Maps, Tour Ideas, City Listings, etc.)

Activity Index...262
(Amusements, Animals & Farms, Museums, Outdoors, State History, Tours, etc.)

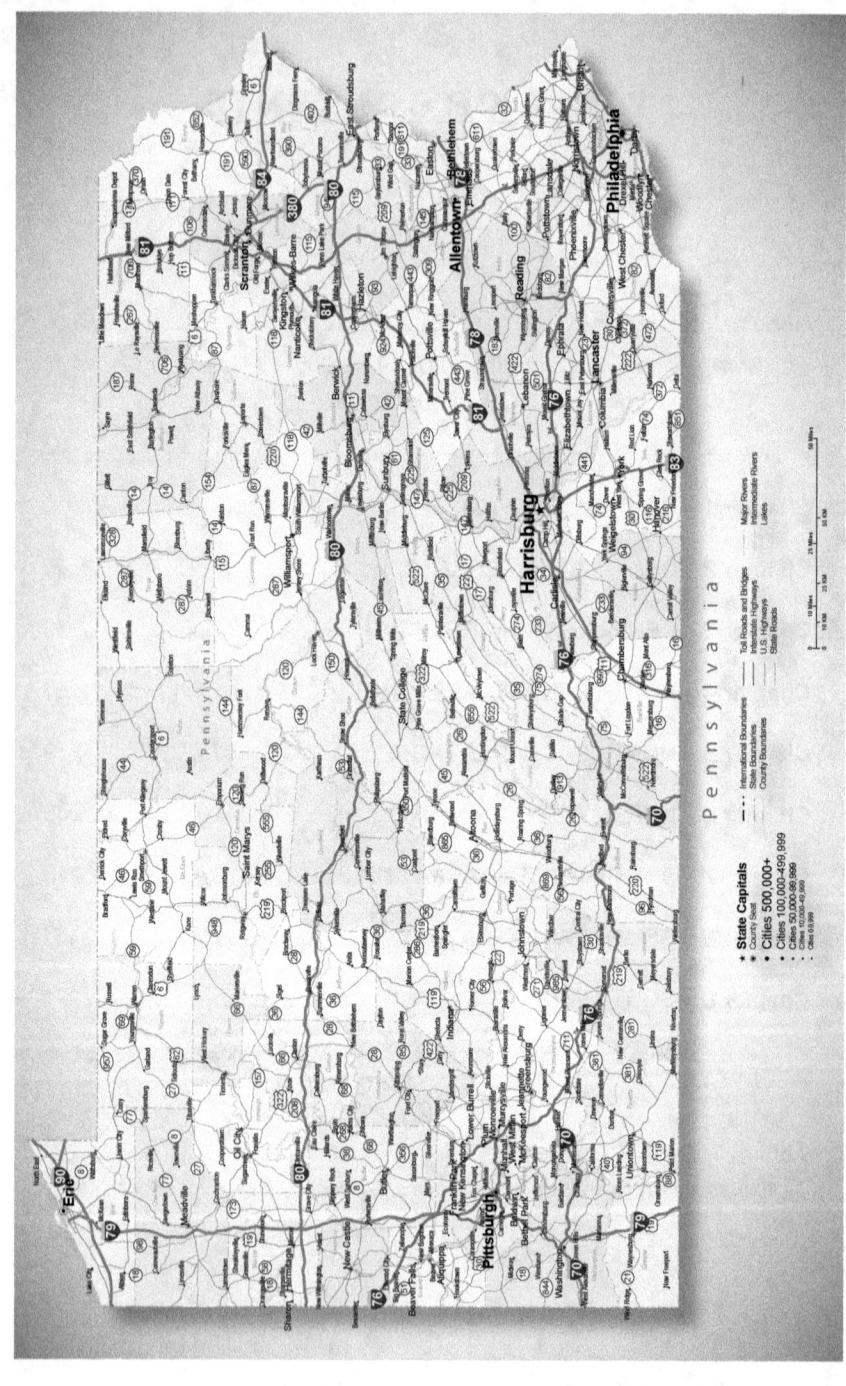

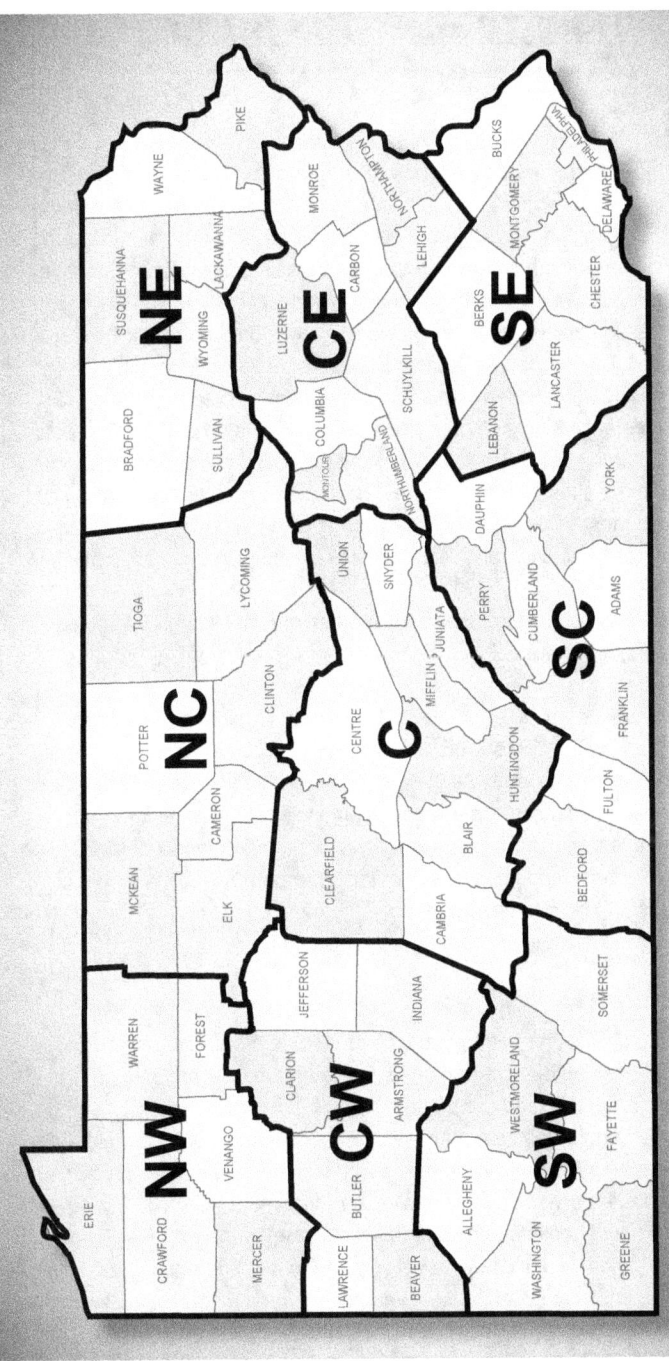

Chapter Area Map

(Chapters arranged alphabetically by chapter name)

HOW TO USE THIS BOOK

(a few hints to make your adventures run smoothly:)

BEFORE YOU LEAVE:

- ☐ Each chapter represents a two hour radius area of the state or a Day Trip. The chapter begins with an introduction and Quick Tour of favorites within the chapter. The listings are by City and then alphabetical by name, numeric by zip code. Each listing has tons of important details (pricing, hours, website, etc.) and a review noting the most engaging aspects of the place. Our popular Activity Index in back is helpful if you want to focus on a particular type of attraction (i.e. History, Tours, Outdoor Exploring, Animals & Farms, etc.).

- ☐ Begin by assigning each family member a different colored highlighter (for example: Daniel gets blue, Jenny gets pink, Mom gets yellow and Dad gets green). At your leisure, begin to read each review and put a highlighter "check" mark next to the sites that most interest each family member or highlight the features you most want to see. Now, when you go to plan a quick trip - or a long van ride - you can easily choose different stops in one day to please everyone.

- ☐ Know directions and parking. Use a GPS system or print off directions from websites.

- ☐ Most attractions are closed major holidays unless noted.

- ☐ When children are in tow, it is better to make your lodging reservations ahead of time. Every time we've tried to "wing it", we've always ended up at a place that was overpriced, in a unsafe area, or not super clean. We've never been satisfied when we didn't make a reservation ahead of time.

- ☐ If you have a large family, or are traveling with extended family or friends, most places offer group discounts. Check out the company's website for details.

- ☐ For the latest critical updates corresponding to the pages in this book, visit our website: www.kidslovetravel.com. Click on *Updates*.

ON THE ROAD:

- ☐ Consider the child's age before you stop at an exit. Some attractions and restaurants, even hotels, are too formal for young ones or not enough adventure for teens. Read our trusted reviews first.

- ☐ Estimate the duration of the trip and how many stops you can afford to make. From our experience, it is best to stop every two hours to stretch your legs or eat/snack or maybe visit an inexpensive attraction.

- ☐ Bring along travel books and games for "quiet time" in the van. (see tested travel products on www.kidslovetravel.com) As an added bonus, these "enriching" games also stimulate conversation - you may get to know your family better and create memorable life lessons.

ON THE ROAD: *(cont.)*

- In between meals, we offer the family snacks like: pretzels, whole grain chips, nuts, water bottles, bite-size (dark) chocolates, grapes and apples. None of these are messy and all are healthy.
- Plan picnics along the way. Many Historical sites and State Parks are scattered along the highway. Allow time for a rest stop or a scenic byway to take advantage of these free picnic facilities.

WHEN YOU GET HOME:

- Make a family "treasure chest". Decorate a big box or use an old popcorn tin. Store memorabilia from a fun outing, journals, pictures, brochures and souvenirs. Once a year, look through the "treasure chest" and reminisce. "Kids Love Travel Memories!" is an excellent travel journal and scrapbook template that your family can create (available on www.kidslovetravel.com).

WAYS TO SAVE MONEY:

- Memberships - many children's museums, science centers, zoos and aquariums are members of associations that provide FREE or Discounted reciprocity to other such museums across the country. AAA Auto Club cards offer discounts to many of the activities and hotels in this book. If grandparents are along for the ride, they can use their AARP card and get discounts. Be sure to carry your member cards with you as proof to receive the discounts.
- Supermarket Customer Cards - national and local supermarkets often offer good discounted tickets to major attractions in the area.
- Internet Hotel Reservations - if you're traveling with kids, don't take the risk of being spontaneous with lodging. Make reservations ahead of time. We don't use non-refundable, deep discount hotel "scouting" websites (ex. Hotwire) unless we're traveling on business - just adults. You can't cancel your reservation, or change them, and you can't be guaranteed the type of room you want (ex. non-smoking, two beds). Instead, stick with a national hotel chain you trust and join their rewards program (ex. Choice Privileges) to accumulate points towards FREE night stays.
- State Travel Centers - as you enter a new state, their welcome centers offer many current promotions.
- Hotel Lobbies - often have a display of discount coupons to area shops and restaurants. When you check in, ask the clerk for discount pizza coupons they may have at the front desk.
- Attraction Online Coupons - check the websites listed with each review for possible printable coupons or discounted online tickets good towards the attraction.

AIRPORTS - All children love to visit the airport! Why not take a tour and understand all the jobs it takes to run an airport? Tour the terminal, baggage claim, gates and security / currency exchange. Maybe you'll even get to board a plane.

ANIMAL SHELTERS - Great for the would-be pet owner. Not only will you see many cats and dogs available for adoption, but a guide will show you the clinic and explain the needs of a pet. Be prepared to have the children "fall in love" with one of the animals while they are there!

BANKS - Take a "behind the scenes" look at automated teller machines, bank vaults and drive-thru window chutes. You may want to take this tour and then open a savings account for your child.

CITY HALLS - Halls of Fame, City Council Chambers & Meeting Room, Mayor's Office and famous statues.

ELECTRIC COMPANY / POWER PLANTS - Modern science has created many ways to generate electricity today, but what really goes on with the "flip of a switch". Because coal can be dirty, wear old, comfortable clothes. Coal furnaces heat water, which produces steam, that propels turbines, that drives generators, that make electricity.

FIRE STATIONS - Many Open Houses in October, Fire Prevention Month. Take a look into the life of the firefighters servicing your area and try on their gear. See where they hang out, sleep and eat. Hop aboard a real-life fire engine truck and learn fire safety too.

HOSPITALS - Some Children's Hospitals offer pre-surgery and general tours.

NEWSPAPERS - You'll be amazed at all the new technology. See monster printers and robotics. See samples in the layout department and maybe try to put together your own page. After seeing a newspaper made, most companies give you a free copy (dated that day) as your souvenir. National Newspaper Week is in October.

PETCO - Various stores. Contact each store manager to see if they participate. The Fur, Feathers & Fins™ program allows children to learn about the characteristics and habitats of fish, reptiles, birds, and small animals. At your local Petco, lessons in science, math and geography come to life through this hands-on field trip. As students develop a respect for animals, they will also develop a greater sense of responsibility.

PIZZA HUT & PAPA JOHN'S - Participating locations. Telephone the store manager. Best days are Monday, Tuesday and Wednesday mid-afternoon. Minimum of 10 people. Small charge per person. All children love pizza – especially when they can create their own! As the children tour the kitchen, they learn how to make a pizza, bake it, and then eat it. The admission charge generally includes lots of creatively made pizzas, beverage and coloring book.

KRISPY KREME DONUTS - Participating locations. Get an "inside look" and learn the techniques that make these donuts some of our favorites! Watch the dough being made in "giant" mixers, being formed into donuts and taking a "trip" through the fryer. Seeing them being iced and topped with colorful sprinkles is always a favorite with the kids. Contact your local store manager. They prefer Monday or Tuesday. Free.

SUPERMARKETS - Kids are fascinated to go behind the scenes of the same store where Mom and Dad shop. Usually you will see them grind meat, walk into large freezer rooms, watch cakes and bread bake and receive free samples along the way. Maybe you'll even get to pet a live lobster!

TV / RADIO STATIONS - Studios, newsrooms, Fox kids clubs. Why do weathermen never wear blue/green clothes on TV? What makes a "DJ's" voice sound so deep and smooth?

WATER TREATMENT PLANTS - A giant science experiment! You can watch seven stages of water treatment. The favorite is usually the wall of bright buttons flashing as workers monitor the different processes.

U.S. MAIN POST OFFICES - Did you know Ben Franklin was the first Postmaster General (over 200 years ago)? Most interesting is the high-speed automated mail processing equipment. Learn how to address envelopes so they will be sent quicker (there are secrets). To make your tour more interesting, have your children write a letter to themselves and address it with colorful markers. Mail it earlier that day and they will stay interested trying to locate their letter in all the high-speed machinery.

General State Agency & Recreational Information

Call *(or visit websites)* for the services of interest. Request to be added to their mailing lists.

CHARTER DAY

Statewide - Free admission to the Pennsylvania Military Museum, Boalsburg; Railroad Museum of PA, Strasburg; Hope Lodge & Mather Mill, Fort Washington and other select Pennsylvania Historical and Museum Commission sites on this date to commemorate the granting of the Charter from Charles II to William Penn which founded "Penn's Woods" in 1681. Go on your favorite PA Historical attraction website to see if they are participating. FREE. (usually second Sunday in March)

- Biking Directory of PA. (717) 787-6746. Free through PENN DOT.
- ExplorePAHistory.com
- PA State Association of County Fairs. (717) 365-3922 or www.pafairs.org
- PA Tourism. (800) VISIT-PA or www.visitpa.com
- PCOA. PA Campground Owners Assoc. Directory. (888) 660-7262. www.pacamping.com
- PA Fish and Boat Commission. (717) 657-4518 or https://www.fishandboat.com. Information on FISH FARMS/HATCHERIES is here. Fun place to tour.
- PA State Forests. (717) 783-7941 or www.dcnr.state.pa.us/forestry/stateforests/
- PA State Parks. (888) PA-PARKS or www.dcnr.state.pa.us/stateparks/index.htm. Junior Naturalist Program and Cabin/Camping Rentals.
- Statewide Fall Foliage Hotline. (800) FALL-IN PA

C Penn State Athletics, State College. Nittany Lions. (800) 833-5533 or (800) 863-1000 tickets or www.gopsusports.com. Baseball, basketball, fencing, field hockey, football, golf, gymnastics, soccer, softball, swimming, tennis, track, volleyball and wrestling.

CE Dam Releases. LeHigh River Area. (717) 424-6050. Releases create whitewater and rapids. Call for rafting outfitters. Late Spring and Early Fall.

NE POCONOS Tourist Information. (800)-POCONOS or www.800poconos.com. Ask about selection of whitewater rafting, canoeing and riding stables.

NW Erie Area CVB. www.visiteriepa.com or (800) 524-3743.

SE Philadelphia. www.visitphilly.com or Visitors Center at Independence Historical Park Center. Check out their FAMILY PHILADELPHIA packages that are truly an economical way to explore some of Philly's best sites while staying at "kid-friendly" hotels in town.

SW Laurel Highlands River Tours. www.laurelhighlands.org

SW Pittsburgh CVB. (888) 849-4753 or www.visitpittsburgh.com.

SW University of Pittsburgh Athletics. (412) 648-PITT or (800) 643-PITT or www.pittsburghpanthers.com.

Chapter 1
Central
Pennsylvania

Altoona
- Fort Roberdeau Historic Site
- Quaint Corner Children's Museum
- Horseshoe Curve Landmark
- Lakemont Park
- Railroader's Memorial Museum

Altoona (Lakemont)
- Altoona Curve Baseball Club

Altoona (Tyrone)
- Gardner's Candy Museum

Boalsburg
- Boal Mansion/Columbus Chapel

Boalsburg
- Pennsylvania Military Museum
- Tussey Mountain Ski Area

Centre Hall
- Penn's Cave

Claysburg
- Blue Knob All Seasons Resort

Gallitzin
- Allegheny Portage Railroad
- Gallitzin Tunnels Park, Caboose And Museum

Hollidaysburg
- Canoe Creek State Park

Howard
- Bald Eagle State Park

Johnstown
- Johnstown Inclined Plane
- Johnstown Children's Museum
- Johnstown Flood Museum
- Johnstown Heritage Center

Johnstown (South Fork)
- Johnstown Flood Nat'l Memorial

Mifflinburg
- R.B. Winter State Park
- Mifflinburg Buggy Days

Milroy
- Reeds Gap State Park

Patton
- Prince Gallitzin State Park

Penfield
- Parker Dam State Park

Philipsburg
- Black Moshannon State Park

Raystown Lake (Entriken)
- Lake Raystown Resort

Raystown Lake (Hesston)
- Seven Points Cruises

Raystown Lake (Huntingdon)
- Greenwood Furnace State Park
- Lincoln Caverns/Whisper Rocks
- Swigart Antique Auto Museum
- Rothrock State Forest

Raystown Lake (James Creek)
- Trough Creek State Park

Rock Springs
- Ag Progress Days

Rockhill Furnace
- Rockhill Trolley Museum

Spruce Creek
- Indian Caverns

State College
- Penn State University Campus
- Stone Valley Recreation Area
- Central Pennsylvania Festival Of The Arts

Sunbury
- Shikellamy State Park

Tipton
- Delgrosso's Amusement Park

Woodward
- Woodward Cave

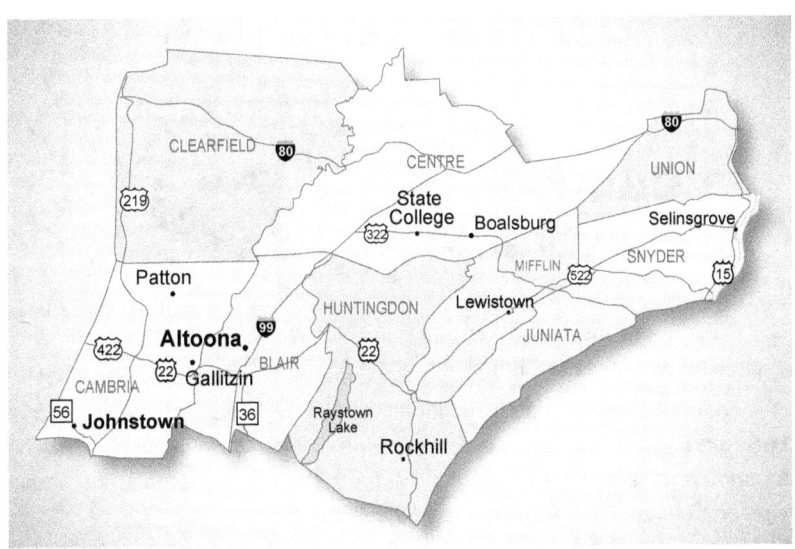

Travel Journal & Notes:

A Quick Tour of our Hand-Picked Favorites Around...

Central Pennsylvania

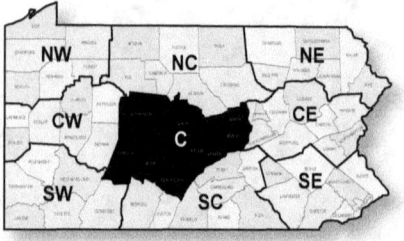

Central Pennsylvania is all about Caves, Curves, a Chapel, a horrible Flood, and a wonderful Campus.

That wonderful campus is found in Happy Valley, at **Penn State University**. Walking around and peeking in the little museums scattered around campus is fun but topping the trip off with a homemade ice cream sundae from the Creamery is always the highlight.

Nearby, in Boalsburg, is an extremely interesting mansion. While the **Boal Mansion** tour is full of hidden corners and stories, what is tucked away in an outbuilding is really magical. A real Spanish Chapel – the **Columbus Chapel** houses one of the best displays of real Christopher Columbus family articles. Kids think his sea chest is cool!

As transportation progressed west, carving out railroads through the mountains proved very difficult. Ingenious engineers decided to climb up or go around the mountainous terrain. **Horseshoe Curve** was developed because, even if a bridge could be built, no locomotive could climb the steep grade – so, they built track around the inside curves. No trains or canals could get through the Allegheny Mountains before the idea of the "incline" was introduced. **Allegheny Portage Railroad National Historic Site** demonstrates solving the problem by using a combo of 10 inclines. It's difficult to imagine until you see the working scale models in both of these railroad museums. Or, go outside and see it for yourself. It's like a giant physics lesson. Plus, the kids love the demonstration model trains – many with interactive features.

The Central PA area is riddled with **Caves**. Some are crystal caverns with Kids' Cave Crawls. Two others are massive – one has the nickname of "the Big One." One cave even features America's only all-water cavern and is a boat tour.

The power of nature was also severely demonstrated in Johnstown. The flood of 1889 left the town a wasteland for a while. The whole town of

Johnstown is one big experiment in survival and culture. Families probably find the best place to start is downtown. While the Flood Museum is more historical and vivid, young families may gravitate to the **Johnstown Heritage Discovery Center**. It now includes a museum on the first floor where you choose a character to follow through various daily life tasks and decisions OR play pretend coal miner or incline operator in the **Children's Museum** on the third floor. They were so clever to disguise history as play or acting, most kids don't even know you've been sneaking in some history lessons.

So that the townspeople never felt trapped by the fear of floods again, they built an incline tram up to the top of the highest point in town. The **Johnstown Inclined Plane** still exists and you can ride it! It's the steepest, yet slowest "roller coaster" ride you can go on in Pennsylvania...

Sites and attractions are listed in order by City, Zip Code, and Name. Symbols indicated represent: 🍽 Restaurants   🛏 Lodging

Altoona

FORT ROBERDEAU HISTORIC SITE

Altoona - RD #3 Box 391 (I-99, Bellwood Exit) 16601. Phone: (814) 946-0048. www.fortroberdeau.org. Hours: Monday-Saturday 10:00am-4:00pm, Sunday 1:00-4:00pm (May-October). Admission: $3.00-$6.00.

A reconstructed 1778 fort with exhibits. Original site of a Revolutionary War fort established to mine lead for the army. The rural 230-acre tract features a reconstructed Revolutionary War stockade surrounding six log cabins. It also includes an 1858 barn containing exhibits and a museum shop, and an education center in an 1860 farmhouse; miners quarters, officers quarters, barracks and blacksmith. A costumed guide will show you around and tell you the story of the Lead Mine Fort. Enjoy the sights and sounds of the past. Hear musket fire, wood chopping, and the daily work of a rangers and craftsmen. Take part in the fort's everyday life. Shoulder a musket, mend clothes, smell the stew, and meet the soldiers. If your kids are antsy, there are 47 acres on the property with 3 nature trails and various habitats. Environmental education programs are available to groups from schools, community organizations, etc. Topics include "Discovery Trail Walk", birds, trees, wild edible plants, reading the landscape, and stream study. Living history re-reenactments. (Summer)

<u>REVOLUTIONARY WAR DAYS</u>

Altoona - Fort Roberdeau Historic Site - Experience danger on the 1778 frontier when British Rangers and Iroquois attack patriots and ruin bullet-making at General Roberdeau's lead mine fort. Admission. (second weekend in July)

QUAINT CORNER CHILDREN'S MUSEUM

Altoona - *2000 Union Avenue (Downtown SR36) 16601. Phone: (814) 944-6830. www.quaintcorner.org Hours: Wednesday, Friday-Saturday 10:00am-5:00pm. Admission: $5.00 general. Note: Quick walk from Altoona Railroaders Museum.*

This is a real Victorian home that kids are allowed to explore - in fact, they're encouraged to snoop around. Probably the cutest and most popular areas are the closets and climbing the ladder into Grandma's Attic at the very top of the house. Make a Spirograph with lasers...in the dark. Draw on the wall in the Craft Kitchen or hug a furry friend and then shop in Market Place. Visit the Pirates Treasure, explore nature in the Audubon Room, and see doll houses and antiques. There's even a sandbox in the basement. Cool.

HORSESHOE CURVE NATIONAL HISTORIC LANDMARK

Altoona - *Horseshoe Curve Road (6 miles West of Altoona) 16602. Phone: (888) 4-ALTOONA. www.railroadcity.org. Hours: Tuesday-Sunday 10:00am-7:00pm, (May-October). November & April, long weekends only.Admission: $5.00 adult, $4.00 senior (65+), military and student, $3.00 child (4-11). Combo Memorial Museum & Horseshoe Curve admission. Note: Train Gift shop. Picnic areas.*

Built with just hand tools and dynamite - wow!

Developed in 1854, the Penn Railroad needed to expand west, but through the mountainous terrain. This curve was developed because, even if a bridge could be built, no locomotive could climb the steep grade. To solve this crossing problem, they built a track around the inside curves of the large mountain range. Inside the Interpretive Center, you can view a video of the curve's history and see a model of what the land looked like before the railroad changed the landscape. Kids like the push button display of train sounds as they make the turn (gaining speed, upgrade and downgrade). The highlight is the funicular ride up to the elevation area (or you can walk up - 200 steps) where you can look out onto the horseshoe track. There's a good chance a train (the railroad still uses this curve) will pass through while you are visiting.

LAKEMONT PARK

Altoona - *700 Park Avenue (I-99 to Frankstown Road) 16602. Phone: (814) 949-PARK or (800) 434- 8006. www.lakemontparkfun.com. Hours: Daily 11:00am-dark (Summers). Weekends only in May and September, Noon-8:00pm. Admission: All day unlimited Splash $9.95 tickets. All day unlimited Splash & Play pass $19.95.*

Lakemont Park, the eighth oldest amusement park in the United States, opened its gates for the first time in 1894 as a trolley park in Altoona. One of Lakemont's most prized possessions is the world's oldest roller coaster, Leap-the-Dips. Over 30 rides and attractions. In addition, the park holds an 18-hole miniature golf course, the Island Waterpark and several other rides to thrill visitors of all ages. Go-Kart tracks, picnic areas and arcade. Kids Mini-Indy and Kiddie Lane.

DECEMBER - Glistening lights. Visit with Santa. Hot chocolate. Freshly baked cookies. Toy/gift shops. Model train display. Weekend entertainment. Admission. (Evenings - late November through New Year's Day)

RAILROADER'S MEMORIAL MUSEUM

Altoona - *1300 Ninth Avenue (off 17th Street on I-99) 16602. Phone: (814) 946-0834. www.railroadcity.com. Hours: Monday-Saturday 9:00am-5:00pm, Sunday 11:00am-5:00pm (early May-October). Weekends only (November & April). Admission: $12.00 adult, $10.00 senior (65+), military and students, $9.00 child (4-11). Combo Memorial Museum and Horseshoe Curve admission. Note: Museum store.*

"Here in Altoona an army of railroaders designed, built, maintained, and moved the Pennsylvania Railroad, the largest railroad in the world...in so doing, they changed the face of America... this is their story!" Why was Altoona chosen to be the heart of construction? (watch a 27 minute film to find out). Listen to the folks  talk about their life at local scenes depicting a home, church, newsstand, and clubs. The "News Boy" is funny to listen to. Learn how railroad workers laid the tracks, worked in shops (the test lab is pretty eye opening) and designed and built locomotives. This museum has less focus on displays of trains and more on the lives and work habits of people involved. Nice change.

ALTOONA CURVE BASEBALL CLUB

Altoona (Lakemont) - *1000 Park Avenue (games played at Peoples Natural Gas Field) 16602. Phone: (814) 943-5400 or (877) 99-CURVE. www.altoonacurve.com.*

The Altoona Curve is the AA affiliate of the Pittsburgh Pirates and has been thrilling local fans with hometown baseball since 1999. The Curve games end with fantastic fireworks displays and popular giveaway events. The team also hosts concerts and other community events. Single game tickets run $6-$15.

GARDNER'S CANDY MUSEUM

Altoona (Tyrone) - *30 West 10th Street (I-99 to SR453 or SR220) 16686. Phone: (814) 684-0857. www.gardnerscandies.com. Hours: Monday-Saturday 9:30am-9:00pm, Sunday 1:00-9:00pm. Admission: FREE*

Gardners is famous for the Original Peanut Butter Melt-away, a creamy, smooth peanut butter dipped in rich chocolate. Many have tried, but none can duplicate the Gardner's family recipe. Take a Nostalgic walk through a penny candy store. Big candy counters with large jars of candy. Also stop in the Candy Kitchen where old-time (mostly brass) equipment is displayed. Take a look at their giant Taffy Hook. Mr. Gardner started "the sweetest place in town" in 1897 and still has licorice whips and candy buttons for sale.

Boalsburg

BOAL MANSION / COLUMBUS CHAPEL

Boalsburg - *300 Old Boalsburg Road (US322 - Business Route) 16827. Phone: (814)466-6210. www.boalmuseum.com. Hours: Tuesday-Sunday 1:30-5:00pm (May- October). Admission: $15.00 adult, $8.00 child (7-17). Educators: an eighth grade unit study is found here: http:// boalmuseum.com/unitplan.htm.*

COLUMBUS CHAPEL: Want to see a real part of Christopher Columbus? On the grounds of the originally furnished mansion is the Columbus Chapel that was brought here from Spain in 1909. They actually have a sea desk once owned by Columbus and many Columbus family heirlooms dating back to the 1400s. The highlight of this place begins with your first step inside the chapel. If you're like us…your mouth will drop wide open in disbelief as you begin to notice the centuries-old heirloom pieces. Many of the artifacts look like movie props (the natural way they have aged makes it hard to believe they are real!) Actual parchment family documents, the family cross, a copy of the family tree and 2 actual pieces of the "true" cross are awesome to see up close. When your family steps into the Columbus Chapel, they step into Spain in the time of Christopher Columbus. Nowhere else in America can they experience this connection both with the Old World and with Columbus himself. It's incredible all of this history is in a small town museum!

BOAL MANSION: The Boal Mansion Museum contains the original furnishings, papers, portraits, tools and weapons of nine generations of this American family. The first exhibit room contains medieval armor, a scale model of the Santa Maria and other family memorabilia. The "Country Life" room contains a beautifully restored 1850s stage coach, a buckboard buggy, farm tools, the 1816 accounts book from David Boal's tavern and many farm and kitchen implements. The Weapons Room contains a large collection of swords, rifles and pistols from the Revolutionary War through World War I, including David Boal's Pennsylvania long rifle from the 1790's and Captain John Boal's officer's sword from the Civil War. Hearing stories about the Boal family and their home can be interesting, too.

PENNSYLVANIA MILITARY MUSEUM

Boalsburg - *51 Boal Avenue (Business Route 322) (US322) 16827. Phone: (814) 466-6263. www.pamilmuseum.org. Hours: Thursday-Saturday 10:00am-3:00pm, Sunday Noon-3:00pm (mid-March-November). Admission: $6.00 adult, $5.50 senior (65+), $4.00 child (3-11) and FREE to uniformed military personnel.*

DID YOU KNOW?

Did you know that this is the birthplace of Memorial Day?

Honoring Pennsylvania's soldiers from Benjamin Franklin's first volunteer unit to Operation Desert Storm. Start your visit viewing the short movie: "Answering the Call: Pennsylvanians in Service to the Nation." Discover why a tank is called a "tank" and how evacuating a patient off the battlefield changed so drastically over the years. Size yourself up against a World War II tank and compare that to other armored vehicles from the 1950s and 60s. Young children enjoy climbing on tanks and cannons outside in the park, but it takes older kids to enjoy the museum especially the World War I trench scene, complete with sound and light effects. The museum only focuses on citizen soldiers – "the men and women of Pennsylvania who served their country in time of war."

WAR ENCAMPMENT

Boalsburg - Pennsylvania Military Museum Parade Grounds. Military units encamped throughout the area. Daily living history demonstrations. Live fire artillery demonstrations. Day-long festivities in nearby Boalsburg. Parking fee only. (Memorial Day Weekend)

TUSSEY MOUNTAIN SKI AREA

Boalsburg - *301 Bear Meadow Road - Route 322 16827. Phone: (814) 466-6266 www.tusseymountain.com.*

Longest Run: 2700 ft.; 8 Slopes & Trails plus snowboarding in winter. Skatepark, driving range, batting cages and par 3 golf in the fall.

Centre Hall

PENN'S CAVE

Centre Hall - *222 Penns Cave Road (SR 192 East, Near I-80, Exit 14) 16828. Phone: (814) 364-1664. www.pennscave.com. Hours: Generally daily 10:00am-5:00pm. Open later summers. Closed January. Weekends Only 11:00am-5:00pm (December & February). Closed Thanksgiving and Christmas Day. Admission: CAVERN: $22.99 adult, $21.99 senior (65+), $12.99 child (2-12). WILDLIFE, FARM AND NATURE TOURS: $24.99 adult, $23.99 senior, $15.99 child (2-12). Combo pricing available. Tours: Cave-1 mile guided tour by motorboat - approximately 1 hour long. Note: Miners Maze (extra fee). There are 48 steps that lead to the cave entrance. Cafe*

America's only all-water cavern and wildlife (1000 acre) sanctuary. Colored lights enhance "The Statue of Liberty", "The Garden of Gods" and "Niagara Falls". The farm and wildlife tour is a guided 90-minute motorized tour over the thousand acres of Penn's Cave forests and fields and a natural habitat for birds, plants, and animals. North American animals, such as deer, elk, wolves, bears, bison, and mustangs are seen, as well as longhorn cattle. Come to Penn's Cave and enjoy both tours. You will be educated about the geology, biology, and geography of Central Pennsylvania.

NITTANY ANTIQUE STEAM ENGINE DAYS

Centre Hall - Penn's Cave. Tractor pulls, antique steam engines, parades, food (made with steam), threshing, baling, cider and apple butter making, hayrides, children's activities, petting zoo & fall crafts. Admission. (first week of September)

BLUE KNOB RESORT/SKI AREA

Claysburg - *PO Box 247 (between Altoona & Johnstown, in north corner of Bedford County) 16625. Phone: (814) 239-5111. www.blueknob.com.*

Activities include skiing/snowboarding, a tubing park, and cross country skiing. In the warmer months, golfing, hiking and trail biking are big attractions. All condos are furnished with fully equipped kitchens and fireplaces. Longest Run: 2 miles; 34 Slopes & Trails.

Gallitzin

ALLEGHENY PORTAGE RAILROAD NATIONAL HISTORIC SITE

Gallitzin - *110 Federal Park Road (US22, Gallitzin exit - follow signs) 16641. Phone: (814) 886-6150. www.nps.gov/alpo/. Hours: Daily 9:00am-5:00pm. Closed winter holidays & winter/early spring weekdays. Admission: FREE. Note: Visitor Center with 20 minute film. Costumed presentations during the summer. Lemon House - restored tavern and business office on premises along with the Engine House and walking trails to the incline site.*

You'll be amazed at the ingenuity of railroad engineers back then! The problem was the Allegheny Mountains. No trains or canals could get through them before the idea of the "incline" was introduced. Called "an engineering marvel" at its opening, travel that took three weeks by wagon took only four days by railroad and canal. It used a combination of 10 inclines and horses or steam locomotives pulling cars on levels in between. A system of inclined planes and a nine hundred foot tunnel carved through solid rock by Welsh coalminers made this feat possible. It's difficult to visualize until you see the working small-scale model in the center of the museum - then it all makes

It's just like
"The Little Engine that Could"

sense (still in amazement of course!). With a hands-on demonstration, you can personally try turning a wheel hooked to balanced and unbalanced weights. This clearly demonstrates the need for balanced (one car up - one car down at the same time) inclines. Park rangers give guided tours in costume while demonstrating log hewing, stone cutting, coal mining and musket firing. Be sure to catch the movie about this special railroad.

GALLITZIN TUNNELS PARK, CABOOSE AND MUSEUM

Gallitzin - *702 Jackson Street (off Route 22 - Follow signs) 16641. Phone: (814) 886-8871. www.gallitzin.info/. Hours: Daily, daylight hours. Museum open Tuesday-Sunday 11:00am-5:00pm, weather permitting. Admission: FREE. Note: there's a video tour of the west slope of the mtn. Rail online on their front page.*

See and feel the awesome power of the trains passing through the Allegheny Tunnel (modified 1854). View the tunnels that were built with picks and shovels using over 300 immigrants to complete it. Twin tunnels, the Allegheny and Gallitzin Tunnels, are the highest and longest on what once was the Pennsylvania Railroad. Because of their integral role in the transportation system, these tunnels were guarded during times of war. Also on site is a PRR walkway and railroad signal and a restored PRR caboose - climb aboard to see the sleeping quarters and pot-bellied stove. This is a cute side trip between visits to the Allegheny Portage Railroad and Horseshoe Curve. The museum shows a video called "Once Upon a Mountain" illustrating the fascinating transportation history of the area - especially trains.

DID YOU KNOW?
Trains run through the tunnels 24 hours a day. Chances are you'll get to see at least one pass by and feel its rubble while you're there.

CANOE CREEK STATE PARK

Hollidaysburg - *RR 2, Box 560 (US 22) 16648. Phone: (814) 695-6807. www.dcnr.state.pa.us/stateparks/findapark/canoecreek/index.htm Admission: FREE however swimming, marina and camping/lodging fees apply.*

The park boasts one of the largest bat colonies in the Eastern US. The visitor center has natural and historical exhibits and information. Modern Cabins: Eight modern cabins overlook the lake. They are within walking distance of the swimming area and are available for year-round rental. Beach, Boat Rentals, Horseback Riding, Sledding, Limestone kilns, Trails, and Cross-Country Skiing. A nine-hole disc golf course begins on the sidewalk near the beach house.

BALD EAGLE STATE PARK

Howard - *149 Main Park Road (off PA Route 150, midway between Milesburg and Lock Haven, it is accessible by I-80) 16841. Phone: (814) 625-2775. www.dcnr. state.pa.us/stateparks/findapark/baldeagle/index.htm. Admission: to PA State Parks is FREE however swimming, marina and camping/lodging fees apply.*

The Nature Inn at Bald Eagle provides full-service accommodations overlooking the lake. The rugged 1,730-acre lake features unlimited horsepower boating, hiking and butterfly trails (1.5 miles long, marked & maintained). An interpretive area provides information and examples of butterfly habitats. In September, migrating monarchs are often seen drinking nectar on the abundant goldenrod. This trail is a popular family hike. Swimming is available at the sand beach. The 1,200-foot long sand and turf beach has a children's playground, a snack bar, changing rooms, public restrooms, and parking. The beach is open from late-May to mid-September, 8:00am to sunset, unless otherwise posted. Boat Rentals, Year-round Education & Interpretation Center, Sledding, Campsites, Hiking, and Fishing.

Johnstown

JOHNSTOWN INCLINED PLANE

Johnstown - *711 Edgehill Drive (off SR56, 403 or 271 & Johns St.) 15905. Phone: (814) 536-1816. www.inclinedplane.org. Hours: Daily 11:00am-9:00pm (April-December). Open til 11pm Friday & Saturday night. Closed Christmas and New Years. Admission: $5.00 adult, FREE senior (65+), $3.00 child (2-12). Round Trip. Note: Gift shop. Visitor's center. Observation deck on top. Ice cream shop & Italian restaurant at the Incline. Educators: here's a complete lesson plan: www. jaha.org/edu/inclined_plane/index.html FREEBIES: Scavenger Hunt: www.jaha. org/edu/inclined_plane/documents/rise_challenge.pdf.*

Brightly lit, it is the world's steepest vehicular inclined plane (71 % grade) with a panoramic view of the city through viewing windows. After the flood, many residents wanted to live up on the hill...but they needed a way to commute.  It was also used as an escape route during subsequent floods. A viewing window looking into the motor room explains the "physics" behind the scenes. Hang on tight to those little ones! Ride on the incline and then grab a snack or ice cream at the top. Spectacular views of the valley and you get to see the largest American flag in the county.

The **JAMES WOLFE SCULPTURE TRAIL** is the first nature trail with sculptures made from steel. It honors the city's steel heritage with ten pieces, eight on the trail. Most photographed and visible is "Steel Floats" (Bottom of the incline).

JOHNSTOWN CHILDREN'S MUSEUM

Johnstown - 201 6th Avenue, Discovery Center, 3rd Floor (Route 56, at the corner of Broad Street and Seventh Ave.) 15906. Phone: (814) 539-1889. www. jaha.org/ChildrensMuseum/virtualtour.html. Hours: Monday, Thursday-Saturday 10:00am-5:00pm. Sunday Noon-5pm. Open Tuesdays and Wednesdays also (April-October). Closed major holidays. Admission: $8.00-$10.00 per person. Includes admission to the Heritage Center.

The third floor of the Johnstown Heritage Discovery Center is fully devoted to kids and play. From the beginning, kids are transported along a colorful timewarp wall of recognizable buildings and landmarks including the Stone Bridge. Wooden toys can be played with or quiet reading at Morley's Dog café. The Water Room gets lots of attention as kids love splashing around water. As the kids "play" with water from rain in the mountains and valleys, they learn the concept of dam-building and why solid, reliable dams are essential to a town. The Inclimber Slide mimics Yoder Hill, including mine tunnels that climb high to the ceiling. When you reach the top, take a "coal chute" slide down, where you'll land in a padded coal car full of foam coal. While you're up hill, you can control the incline or dress up like coal miners, including hard hats with lights, orange vests and coal picks. Now you can choose to work in a Steel Mill - trying your hand at making molds or being a boss. Kids can "cook" in The Kitchen or pretend "shop" in the General Store. Other interactives include a Fashion studio and a Music Mix-Master studio. During mild weather, The Overlook Garden is a rooftop delight. Kids can see displays of native Pennsylvania plants. A rain meter keeps track of how much rain we get each month. Enjoy the spectacular view of Cambria City and the Conemaugh Gap -- and use the telescope to take a closer look.

JOHNSTOWN FLOOD MUSEUM

Johnstown - 304 Washington Street (off SR56 West to Walnut Street Exit) 15907. Phone: (814) 539-1889. www.jaha.org/ FloodMuseum/. Hours: Monday, Thursday-Saturday 10:00am-5:00pm. Sunday Noon-5pm. Open Tuesdays and Wednesdays also (April-October). Closed major holidays. Admission: $8.00-$10.00 (age 6+). Note: Museum store. Film shown hourly (25 minutes long). Film has some shrill screaming that may frighten young children. Educators: middle school students may benefit from their extensive Teacher's Guides downloadable here:

www.jaha.org/edu/index.html.

On May 31, 1889, a neglected dam and a phenomenal storm led to a catastrophe in which 2,209 people died, tens of thousands were left homeless, and a prospering city became a wasteland. Hear and see the story of the infamous disaster of 1889 focusing on both the tragedy and triumph of the human spirit. View the Academy Award Winning "The Johnstown Flood" documentary film with multi-media exhibits including an animated map with sound and light effects showing water movement. ... "it was a roar and a crash and a smash...". In 2000, an original "Oklahoma" house, one of the first types of temporary houses erected to shelter the people left homeless by the flood, was installed. Originally manufactured for homesteaders in the Oklahoma Territory, these buildings were a very early example of prefabricated housing. Many Johnstown families combined one large and one small Oklahoma to accommodate their needs. The houses were not attractive -- nor were they suitable for the harsh Southwestern Pennsylvania winters. The Oklahoma House was moved from the Moxham neighborhood and placed on an existing patio adjacent to the museum. It is a telling display of how survivors deal with disaster. Other exhibits include: A Quilt - used as a rescue rope, A Wall of Wreckage in 3-D (17 feet tall - flood wall was actually 40 feet tall). It really captures the horror of the moment, yet is subtle enough to not scare school-aged children.

JOHNSTOWN HERITAGE DISCOVERY CTR

Johnstown - (Route 56, at the corner of Broad Street and Seventh Ave.) 15907. Phone: (814) 539-1889. www.jaha.org. Hours: Hours: Monday, Thursday-Saturday 10:00am-5:00pm. Sunday Noon-5pm. Open Tuesdays and Wednesdays also (April-October). Admission: $8.00-$10.00 (age 6+). ticket includes admission to the Children's Museum. Note: Café. Educators: downloadable elementary aged Teachers Guide is online here: www.jaha.org/edu/discovery_center/index.html.

All Johnstown's immigrants were history-makers - ordinary men, women, and children who made a contribution to the rise of industrial America. When you visit the museum, you will be able to assume the persona of such immigrants as Josef and Maria (as well as Prokop, Katerina, Andrej, and Stefan) as you journey through the exhibit that examines the world the immigrants made in Johnstown, Pennsylvania. The visitor will be able to see and touch the environments - you will feel the sharpness of the coal mine walls and smell the scent of incense in the church. One coal-mining exhibit depicts a mining accident, while another gives you the chance to try working at the picking tables, separating rock from coal.

You'll see the flames and sparks in the open-hearth steel furnace exhibit and become bystanders to an argument between management and an immigrant worker expressing his mounting frustration with immigrant working conditions. You will hear the thoughts of a young immigrant girl as she sells eggs and butter on the street to help the family's finances. Play "History Jukeboxes" -You sit down in front of the computer and tell your story. The "jukebox" records your voice and image. Rather than simply looking at artifacts, you'll actually experience the sights, sounds and even the smells of immigrants' daily lives, and come away with a more complete understanding of the sacrifices and achievements of these Americans in the making.

JOHNSTOWN FLOOD NATIONAL MEMORIAL

Johnstown (South Fork) - 733 Lake Road (US219 to St. Michael Exit - SR869east) 15956. Phone: (814) 495-4643. www.nps.gov/jofl. Hours: Daily 9:00am-5:00pm. Closed winter holidays. Admission:FREE. Educators:a complete lesson plan about the Flood is found here: www.nps.gov/history/nr/twhp/wwwlps/lessons/5johnstown/5johnstown. htm.

The flood began here - see what little is left of South Fork Dam. It is operated by the National Park Service and features exhibits an actual size "debris wall" which dramatically illustrates the wall of water that devastated Johnstown. The film Black Friday chillingly recreates that day in 1889 - a little frightening for youngsters. Remember over 2200 people died in about 10 minutes. In addition, visitors can enjoy a picnic area, hike nearby trails around the dam's remains, take part in the park's interpretive program journey hikes or view exhibits created by the South Fork Fishing and Hunting Club. Other recreational activities available: bird watching and cross country skiing.

R.B. WINTER STATE PARK

Mifflinburg - RR 2, Box 314 (on PA Route 192, 18 miles west of Lewisburg) 17844. Phone: (717) 966-1455. www.dcnr.state.pa.us/stateparks/findapark/ raymondbwinter/. Admission: FREE however swimming, marina and camping/ lodging fees apply.

This park is situated in a narrow valley surrounded by oak forests on steep mountain ridges. A spring-fed mountain stream flows through the valley. Beach, Visitor Center, Year-round Education & Interpretation Center,

Campsites, Camping Cabins, Trails, and Winter Sports. The swimming beach features 300 feet of white sand. The beach is open from late-May to mid-September,   8:00am to sunset. Halfway Run Environmental Learning Center is equipped with many educational tools and features a hands-on science area, a computer center with environmental software, a library of field guides, classic environmental works and children's books, and displays of native wildlife. Visitors can test their knowledge of lumber on the Wall of Woods display. Others enjoy sitting at the center's observation window listening to birds gathered at the microphone- equipped feeding station. Large porches provide opportunities to relax and enjoy the surrounding forest scenery.

RAVENSBURG STATE PARK: This pretty valley is especially beautiful when the mountain laurel blooms in late June and during the fall foliage of October.

MIFFLINBURG BUGGY MUSEUM DAYS
Mifflinburg - 598 Green St, SR 45, Downtown www.buggymuseum.org. Explore the actual home, carriage house, and workshop of the Heiss Coach Works, the only operation rescued from almost 50 different buggy works in the area (early 1900's). It looks as it did before the Heiss family left. Working demonstrations and buggy rides. Donations. (first Thursday in April thru last Sunday in October)

REEDS GAP STATE PARK

Milroy - *1405 New Lancaster Valley Road (U.S. Route 322 from Milroy by following park signs for seven miles) 17063. https://www.dcnr.pa.gov/StateParks/FindAPark/ ReedsGapStatePark/. Phone: (717) 667-3622. Admission: to PA State Parks is FREE however marina and camping/lodging fees apply, with reservation or entrance.*

The Self-guiding Interpretive Trail is a 1.1-mile trail following the scenic banks of Honey Creek. Interpretive waysides focus on the various ecological communities. This green-blazed trail starts at the kiosk beside the snack bar and follows parts of Blue Jay and Honey Creek trails. Also: Two, free, guarded swimming pools, Sledding, Campsites, Fishing, Winter Sports.

POE PADDY STATE PARK is located at the confluence of Big Poe Creek and Penns Creek, a trout angler's paradise featuring the nationally recognized green drake mayfly hatch in June. You can hike through the 250-foot long Paddy Mountain Railroad Tunnel on the Mid State Trail by following the trail upstream along Penns Creek, crossing a pedestrian bridge and then going to the tunnel. POE VALLEY STATE PARK's hiking trail system connects to the extensive trail network of Bald Eagle State Forest. The hiking trails vary from easy hiking to very rugged, steep trails. Boating, Fishing, Swimming with beach, Hiking, and Winter Sports.

Patton

PRINCE GALLITZIN STATE PARK

Patton - *966 Marina Road (SR 1021) (reached by PA Routes 36 and 53 and U.S. Route 219) 16668. Phone: (814) 674-1000. https://www.facebook.com/ PrinceGallitzinSP   Admission: to PA State Parks is FREE however swimming, marina and camping/lodging fees apply, with reservation or entrance.*

The major attractions to the park are the 1,600-acre Lake Glendale and the large campground. Beach, Visitor Center, Boat Rentals, Horseback Riding, Sledding, Campsites, Modern Cabins, Fishing, Trails, & X-Country Skiing.

Penfield

PARKER DAM STATE PARK

Penfield - *RD 1, Box 165 (I- 80, take Exit 18 onto Route 153 North, Turn right onto Mud Run Road) 15849. Phone: (814) 765-0630. https://www.facebook.com/ ParkerDamStatePark/   Admission: to PA State Parks is FREE however swimming, marina and camping/lodging fees apply, with reservation or entrance.*

This rustic, remote park in the heart of **MOSHANNAN STATE FOREST** is almost entirely wooded and offers picturesque areas of forest and swamp meadows. The CCC Interpretive Center interprets the Civilian Conservation Corps. Parker Dam is a good base to explore the surrounding state forest. The swimming area in Parker Lake features a beautiful sand beach and is open from late-May to mid-September, 8:00am to sunset. Beach, Visitor Center, Boat Rentals, Sledding, Campsites, Rustic Cabins, Hiking Trails, and Cross-Country Skiing. Of all the hiking trails, we think the Logside Trail (0.5 mile) is easy and takes you by an authentic repro of a logslide, used at the turn of the century to haul logs out of the forest. Other shorter trails are labeled Stumpfield or Tornado Alley - can you guess why? Wayside exhibits interpreting the tornado are located outside of the Cabin Classroom.

A small-scale, interpretive maple sugaring operation runs throughout March. Apple-cidering is demonstrated each October. A visitor center attached to the park office offers interpretive displays, games and resource and children's' books. It is open during park office hours.

S.B. ELLIOTT STATE PARK is a quiet, rustic, mountaintop recreational area just off of I-80 near the mid-point of the state. This 318-acre park, in the heart of the Moshannon State Forest, is entirely wooded and offers picturesque areas of forest and swamp meadows and typical second growth mixed hardwood and oak timber. Camping, Rustic Cabins and Winter Sports.

WOODHICK WEEKEND

Penfield - Parker Dam State Park. A hands-on competition in old logging events to see who is the best woodhick of the year. X-cut sawing, log rolling, shoe pitching, seed spitting, and more. FREE. (Sunday of Labor Day Weekend)

BLACK MOSHANNON STATE PARK

Philipsburg - RR 1, Box 185 (PA Route 504) 16866. Phone: (814) 342-5960. https://www.facebook.com/BlackMoshannonStatePark/. Admission: to PA State Parks is FREE however swimming, marina and camping/lodging fees apply, with reservation or entrance.

Black Moshannon State Park features the Black Moshannon Bog Natural Area. Trails and a boardwalk help people explore the birds and plants of the bog and surrounding forests. According to local tradition, American Indians called this watershed "Moss-Hanne," meaning "moose stream," thus the origin of the park's name. Appropriately, the "black" in the park name describes the tea-colored waters. Beach, Mountain Biking, Boat Rentals, Campsites, Modern Cabins, Trails, and Cross-Country Skiing. One of their trails is accessible and takes you on a boardwalk to explore wetlands (Bog Trail, .3 mile).

Raystown Lake

LAKE RAYSTOWN RESORT

Raystown Lake (Entriken) - 100 Chipmunk Crossing (Route 994) 16638. Phone: (814) 658-3500. www.raystownresort.com.

The Resort is located between Harrisburg and Pittsburgh in Entriken on Pennsylvania's largest inland lake with 118 miles of scenic shoreline and thousands of acres of pristine woodlands and streams. Lodge rooms, boating and boat rentals, Hiking, Biking and Fitness Trails, Camping and Cottages, Swimming and Beach Areas. Other attractions:

- **PROUD MARY TOURBOAT**: Sightseeing cruises. Food available. Scheduled departures by season (April - October). Admission: Adults $9.95+, Children (under 6) 50% off Adult pricing, (for most cruises). Breakfast Bingo Cruise for kids is $17.95 for everyone.
- **WILDRIVER WATER PARK**: Speed slides, twisting slides, whitewater tubing slides, Children's splash pool and mini-golf. $6.00-$13.00 depending on activity.

SEVEN POINTS CRUISES

Raystown Lake (Hesston) - RD #1, Route 26 (Seven Points Marina) 16647. Phone: (814) 658-3074. www.7pointsmarina.com. Hours: May - mid-October. Admission: Pontoon boat rentals start @ $100. Dog friendly.

Reserve a boat and cruise where you can view wooded shoreline (esp. cedar trees), wild turkey, deer, beaver, bald eagles, and ravens. Close to Lake Raystown Resort (waterpark and activities).

RAYSTOWN REGATTA

Raystown Lake (Entriken) - (888) RAYS-TOWN. www.raystown.org. Boat racing, concerts, kids' activities, area Pow Wows, & fireworks. (June weekend)

GREENWOOD FURNACE STATE PARK

Raystown Lake (Huntingdon) *- RR 2, Box 118 (SR 305 North) 16652. Phone: (814) 667-1800. https://www.facebook.com/greenwoodfurnaceSP/. Admission: to PA State Parks is FREE however swimming, marina and camping/lodging fees apply, with reservation or entrance.*

Relive the 1800s by visiting this 423-acre park, site of an active iron furnace community. Greenwood Furnace was the site of an active iron furnace community from 1834 to 1904. The visitor center is a restored blacksmith shop and provides historical programming. Along the Mid-State Trail to the Greenwood Forest Fire Lookout Tower, you can view charcoal hearths where wood was made into charcoal.

- GREENWOOD HISTORIC WALKING TOUR: Greenwood Furnace was once a thriving ironmaking village. Today, only a handful of its 127 buildings remain. This walking tour explores a portion of the historic district and includes parts of the town, tramway, historic roads and charcoal hearths. A free guide to the historic district is available at the park office and visitor center.

- BLACKSMITH SHOP: This historic building has displays on the history of the park and offers blacksmithing demonstrations in the summer. It is open Wednesday, Friday, Saturday and Sunday through the summer months and weekends in May, September and October.

- VISITOR CENTER / PARK OFFICE: The Visitor Center/Park Office is open 8:00am-4:00pm, Monday through Friday and seven days a week from Memorial Day to Labor Day. There are temporary exhibits on display. Campsites. A 300-foot sand beach is open from May to mid-September, 8:00am to sunset.

LINCOLN CAVERNS & WHISPER ROCKS

Raystown Lake (Huntingdon) *- RR#1 Box 280 (I-76 to US 522 north to US 22 west) 16652. Phone: (814) 643-0268. www.lincolncaverns.com. Hours: Daily 9:00 am-4:00pm (December - Weekends only). Admission: $20.98 adult, $19.98 senior (65+), $12.98 child (4-12). Child Combo Ticket: $18.98 Includes Cave tour and regular bag of mineral rough to pan for gems - available mid-March thru mid-November. Note: Gift shop, nature trails, gem panning. They also have Fall festivals and winter Batfests. Educators: They provide lesson plan packets with* *each group reservation.*

Nature's handiwork has been protected and preserved for your visit since they were first discovered in 1930 and 1941. Two crystal caverns - Lincoln and Whisper Rock have winding passages, large "rooms" with massive and delicate flowstones, pure white calcite and crystals. The interpretive tours of two spectacular crystal caverns features history, geology, bat facts, and trivia, while offering guests plenty of time for questions and picture taking. The caverns are a comfortable 50 year round, making them the ideal place to spend a hot summer afternoon. Ask about seasonal "Kids' Cave Crawls". Kids can suit up like a real spelunker and move through the simulated Kids Cave Crawl.

SWIGART ANTIQUE AUTO MUSEUM

Raystown Lake (Huntingdon) - *12031 William Penn Highway (US22 East) 16652. Phone: (814) 643-0885. www.swigartmuseum.com. Hours: Daily 9:00am-5:00pm (Memorial Day weekend- October). Admission: $4.00-$8.00 (age 6+).*

See over 40 cars on display and the world's largest collection of cars, toys, license plates, bicycles and clothing. The 1908 Studebaker Electric sits in mint condition. It is one of two that belonged to the United States government and were used to transport people in the tunnel between the House and the Senate in Washington, D. C. The 12-passenger vehicle was designed with two front ends so it could reverse direction without turning around. Fun for nostalgic boys and grandparents.

ROTHROCK STATE FOREST

Raystown Lake (Huntington) - *Rothrock Lane - Box 403 16652. Phone: (814) 643-2340. www.dcnr.state.pa.us/forestry/stateforests/rothrock/.*

Vistas or scenic overlooks are a major attraction for many forest visitors. The best known and most easily accessible is the well-known overlook atop Tussey Mountain along PA Route 26 at the Centre/Huntingdon County line. 93,349 acres of Fishing, Camping, Hiking, Cross-Country Skiing, Snowmobile and Bike Trails, and Picnic Areas.

TROUGH CREEK STATE PARK

Raystown Lake (James Creek) - *16362 Little Valley Road (PA Route 994) 16657. Phone: (814) 658-3847. www.dcnr.state.pa.us/stateparks/findapark/troughcreek/. Admission: to PA State Parks is FREE however swimming, marina and camping/ lodging fees apply, with reservation or entrance.*

Located along a scenic gorge where Great Trough Creek cuts through Terrace Mountain and empties into Raystown Lake. Rugged hiking trails lead to wonders like Balanced Rock and Rainbow Falls. Rothrock State Forest and Raystown Lake Recreation Area border the park, making a large, contiguous area of public land for recreation Campsites, Modern Cabins, Fishing and Hiking. IN the winter, the park serves as a trailhead for snowmobiling in nearby Rothrock State Forest lands.

WARRIORS PATH STATE PARK About 12 miles southwest of Trough Creek State Park in Saxton, Bedford County, the park is just off of PA 26. Natural cliffs, boating, and part of Raystown Lake area.

AG PROGRESS DAYS

Rock Springs - Larson AG Research Center. http://apd.psu.edu. AG museum (open mid-April to Mid-October). One of the largest agricultural shows in the country features a petting zoo, live animal expos, games and food, and farming technology demos. Kids Climb a 25 foot tree, fishing center, corn maze and ImAGination Station with other fun things for kids. FREE (Tuesday – Thursday, mid-August)

Rockhill Furnace

ROCKHILL TROLLEY MUSEUM

Rockhill Furnace - PO Box 203 (PA Turnpike, exit 13 to US522 North to Route 994 - Meadow Street) 17249. Phone: (814) 447-9576 (weekends only) (610) 437-0448. www.rockhilltrolley.org. Hours: Weekends and Holidays 11:00am-4:00pm (Memorial Day-October). Special events only in November and December. Admission: $10.00 adult, $8.00 child (2-12). Tours: Every 1/2 hour service. Note: Pennsylvania Transportation Museum and restoration shop where volunteers are always working on new projects.

Take the 2 1/2 mile trolley rides along with a motorman on an antique streetcar - unlimited rides on many different varieties of streetcars. Even though they run on a standard railroad track, streetcars or "interurbans" (city to city) are powered by electricity. Wires running along the length of main streets were connected to rods moving along a set track. The grandparents will remember this form of transport and have fun memories to share of the friendships that freely developed on the way to work or to the movies.

PUMPKIN PATCH TROLLEY

Rockhill Furnace - Rockhill Trolley Museum. Visit the Pumpkin Patch while riding aboard a historic trolley. All children 12 years and under receive a free pumpkin with their paid fare. All riders are welcome to ride as often as they like all day long. Admission. (weekends in October)

POLAR BEAR EXPRESS & SANTA'S TROLLEY

Rockhill Furnace - Rockhill Trolley Museum. Polar Bear Express - Ride to Blacklog Narrows aboard a closed or open trolley during the evening and see lighted decorations along the trolley line. Rides operate from 6:30-9:00pm. (last weekend in November, first weekend in December). Santa's Trolley - Ride aboard a real trolley car, where each child will personally visit with Santa and receive a gift. Rides from 10:00am-4:00pm. (first Saturday in December)

State College

PENN STATE UNIVERSITY PARK CAMPUS

State College - *(Hetzel Union Building) (off US322) 16801. Phone: (800) PSU-TODAY. www.psu.edu/visitors-and-neighbors.   Hours: Mostly weekdays. Some museums also open Saturday & Sundays - Call first.   Tours: Call for reservations.*

Things you can see:

- NITTANY LION SHRINE - The 13 ton block of Indiana limestone shaped like the mascot, Nittany Lion.

- FOOTBALL HALL OF FAME - Greensburg Sports Complex, (814) 865-0411. Nittany Lion football greats. Greenberg Sports Complex, along with containing the ice rink, houses the PSU Football Hall of Fame and the Football offices. Greenberg's ice pavilion is open to students and the public and is very popular year round.

- FROST ENTOMOLOGICAL MUSEUM - (814) 865-2865. 250,000 insects!

- EARTH & MINERAL SCIENCES MUSEUM - (814) 865-6427. Steidle Building. Minerals and paintings depicting Pennsylvania's mineral industries.

- PALSNER MUSEUM OF ART - (814) 865-7672.

- PENN STATE BOOKSTORE - (814) 863-0205.

- COLLEGE OF AGRICULTURAL SCIENCES - Dairy, beef and sheep research center, deer pens. Look for Coaly the mule.

- <u>THE CREAMERY</u> - www.creamery.psu.edu. west on Bigler Road (814-865-7535). 500,000 cones of ice cream are sold here each year. Most visitors to the Creamery at Penn State know only of its famous ice cream, sherbet, and cheeses sold at the store or over the Internet, but what they don't know is that it is the largest university creamery in the nation. Each year, approximately 4.5 million pounds of milk pass through the Creamery's stainless steel holding tanks. These dairy products are produced in the Food Science Lab, located directly behind the Creamery, and then used throughout the campus. Ben and Jerry actually took a correspondence course through Penn State to learn about ice cream production.

STONE VALLEY RECREATION AREA

State College - *(CR1029 - off SR26 South) 16801. Phone: (814) 863-1164. Center - (814) 863-2000. https://studentaffairs.psu.edu/campusrec/stonevalley. Hours: Dawn - Dusk (AREA). Daily 10:00am-5:00pm (CENTER). Closed mid-December through January. Admission: FREE Note: be sure to check status of dam repairs before planning water activities.*

Boating, fishing, hayrides, ice skating, sledding, cross-country skiing, hiking, equipment rental for most sports, and cabins. Hikers enjoy many trails around Lake Perez, including the boardwalk over the wetlands at the head of the lake. The trails are also used for mountain biking and, in the winter, snow shoeing and cross-country skiing. Vertical Adventures challenge course.

SHAVER'S CREEK ENVIRONMENTAL CENTER - www.shaverscreek. org. Raptor Center (rehabilitate injured large birds) and Day Camps. FREE Admission. Fees for rentals. Explore discovery rooms, tour the raptor center, walk the network of trails, and visit the gardens and the Pennsylvania nature book and gift shop. Explore animal tracks, constellations, and other cultural and natural history games. Under the Children's Loft, you will find live Pennsylvania frogs, toads, turtles, and snakes, just waiting for your visit.

MAPLE SUGARING

State College - Stone Valley Recreation Area. Actual tapping of trees. Syrup making. Demos of coopering&sugaring off in a realistic sugar camp. Pancakes & syrup served.

CENTRAL PENNSYLVANIA FESTIVAL OF THE ARTS

State College - Downtown & PSU Campus. www.arts-festival.com. The first day is usually Children and Youth Day featuring art creations of local kids ages 8-18. Art and mask parade with costumed characters, storytelling, marionettes, and concerts. (second Full Week of July, Monday - Friday)

SHIKELLAMY STATE PARK

Sunbury - *Bridge Avenue (Blue Hill is reached from the town of Shamokin Dam on US 11north. Marina off of PA 147) 17801. Phone: (717) 988-5557. https://www. dcnr.pa.gov/StateParks/FindAPark/ShikellamyStatePark/Pages/default.aspx. Admission: FREE however swimming, marina and camping/lodging fees apply, with reservation or entrance.*

The marina provides access to unlimited horsepower boating on Lake Augusta that is formed by an inflatable dam on the Susquehanna River. The Blue Hill area is across the river from the Marina and provides panoramic views of the confluence of two branches of the Susquehanna River. Paved paths encircle Shikellamy Marina. A walk around the one-mile nature trail on Shikellamy Overlook can reveal the wildlife that abounds in the park, like deer, songbirds and wildflowers. Unique geologic formations can be studied in the park and on the eastern boundary cliff trail extension. Bicycling: A one-mile, paved hiking and biking path encircles Shikellamy Marina. Bicycle rentals are available at the boat rental during the summer.

DELGROSSO'S AMUSEMENT PARK & LAGUNA SPLASH

Tipton - *Old Route 220 (I-99 North, Exit Grazierville or Bellwood) 16684. Phone: (814) 684-3538. www.delgrossos.com. Hours: Daily (Summer). Weekends in May and September. Open at 11:00am. Admission: FREE. (All-day passes, ~$24.95-$36.95 and individual ride prices, ~50c each available). Mini golf and go karts extra fee per ride. All water park guests must have a Fun Pass Wristband to enter.*

North of Altoona sits DelGrosso's Amusement Park, originally established in 1919, it is a perfect example of a vintage amusement park. Offering "America's best amusement park food," the park is home to the famous, award-winning DelGrosso's spaghetti sauce, Murf's famous potato salad and their fresh-made pizza. Visitors can also take a ride on the antique Carouselle. Today, more than six decades after they started a spaghetti sauce company, Mafalda's and Fred's seven sons and daughters, 22 grandchildren and 20 great-grandchildren make millions of jars of spaghetti sauce and host hundreds of thousands of guests at their amusement park. 30 rides and attractions. Most of the rides are old-fashioned spinning rides and roller coasters. Take a float on the lazy river and enjoy the feel of the ocean in the wave pool in the waterpark. Mini-golf - (18 holes with lakes & waterfalls), Go-Karts, mini-train rides and an water park. Free concert series during the summer. This pay-by-ride park offers free admission, free parking and free live entertainment.

WOODWARD CAVE

Woodward - *SR 45 (US 22 east to Water Street, then SR 45 east) 16882. Phone: (814) 349-9800. www.woodwardcave.com. Hours: Generally Daily 9:00am-4:30pm (Summer). Friday-Sunday 10:00am-4:00pm (Spring, Fall). Admission: $6.00-$12.00 (age 2+). Tours: 50 - 60 minutes, guided*

Experience spectacular Woodward Cave, nicknamed "The Big One". One of the largest caverns in Pennsylvania, its nickname reflects its five spacious rooms, one of which, "The Hall of Statues" is 200 feet long. Experienced guides conduct a well explained, easily walked tour. Five big, well-lit rooms include the "Ball Room", "Square Room". "Hanging Forest", "Tower of Babel" (largest stalagmites in U.S.) and "Upper Room" (cathedral ceiling). Indian burial room and the passageways are wide and flat. On tour, did you notice any cave pearls? Your guide might even sneak in some cave chemistry - you'll feel smarter afterwards.

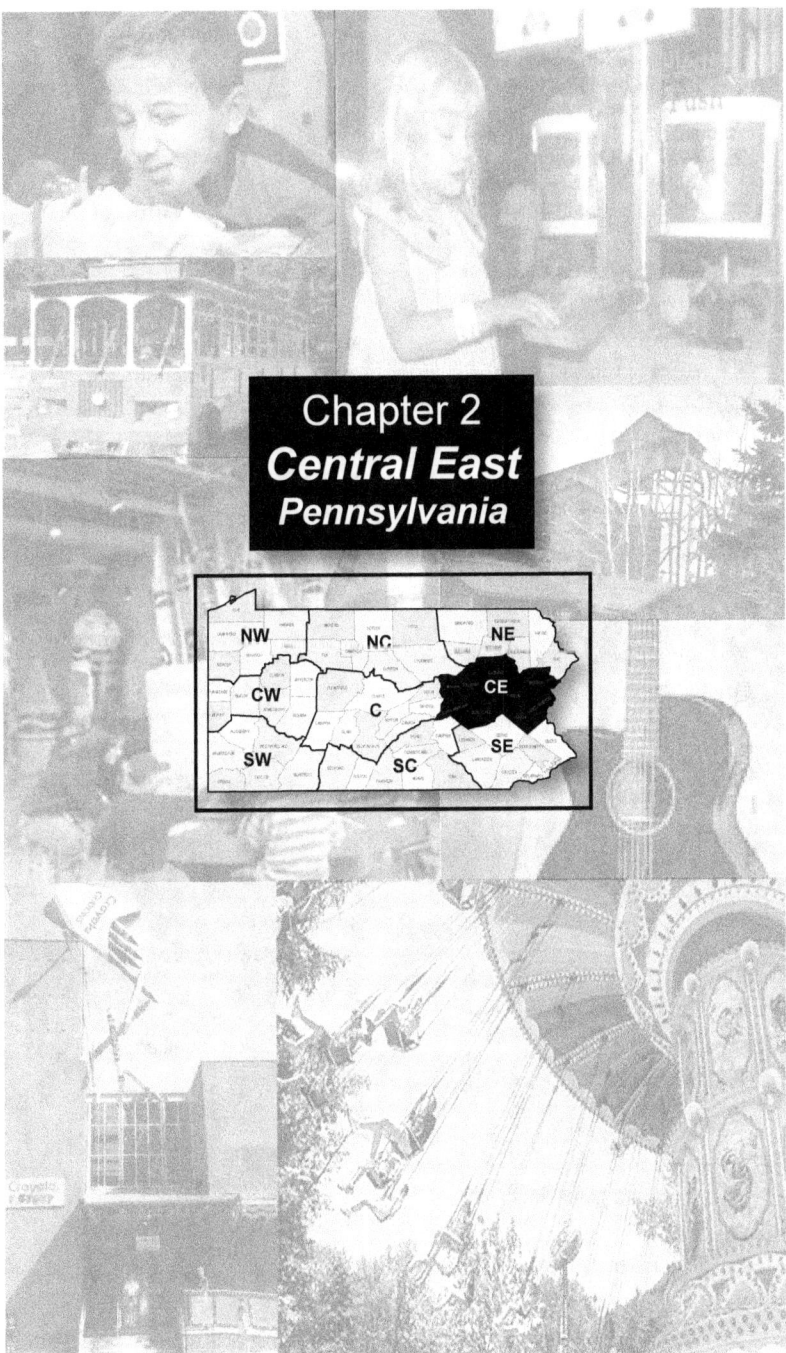

Chapter 2
Central East
Pennsylvania

Allentown
- Allentown Art Museum
- Lehigh Valley Heritage Center
- America On Wheels
- Da Vinci Science Center
- Museum Of Indian Culture
- Dorney Park & Wildwater King
- Lehigh Valley Ironpigs
- Lights In The Parkway

Allentown (Schnecksville)
- Lehigh Valley Zoo

Ashland
- Pioneer Tunnel Coal Mine

Barnesville
- Tuscarora State Park

Benton
- Ricketts Glen State Park

Bethlehem
- Pennsylvania Youth Theatre
- Bethlehem Historic Area
- Blueberry Festival
- Celtic Classic Highland Games

Bloomsburg
- Children's Museum, The

Breinigsville
- Grim's Corny Maze

Catawissa
- Pumpkin Fall Festival

Danville
- Iron Heritage Festival

Delaware Water Gap
- Water Gap Trolley

Easton
- Crayola Factory
- Hugh Moore Canal Ride Park
- National Canal Museum

Elysburg
- Knoebel's Amusement Resort

Hellertown
- Lost River Caverns

Jim Thorpe (Summit Hill)
- Mauch Chunk Lake Park & Environmental Education Center

Lake Harmony
- Split Rock Resort

Lehighton
- Beltzville State Park

Minersville
- Big Diamond Raceway

Nazareth
- Martin Guitar Company

Palmerton
- Blue Mountain Ski Area

Poconos (Blakeslee)
- Jack Frost Mountain & Big Boulder Ski Areas

Poconos (Marshalls Creek)
- Pocono Snake & Animal Farm

Poconos (Scotrun)
- Great Wolf Lodge Resort & Indoor Waterpark

Poconos (Shawnee-On-Delaware)
- Shawnee Mountain Ski Area

Stroudsburg
- Quiet Valley Living Historical Farm

Swiftwater
- Delaware State Forest

Tannersville
- Camelback Beach Water Park (Camelback Ski Area)

Weatherly
- Eckley Miners' Village

White Haven
- Hickory Run State Park

Wind Gap
- Jacobsburg Park
- Lenape Nation Pow Wow

Wyoming
- Frances Slocum State Park

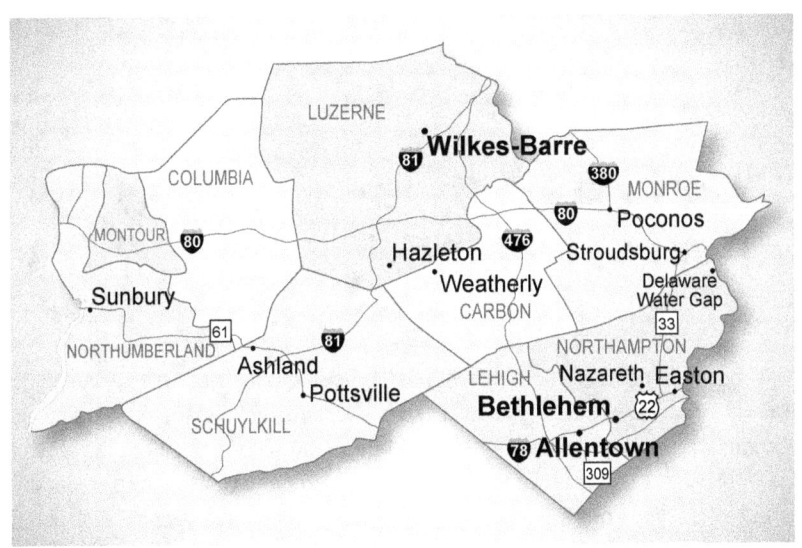

Travel Journal & Notes:

A Quick Tour of our Hand-Picked
Favorites Around...

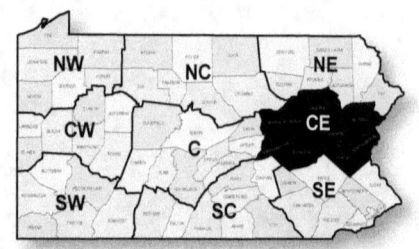

Central East
Pennsylvania

See how some of the region's most famous products are made, including **Martin Guitars** and **Crayola** crayons. Be sure you're in the creative mode because both of these "factory tours" engage the hidden spirit of creativity in all of us. What a great way to introduce your kids to the Arts – music, artistry and crafts. Who knows, someone in your family may have talent?

No matter what time of year, the **Pocono Mountains** are full of activity. Beat the winter blues by skiing fresh powder or splashing indoors at a waterpark. Dive into summer by rafting, kayaking or canoeing in the Delaware and Lehigh rivers or take a bike ride through one of the area's state parks. Next, cool off at an outdoor waterpark or resort pool; visit the petting zoo or go-carting at one of their numerous family fun parks.

Many hard-working immigrants landed jobs in this part of the country. Early transport of goods was done using canals. Try your hand at packing for a trip at the **National Canal Museum**. Your admission to the Crayola Factory includes this museum (parents note: a nice, quiet diversion from the chaos upstairs). Now, head down the road and actually have a chance to ride a real canal boat – kids may even get a turn at steering. Other immigrants performed super-human feats coal mining. With poor conditions, these miners chiseled through rock all day to find veins of precious coal. A "ghost town" workers village is found at **Eckley Miners' Village** in Weatherly and an actual "train" tour of an underground mine is offered at **Pioneer Tunnel Coal Mine** in Ashland. All these transportation options are grand adventures for kids!

Sites and attractions are listed in order by City, Zip Code, and Name. Symbols indicated represent:

🍽 Restaurants   🛏 Lodging

Allentown

ALLENTOWN ART MUSEUM

Allentown - *31 North Fifth Street (5th & Court Streets) 18101. Phone: (610) 432-4333. www.allentownartmuseum.org. Hours: Thursday-Sunday 11:00am-4:00pm. Free Museum admission. Art Ways is always open during regular Museum hours, free with Museum admission.*

European to architecture of Frank Lloyd Wright to American art. Gem Collection, photography, textiles, museum shop. In Art Ways, a unique interactive learning center, throw caution to the wind and invite your family to look, learn, play, read, create, and yes, even touch together!

LEHIGH VALLEY HERITAGE CENTER MUSEUM

Allentown - *432 West Walnut Street (US-22 take PA 145 south 1.8 mi. to Walnut St. Turn left on Walnut .2 miles to 5 th St.) 18101. www.lchs.museum. Phone: (610) 435-1074. Hours: Tuesday-Saturday 10:00am-4:00pm. Admission: $8.00 adult, $3.00 child (2-11). Note: Geology Garden adjacent. Educators: online exhibit and lesson plans here: www.lchs.museum/ww2/teachers.htm.*

Here you can trace the main lines of the county's story: from the region's indigenous peoples, through the rural life of early Pennsylvania German immigrants, to the developments that made Lehigh County a birthplace of the American Industrial Revolution. Take a trip into the world of the Pennsylvania Dutch rural community and tour the:TROXELL-STECKEL HOUSE (PA-German farmhouse), Claussville One-Room School, and Haines Mill. Or learn how Lehigh County served as a birthplace of the American Industrial Revolution as you view the soaring remains of the Lock Ridge Iron Furnace and Saylor Cement Kilns. Other properties worth a look in this county are: (small adult fee required to tour) CLAUSSVILLE ONE-ROOM SCHOOLHOUSE- 2917 Rte. 100; SAYLOR CEMENT INDUSTRY MUSEUM - 245 N. 2nd. On site, 9 cement kilns from beginnings of cement industry; HAINES MILL MUSEUM - 3600 Dornay Park Road. Operating gristmill built in 1760 shows milling techniques; LOCH RIDGE FURNACE MUSEUM (Alburtis) - 525 Franklin. Iron furnaces, industry park. Most of these are only open weekends (May-September).

AMERICA ON WHEELS

Allentown - *5 North Front Street 18102. www.americaonwheels.org. Phone: (610) 432-4200. Hours: Wednesday-Saturday 10:00am-3:00pm, Sunday Noon-3:00pm. Extended close each summer. Admission: $13 adult, $10 senior (62+), 8 students (6-16).*

Start a rainy morning trip to Allentown with a visit to the America On Wheels museum to see the Mack Trucks archives and learn how these world-famous trucks were made in the region for decades. Much more than just cars, the museum features everything on wheels, from racing lawn mowers and bicycles, to carriages and trucks. It has over 23,000 sq. ft. of exhibit space in three exhibit areas including subjects such as the American trucking industry, and also has a long-term education exhibit on alternative fuels. Nice place to get some ideas for kids' science reports about future fuels.

DA VINCI SCIENCE CENTER

Allentown - *3145 Hamilton Blvd. Bypass, Cedar Crest College (corner of the Hamilton Blvd. Bypass and Cedar Crest Blvd.) 18103. Phone: (484) 664-1002. https://www.davincisciencecenter.org/. Hours: Monday-Saturday 10am-5:00pm, Sunday Noon-5:00pm. Closed only Christmas Day and New Years Day. Admission: $12.95 general, children under 3 are free.*

This center is based on the understanding that each young person, like Leonardo da Vinci, is insatiably curious about the world around them, uses multiple modes of investigation, embraces creativity, and seeks to make connections among all the things they are learning. The Center contains more than 200 fun, interactive, hands-on exhibits. Learn what makes the Earth work and become a real weather forecaster. Investigate forces and discover how machines make work easier. Can you lift 1,000 pounds? Some lab experiments encourage you to get "shocked" or messy Other Family favorites:

WHAT HURTS? When your body is hurt or sick, it provides clues to what is wrong. You can use these clues to figure out the problem and how to fix it.

WATTS UP? Experiment with energy as you explore light, electricity, and magnetism. Enjoy images from deep space and dance in the Shadow Room.

WHAT'S THE MATTER? Atoms can join together in many unique, but predictable, ways to form new materials with new properties. Have you

...watch water freeze

ever rearranged some atoms?

MUSEUM OF INDIAN CULTURE

Allentown - 2825 Fish Hatchery Road (I-78 exit Cedar Crest Blvd. Take Rte. 29 south and then left on Fish Hatchery) 18103. www.lenape.org. Phone: (610) 797-2121. Hours: Friday-Sunday 10am-4:00pm. Plus summer Thursdays. Admission: $4.00-$5.00 (over age 12).

Hands-on exhibits enhance the learning of the Native American culture. Pretend you're walking in an Indian's moccasins and head dress as you look at exhibits of their crafts and tools. Special events include corn planting in May and Time of Thanksgiving in October.

DORNEY PARK AND WILDWATER KINGDOM

Allentown - 3830 Dorney Park Road (I-78 West to Exit 16 B) 18104. Phone: (610) 395-3724. www.dorneypark.com. Hours: Daily (Memorial Day-Labor Day), Weekends (May and September). Admission: $39.99 (starlight/junior) to $42.99 general (includes wet and dry park rides). Parking $10.00.

This old-fashioned amusement park may be smaller, but it's full of good rides. Dorney Park & Wildwater Kingdom is home to more than 100 rides and attractions, including eight roller coasters and dozens of state-of-the-art thrill machines. Steel Force is the longest, tallest, fastest coaster in the East. Hang Time - "hang out" thrill ride and Water Works interactive aquatic play ride. Also, high energy live shows.

* PLANET SNOOPY — Dorney Park & Wildwater Kingdom is the only place on the East Coast where families can visit Snoopy, Charlie Brown and the PEANUTS™ gang.

* WILDWATER KINGDOM — Splash around and beat the heat in one of the country's best-ranked water parks. . . Includes 18 water slides, a giant wavepool and Lollipop Lagoon for little kids. Aquablast is the longest elevated water slide (701ft.) in the world.

LEHIGH VALLEY IRONPIGS

Allentown - Coca-cola Park, 1050 IronPigs Way 18109. Phone: (610) 841-PIGS. www.ironpigsbaseball.com. AAA Minor League baseball team. Affiliated with Philadelphia Phillies. The name is a reference to pig iron, used in manufacturing steel, for which the Lehigh Valley region of is world-renowned. The giant Coca-Cola bottle on top of the videoboard, towering 90-feet above ground level, shoots fireworks and illuminates the sky. Kids Zone features a free playground area - a number of games, including speed pitch, slides and more.

LIGHTS IN THE PARKWAY

Allentown - LeHigh Parkway. www.lightsintheparkway.com. This drive-through light display covers more than a mile of one of Allentown's most beautiful parks (Lehigh Parkway) and features lighted trees, light tunnels and animated displays. Horse-drawn wagon rides. The Gift Barn features fine crafts and unique gift ideas for everyone on your holiday shopping list as well as refreshments and Lights In The Parkway souvenirs. Visit with Santa. Admission. (evenings mid-December thru New Years weekend)

LEHIGH VALLEY ZOO

Allentown (Schnecksville) - *5150 Game Preserve Road (I-78 follow SR309 north) 18078. Phone: (610) 799-4171. www.lvzoo.org. Hours: Daily 10:00am-4:00pm (Late April - October). Daily 10am-3pm (November-March). Admission: $12.50-$14.50 (age 2+). Reduced winters.*

Founded by General Harry C. Trexler, a local industrialist, the Game Preserve played a significant role in saving the North American Bison from extinction. Native, exotic birds, and petting zoo inhabit a 25 acre zoo. The zoo's newest attraction is the addition of penguins moving around an open space with a rock border. The zoo skips the large animals like tigers, elephants or giraffes and instead focuses on onyx, zebra, bobcats, prairie dogs, river otter, kangaroo, owl, etc. Investigation Station: Become an Investigative Agent and solve eco-crimes or solve the earth's dilemmas. Catch live animal presentations daily (look on the announcement board). Conserving species of endangered animals is a specialty. Look for their mascot bison, Wooly Bully. Because the zoo is small, you can get very close to the animals and the zoo is rarely crowded.

PIONEER TUNNEL COAL MINE

Ashland - *2001 Walnut St, 19th & Oak Streets (SR61 North to Downtown Area - Follow signs off Center Street SR61) 17921. Phone: (570) 875-3850. www.pioneertunnel.com. Hours: Daily 10:00am-6:00pm (Summer). Weekdays 11:00am, 12:30pm, 2:00pm and Weekends 10:00am-6:00pm (May, September, October). Weekdays only in April. Some reserved group tours in November. Admission: $8.00-$11.00 adult, $7.00-$9.00 child (each activity). Save money purchasing the combo. Tours: Approximately 35 minutes long, given by real coal miner guides. Note: Snack bar, Gift shop where most novelties are made from coal. Wooden "train" playground.*

Two tour options are available and we highly recommend both. (Pre-schoolers may find the mine tour frightening due to darkness, dampness, and confined areas...but will love the lokie train tour).

- <u>COAL MINE TOUR</u> - Watch you children's eyes light up with fascination as you enter and travel 400' deep into a real working coal mine! Though closed in 1931 (because of the Great Depression), you will see and have explained all the features of a real mine. Learn how and why tunnels were built to access the coal. See the Mammoth Vein (the largest in Pennsylvania) and learn why all miners carried a safety lamp (not for light, but for safety from dangerous gases). Our guide was a real miner who carefully explained what we were seeing. He even turned out all of the lights to show how dark a real mine is! If you're concerned, the mine is inspected regularly by the state to insure its safety. If your parents or grandparents were miners, this will surely bring their stories to life. A top 10 Pennsylvania tour and we definitely agree!

- <u>TRAIN RIDE - OPEN COAL FIELD TOUR</u> - A "lokie" (steam locomotive) called the "Henry Clay" takes real mine cars to show you strip mining - where a "vein" of coal is discovered and dug out of the side of a mountain. Also stop by a relic "bootleg" coal mine where men risked life and the law during the Great Depression. They used these small illegal mines to get bags of coal to sell and heat their homes.

TUSCARORA STATE PARK

Barnesville - *687 Tuscarora Park Road (Off I-81, exit 131A, Hometown) 18214. Phone: (717) 467-2404. www.dcnr.state.pa.us/stateparks/findapark/tuscarora/ index.htm Admission: to PA State Parks is FREE however swimming, marina and camping/lodging fees apply, with reservation or entrance.*

This popular camping spot is heavily forested and the only cleared area is the 52-acre lake. Nestled against Locust Mountain, visitors will find many year-round recreational opportunities like boating and fishing, and opportunities to see wildlife. The hiking trails are short enough (most well under one mile) for younger ones to follow. A seasonal beach, swimming and boat rentals are available, too.

<u>LOCUST LAKE STATE PARK</u> is six miles upstream from Tuscarora. The park was developed as a family tent and trailer campground and has 282 campsites. Additional camper facilities include modern restrooms, swimming beach, boat rental, campstore, bicycle trail, hiking trails, fishing, playgrounds, and nature programs.

RICKETTS GLEN STATE PARK

Benton - *RR 2, Box 130 (PA Route 487) 17814. www.dcnr.state.pa.us/stateparks/ findapark/rickettsglen/. Phone: (717) 477-5675. Admission: to PA State Parks is FREE however swimming, marina and camping/lodging fees apply.*

A series of trails, covering a total of five miles, parallel the streams as they course down the Glens. A shorter hike of 1/2 mile, the Evergreen Trail, offers an excellent view of the final series of falls as it meanders through a majestic stand of giant hemlocks and white pine. Twenty-one waterfalls are along the Falls Trail within the Glens Natural Area, while one (Adams) is only a few hundred feet from the Evergreen Parking Lot off of PA 118. Take the Falls Trail and explore the Glens which boasts a series of wild, free-flowing waterfalls, each cascading through rock-strewn clefts in this ancient hillside. The 94-foot Ganoga Falls is the highest of 22 named waterfalls. Beach Trail: 0.8-mile, easiest hiking. Campers in both camping areas can access the Lake Jean day-use and swimming areas without having to travel on a road. Beach/ Swimming, Boat Rentals, Horseback Riding, Campsites, Modern Cabins.

Bethlehem

PENNSYLVANIA YOUTH THEATRE

Bethlehem - *211 Plymouth Street 18015. Phone: (610) 332-1400. www.123pyt.org.*

Pennsylvania Youth Theatre (PYT) is a nonprofit performing arts organization with the mission of educating, entertaining, and enriching the lives of young people and their families through the art of theatre. Productions for/by youth like Cinderella, Babes in Toyland and Charlie and the Chocolate Factory.

BETHLEHEM HISTORIC AREA

Bethlehem - *459 Old York Road (off SR378 - Historic area) 18018. Phone: (800) 360-8687. www.historicbethlehem.org. Hours: Daily, except Tuesdays & Christmas Admission: FREE (Walking self-guided tours). Guided, scheduled tours are $12.00-$20.00/person. Note: Best to visit during re-enacted history festivals around Christmas, Bach Festival in May, Celtic Festival in September or Musicfest in August.*

Points of interest include:

- <u>VISITORS CENTER</u> - Learn about Moravian Missionaries who first developed this town using pre-Revolutionary German architecture. Watch a video before you take a self-guided walking tour. Open daily until 5:00pm.

- <u>MORAVIAN MUSEUM</u> - 66 West Church Street. Can you imagine a 5 story log cabin, built without nails? Once used as a church, dorm and workshop, now it's a Moravian historical museum. (open Thursday-Sunday)

- <u>INDUSTRIAL QUARTER</u> - Start at the Luchenbach Mill (HistoryWorks! Children's interactive gallery located on the first floor), stop at a 1761 tannery or 1762 waterworks - the first pumped municipal water system in the colonies.

CHRISTMAS OPEN HOUSE

Bethlehem - Bethlehem Historic Area. Tours of decorated, historical buildings. Refreshments and musical entertainment. Admission. (Thanksgiving weekend thru weekend after New Years)

BLUEBERRY FESTIVAL

Bethlehem - Burnside Plantation, Schoenersville Road. www.historicbethlehem.org. Enjoy blueberry delights galore on a 250 year old restored Moravian farm. Crafts, demonstrations, children's activities, and special tours are featured. Petting Zoo, Pony Rides, Horse Drawn Carousel, RCN Pie eating contests, Colonial Games. Admission. (third weekend of July)

CELTIC CLASSIC HIGHLAND GAMES & FESTIVAL

Bethlehem - Historic Downtown Area. www.celticfest.org. Exciting & educational weekend celebrating the cultures of Ireland, Scotland, and Wales. Music, dance, bag piping, athletic competition, children's activities, and authentic vendors. FREE. (last full weekend of September)

CHILDREN'S MUSEUM, THE

Bloomsburg - *2 West Seventh Street 17815. www.the-childrens-museum.org. Phone: (570) 389-9206. Hours: Monday-Saturday 10:00am-4:00pm. Admission: $7.00 ages 3+. No admission fee for children two years old and younger.*

Explore, discover and have fun while learning with over 50 different interactive exhibits. Walk into an Egyptian Tomb, set jet balls in motion, track rain, snow, sleet and hail by radar (then give your own live TV broadcast), crawl underground, build a body, try on a spacesuit, brush some giant teeth, or go outside to the Butterfly Garden (seasonal). Although it's a children's museum, some areas focus on interactive history: explore a full-sized longhouse, sit in a classroom with a wood stove, pretend you're a pioneer at the general store and then take a tour of a mini-coal mine.

GRIM'S CORNY MAZE

Breinigsville - 9941 Schantz Road. www.grimsorchard.com. 4 acre maze. FREE Straw maze and corn box. Hayrides. Admission for maze. (Weekends, last week of September - last week of October)

PUMPKIN FALL FESTIVAL

Catawissa - Rohrbach's Farm Market. www.rohrbachsfarm.net. Petting zoo, refreshments, pumpkin patch, corn maze, pony or wagon rides. Flashlight nights too. (Corn Maze begins Labor Day weekend. Pumpkin Patch weekends in October)

IRON HERITAGE FESTIVAL

Danville - www.vanwagnermusic.com/danvilleheritage.html The Iron Age, 1829 thru 1950 and Danville, PA are truly synonymous. In 1829, the first Iron foundry was established in Danville to manufacture wagon boxes, plowshares, andirons sadiron and griddles. In 1839-1840 Iron Ore started to be mined locally and in 1840 the first Anthracite furnace to efficiently produce iron was opened in Danville. On October 8, 1845, the first T-rail in America was rolled out at the Montour Iron Works, the largest iron manufacturing plant in the United States. The T-rail made it possible for Pennsylvania and America to become the leader in the industrial revolution. This festival is a celebration of America's ingenuity.. Charcoal pit and iron ore tours and demonstrations, parade, costumed crafters and demos. Admission. (mid-July weekend)

WATER GAP TROLLEY

Delaware Water Gap - *Historic Castle Inn, 20 Delaware Ave, Rte. 611 (I-80, exit 310) 18327. Phone: (570) 476-9766. https://poconodaytripper.com/ Hours: Daily 10:00am-4:00pm (April-November). Admission: $25 adult, $20 child (2-12). Tours: All weather trolleys, narrated scenic, historical tour of area. 1 hour long. Trolley leaves every 1 1/2 hours (generally) Note: Picnic areas and miniature golf on premises to play as much as you want. Hole in 1 on 10 is a FREE Ice Cream.*

Replica streetcars take a relaxed tour of the Water Gap - Shawnee area where you can learn about Indians, early settlers, and some history. The first half of tour may be boring to kids but the second half stops at Chief Taminy's face formed from rough edges in the mountain rocks (like a natural profile - Mt. Rushmore). Also stop at the Cold Air Cave (regardless of the outside temperature; the air rushing out of the entrance to the small cave is always 38 degrees F. – your kids will say – really cool!). Now that you have a feel for the area, go wander back to some attractions you'd like to visit further or just have a picnic and play mini-golf.

Easton

CRAYOLA FACTORY

Easton - 30 Centre Square, Two Rivers Landing (Look for giant box of crayons on top at Two Rivers Landing) 18042. www.crayola.com/factory. Phone: (610) 515-8000. Hours: Monday-Friday 10:00am-4:00pm, Saturday-Sunday 10:00am-6:00pm. Closed Christmastime, New Years, Easter and Thanksgiving & first two weeks of January. Admission: $28.99 general (3+). Online discounts. Note: The Crayola Store - Colorful collection of anything using color to create is sold. Also area to try new products. Crayola Cafe eatery on premises. To get the most benefit from the full admission price, be prepared to do most of all of the activities (that includes you Mom & Dad)

The Crayola Factory is not the real manufacturing plant. Instead, it is a family

hands-on discovery center that not only provides live demonstrations on how Crayola Crayons and Markers are made but also has more than a dozen hands-on art activities for guests to create mementos of their visit. Each person is asked to learn and think "Outside the Lines" here. Do you know what celebrity molded the 100 billionth crayon? "Color on the Wall" - Go ahead, it's glass and is wiped clean easily. You can color, draw and create with the latest Crayola® product without the worry of cleanup afterwards. Hurry kids, this may be your only chance to break the rules! Everyone creates "their own souvenirs to take home".

Especially great is the Factory Floor exhibit where a worker mixes melted wax and colors to help you make your own souvenir crayons to take home. The most favorite color is red and our kids got to help put the wrappers on real (just manufactured) crayons. The Meltdown area allows you to actually paint with melted crayons or re-create Prints, Stamps and Sculptures in another exhibit. The Color Playground has a section for preschoolers that includes a ball play area with a series of tubes and bins that collect, sort and move colored balls from one location to another; and a soft play area for children ages two and under that includes a crawl space, oversized puzzle pieces and interactive panels. Older kids will like the Doodle in the Dark area where you experiment with color and light combinations.

Silly Selfies: Take selfies to a whole new level - become a robot unicorn, rockstar parrot or a zany pirate bunny. The Crayola Factory went through a redesign, adding two Animation Stations, a manufacturing theatre and new exhibits to give visitors an improved experience. Parents, it does get crazy in here, but if you go with the flow and start creating yourself...you CAN survive and have FUN!

HUGH MOORE CANAL RIDE PARK

Easton - 2750 Hugh Moore Park Road (off I-78 or off US22 to Lehigh Drive) 18042. Phone: (610) 559-6613. https://canals.org/visit/attractions/ Hours: Wednesday-Sunday 11:00am-4:30pm (April - September).
Weekends only in October & early June. Admission: $15 adult, $14 senior, $11 child (3-15). Tours: Costumed interpreter guides you on a 45- minute ride. Note: Canoes and pedalboats can be rented at the canal boat boarding area for use on the canal. Trails, picnic, boat rentals, gift shop.

The mule-drawn canal boat Josiah White II rides is on a restored section of the LeHigh Canal. The large boat and costumed drivers are carried by a mule or two (Hank & George). Why are mules better to use than horses or donkeys? Visit the Loctender's House Museum - lifestyle of his family and also a great view of the dam, lock, and bridge. You can also view the piers and cables of the Change Bridge, including the oldest machine-made wire rope in America.

Admission includes entrance to the EMRICK TECHNOLOGY CENTER. The Technology Center explores the Lehigh Valley's rich industrial heritage. Visitors will see the 26-ton stationary steam engine once used to power the Buehler Furniture Factory; learn the history of the paper drinking cup, the Dixie Cup Company and its founder, Hugh Moore; and view a World War I cannon produced by Bethlehem Steel.

LOCKTENDER'S HOUSE - Where the life and work of a locktender's family is shown by period room exhibits and costumed interpreters. You can also view the piers and cables of the Change Bridge, including the oldest machine-made wire rope in America.

CANAL FESTIVAL

Easton - Hugh Moore Canal Ride Park. Annual canal festival featuring canal boat rides, 19th century living history encampments and reenactments, Locktender's House tours, continuous music and entertainment, food. Parking $5.00. (last Sunday of June)

NATIONAL CANAL MUSEUM

Easton - *30 Centre Square (I-78, Easton exit & US22 - 3rd floor - Two Rivers Landing) 18042. Phone: (610) 559-6613. www.canals.org. Hours: Wednesday-Sunday 11:30am-4:30pm (mid-June thru September), Weekends only early June & October. Admission: Admission: $8 adult, $7 senior (65+), $6 child (3-15). Admission includes the Emrick Technology Center. Educators: Video on canals is online: www.delawareandlehigh.org/talesofthetowpath/*

The National Canal Museum is the only museum in the country dedicated to telling the story of America's historic towpath canals. Visit a short time in history before railroads, highways, and airplanes. Follow the story lines of immigrants and locals who built and ran the canals. Hear the boatman tell stories and sing canal songs. Walk through the middle of a full size replica boat. Hands-on exhibits help kids understand this mode of transport. Load up your cargo and take a journey down a 90-foot long model canal featuring locks and incline planes!

Actually operate a lock model and pilot your play boat through it. Don't miss the miniature train display and the interactive water table. Find out how boats float and how mules were able to pull boats weighing over 100 tons. Then dress up

Waterworks lock experiments

as socialites traveling the canal in luxury with Mr. Tiffany (of Tiffany glass in 1886). The Molly Polly Chunker was a luxury liner canal boat decorated in Victorian fashion. This is the best interactive way to truly understand canals and this brief era of time.

KNOEBEL'S AMUSEMENT RESORT

Elysburg - *391 Knoebels Blvd. (I-80 West to Bloomsburg exits 232, 236, 241. Rte. 232, PA 42 South to Catawissa & SR 487) 17824. www.knoebels.com. Phone: (800) ITS-4-FUN. Hours: Daily 11:00am-10:00pm (Summer). Weekends only (May & September). Admission: FREE. Pay-One-Price Plans are available for $1-$5.00 per ride. Ticket books save 10-15%. Would rather Pay-One-Price? For $34.00-$50.00, you can get a pass to nearly all the rides. Note: Pool and water slides. Games, entertainment. Restaurants. Gift shops. Mini-golf. Swimming and Camping. Overnight Cabin rentals.*

This is America's largest FREE admission park! Designed to allow every style of family to enjoy (and pay for) the rides they like best with 41 rides including the "Phoenix" - rated one of America's 10 best roller coasters. Knoebels recently built their own version of a "Classic" wooden ride called Flying Turns. This is a roller coaster like ride where you sit in a train and roll down a wood track much like a bobsled run. Just as many family rides as thrill or kiddie rides. Ride in the Antique Cars or get a birds-eye view from the Giant Wheel. Want a little more action? Try the Whipper or shriek in the Haunted Mansion. Compose yourself with a nice quiet ride on the Pioneer Train before you return home from a fun filled day at Knoebels. An extremely family-friendly, old-fashioned attraction!

Museums have been added to the park (free admission):

- KNOEBELS COAL MINING MUSEUM. Free admission to Knoebels' tribute to the anthracite coal mining industry.

- KNOEBELS HISTORY MUSEUM - View a time line and photo exhibit detailing the history of Knoebels. Located in the rear of the Mining Museum.

- KNOEBELS CAROUSEL MUSEUM - Learn about the history of the carousel in America and see examples of the work of all of the major carousel carvers.

LOST RIVER CAVERNS

Hellertown - *726 Durham Street (I-78, Exit 21, Rt. 412 South) 18055. Phone: (610) 838-8767. https://lostcave.com/ Hours: Year-round. 9:00am-6:00pm (Memorial Day-Labor Day), Rest of year closes at 5:00pm. Closed Thanksgiving, Christmas, and New Year's Day. Admission: $14.50 adult, $9.50 child (3-12).*

Lost River Caverns is a natural limestone cavern. It was discovered in 1883 by a limestone quarry operation which was digging where the parking lot now stands. At that time, the operation accidentally created the entrance to the cave. Since that is the only entrance to the caverns, they don't have any bats, rats or snakes or any Native Americans, dinosaurs or cavemen in the cave. Experience the wonder of abundant crystal formations, an underground river and five unique chambers. Moving through the cavern is the Lost River, whose clear waters mysteriously originate from an unknown source, then disappear once more beneath the earth's surface. One of the cavern rooms is a dedicated chapel, so visitors can even book Lost River for underground weddings or events. Guided walking tours take guests through beautiful crystal formations. Indoor tropical garden, rock museum and gift shop are on the premises.

MAUCH CHUNK LAKE PARK & ENVIRONMENTAL EDUCATION CENTER

Jim Thorpe (Summit Hill) - *151 E. White Bear Dr. 18250. Phone: (570) 645-8597. www.carboneec.org. Hours: Monday-Friday 8:00am-4:30pm. Park trails and raptor cages are open daily from dawn to dusk.* FREE

Located on the outskirts of historical Jim Thorpe, this County Park is perfect for that family getaway. While lodging at the park you can enjoy the art of Mother Nature on the 2.8 mile Mauch Chunk Lake, walk or bike the renovated Switchback Gravity Railroad and many other trails throughout the park, rent a boat, hike or stroll through the woods to the Environmental Center to see the birds of prey. Then unwind on the parks sandy beach.

Every visit brings you to the CARBON COUNTY ENVIRONMENTAL EDUCATION CENTER, where you'll see a spectacular collection of live birds of prey. This attraction is also a Pennsylvania-licensed wildlife rehabilitation center, so you may have an opportunity to see some of the state's wild residents up close while they recuperate. The center is housed in an old converted dairy barn; it occupies about 70 acres of woodland, wetland, and meadow habitat within Mauch Chunk Lake Park, so you're sure to see a good cross-section of Pennsylvania wildlife.

SPLIT ROCK RESORT

Lake Harmony - *1 Lake Drive (I-80 East to Exit 277 or I-476 to exit 95, follow Rte.940 East 18624. Phone: (717) 722-9111. (800) 255-ROCK (Lodge). Snow Report: (717) 722-9111. www.splitrockresort.com.*

Lodge with 2 indoor pools, whirlpools or sauna, 18 hole championship golf course, sail on beautiful Lake Harmony, mountain bike or hike to Hickory-Run State Park, or do some skiing. Three restaurants, a pizza parlor and water park snack bar provide multiple dining options. Longest Run: 1700 ft.; 7 Slopes & Trails.

H2O.O.O.O.H.H Indoor Family Waterpark is located adjacent to the Galleria at Split Rock Resort in Lake Harmony, PA. This complete indoor water park features attractions for all ages, including the Komodo Dragon - Pennsylvania's 1st indoor flow rider. Daredevils will want to try the Viper, Piranha And Amazon Blast slides, which drop 4 stories. The little ones will have a great time at the jungle falls & leapin' lizards play areas. The water park is open to the general public. Overnight accommodations are not required for use of the waterpark. Please bring your own towels...they do not supply them. Separate admission: ~$38.00 Adult, ~$33.00 Kids under 42 inches tall. $18.00 Passes for observers and seniors.

BELTZVILLE STATE PARK

Lehighton - *2950 Pohopoco Drive (US 209) 18235. Phone: (215) 377-0045. www.dcnr.state.pa.us/stateparks/findapark/beltzville. Admission: to PA State Parks is FREE however swimming, marina and camping/lodging fees apply, with reservation or entrance.*

Beltzville Lake is seven miles long and features fishing, swimming, water sports and unlimited horsepower boating. Along the shore, you can sometimes find fossils. A 525-foot sand beach is open from late-May to Labor Day, 8:00am to sunset. A hike along Wild Creek Trail leads to waterfalls and Sawmill Trail wanders through forests and by a creek. Beach, Boat Rentals, & Cross-Country Skiing.

BIG DIAMOND RACEWAY

Minersville - *(Near Forestville, off Rt. 901) 17901. www.bigdspeedway.net. Phone: (570) 544-6434. Hours: Fridays at 8:00pm (April-Labor Day). Nationals end of September weekend.*

Wide, banked, 3/8-mile clay oval located In Forestville, hosts NASCAR Series for Modifieds, Sportsman and Roadrunners. NASCAR - Winston Series Stock Car Racing.

Nazareth

MARTIN GUITAR COMPANY

Nazareth - *510 Sycamore Street (I-80 to SR33 South to SR191 South to North Broad to Beil St - Follow Signs) 18064. www.martinguitar.com. Phone: (610) 759-2837. Hours: Monday-Friday 8:00am-5:00pm (shop and museum). Closed Holidays and week of Christmas. Public Tours: Conducted at regular intervals between 10:00am and 2:00pm, Monday through Friday. First-come, first-served basis. $5.00 per person. Lasts one hour. Recommended for school-aged children and above because of length of tour. Note: Store w/ memorabilia, strings, & accessories.*

Founded in 1833, Martin guitars are known as "America's guitar". Used by many legendary performers, you'll start your tour in the museum shop of vintage guitars. Children are encouraged to "gently play" several guitars in the waiting area. If any of your children play the guitar, they will be especially interested in all the posters of famous performers who use Martins. Follow a guitar from rough lumber to a finished product which requires more than 300 steps to complete. The tour shows step-by-step production and is very educational. See the types of wood (cured for 4 months prior to production) used - from the usual to the exotic. Watch how each piece is computer-routed or bent in special jigs. Martin even makes their own strings to insure that "one of a kind" Martin sound. They've even produced a $50,000 custom order guitar with diamonds in the guitar neck! Sometimes famous performers stop by the Martin plant...maybe even on your tour!

> **DID YOU KNOW?**
> The company is the oldest surviving maker of guitars in the world.

BLUE MOUNTAIN SKI AREA

Palmerton - *1600 Blue Mountain Drive 18071. Phone: (610) 826-7700. Snow report: (800) 235- 2226. www.skibluemt.com.*

Since its opening in 1977, Blue Mountain has grown into one of the premiere skiing and snowboarding destinations in the Pocono area. The ski and snowboard area boasts the highest vertical in Pennsylvania, a half pipe, two terrain parks and night skiing. 1,082-foot vertical, plenty of trails for ALL abilities plus a half-pipe and two terrain parks. Longest Run: 6400 ft.; 29 Slopes & Trails plus snowboarding.

Poconos Area

JACK FROST MOUNTAIN & BIG BOULDER SKI AREAS

Poconos (Blakeslee) - *PO Box 707 (I-476 exit 95 or I-80 exit 284, head north to Jack Frost, head south to Big Boulder) 18610. www.jfbb.com. Phone: (800) 468-2442. Admission: per activity Note: Baby sitting provided. Choose from Poconos resorts' townhouses, condominiums, cabins, or campsites. SnowMonsters skiing and snowboarding programs are geared towards kids to teach them basic techniques and important safety tips in a fun environment! Chairlifts and SkiCarpets (make it easier for younger skiers to move up the mountains).*

Big Boulder was built on the site of the first commercial ski resort in Pennsylvania, and it was here that snowmaking was first used successfully in a commercial application. Five parks make Jack Frost/Big Boulder the premier destination for skiers and riders to come and test their skills. Visitors can ski two mountains for the price of one when they purchase a lift ticket.

- BIG BOULDER SKI AREA - Longest Run: 2900 ft.; 14 Slopes & Trails. Five family and seven single tubing chutes.
- JACK FROST SKI AREA - Longest Run: 2700 ft.; 21 Slopes & Trails.

POCONO SNAKE AND ANIMAL FARM

Poconos (East Stroudsburg) - *424 Seven Bridge Road. Route 209 (I-80 exit 309, US209 Northeast) 18335. Phone: (570) 223-8653. http://poconoanimals.com. Hours: Daily Noon-5:30pm, weather permitting. Admission: $8.00 to $12.00 (age 2+).*

Visit the "Great Little Zoo". They have over 100 animals including a giant Anaconda, Alligators, Emus, and Mountain Lions. Some of the most popular attractions include a 100 year old, 150 pound Alligator snapping turtle (ugly!), a giant python, Grey Wolves, and the beloved wolf Max whose best friend for over 13 years is a bear - watching them play is an unforgettable experience. Many of the animals are extra large for their species. The antics of the monkeys, or more engaging pot belly pigs, may make your kids "squeal". Petting and bottle-feeding areas, too. It's worth it to get the $2.00 cup of peanuts and fruit to feed the monkeys. Each visit is different as you never know what new animal may appear on the scene (or be left on their doorstep). They are designed to be visited in about an hour's time, a perfect interval for children.

GREAT WOLF LODGE RESORT & INDOOR WATERPARK

Poconos (Scotrun) - *1 Great Wolf Drive (just off I-80, Scotrun exit, Route 611 north) 18355. Phone: (800) 905-WOLF. www.greatwolflodge.com. Admission: Rates (include admission to waterpark) for lodging run $169-$300 per night depending on package. Note: want to save money? Check for off peak season specials and use the micro/frig in your room to prepare at least one meal per day.*

The 401-suite Great Wolf Lodge has an array of amenities including: a huge indoor Waterpark, an Arcade, Cub Club activity/crafts room, Spa, Fitness Room, the Camp Critter Bar & Grille, The Loose Moose Cottage gourmet buffet and food court, Claw Café confectionery and an animated Great Clock Tower to greet you. The Pocono Great Wolf indoor waterpark is the largest of any in the chain. They have a new, state-of-the-art water roller coaster ride that defies the law of gravity, winding up and down hill, and the cannon bowl tube ride, which offers a whirling water ride.

SNOWLAND

Poconos (Scotrun) - Great Wolf Lodge Resort. The lodge is decorated in a winter scene. It snows 3x daily, hot cocoa, live music, sing along, Storytime. North Pole University for Elves. Admission (includes lodging and indoor waterpark passes). (month-long in Dec)

SHAWNEE MOUNTAIN SKI AREA

Poconos (Shawnee-on-Delaware) - *PO Box 339 (Exit 309, Off I-80) 18356. Phone: (570) 421-7231. (800) VILLA-4-U. (Lodge). Snow Report: (800) 233-4218. www.shawneemt.com.*

SKIwee Bowl Teaching Area: This exclusive contoured teaching terrain, located between lower Bushkill Trail and Little Chief Slope, features new extended carpet lifts, colorful teaching aides, and automated snow-making.

- INCUBATOR TERRAIN PARK: The Incubator Park serves as a learning area for those Riders and Skiers not yet at a comfortable skill level to challenge the Bushkill Park.

- TANDEM SNOW TUBES: Shawnee's Pocono Plunge Snow Tubing Park has two person snow tubes able to accommodate one adult and one small child in the same snow tube.

22 Trails, Terrain Park, Snowboarding, "Pocono Plunge" Snow Tubing Park & Half-Pipe. Open Day & Night. Longest Run: 5100 ft. Comfortable rooms, dining, indoor pool/jacuzzi, & the only full-size indoor ice rink in the region.

Stroudsburg

QUIET VALLEY LIVING HISTORICAL FARM

Stroudsburg - *347 Quiet Valley Road (I-80 to exit 304, US209 SW (Bus Rte), right at Shafer's School House Road, left on Business Route 209. 18360. Phone: (570) 992-6161. www.quietvalley.org. Hours: Tuesday-Saturday 10:00am-5:00pm, Sunday 1:00-5:00pm (June 20-Labor Day). Admission: $10.00 adult, $5.00 child (3-12). Tours: 90 minute, costumed guided. Last tour leaves at 4:00pm. Educators: you'll find so many pre-and-post visit activities here: www.quietvalley.org/programs/schoolprograms/resources.htm. Even lesson plans, crosswords, quizzes, a story to tell and a field trip workbook.*

Meet a Pennsylvania Dutch family as they go about their numerous daily chores – pretend the time is the early 1800s. "Family" guides in period clothing share the daily routine of a typical Pennsylvania German family and its descendants who lived at this location from 1765 to 1913. There are fourteen buildings, including original and reconstructed, on the farm. Daily activities include spinning, weaving, smoking and drying meats, vegetables and fruits; cooking, gardening, and tending to animals. Kids can touch barnyard animals and jump in a giant haystack! Usually one craft is highlighted weekly - ex. quilting, butter churning, candle dips, basket making, natural wool dying (how do they get color naturally?) and blacksmithing. Actual aunts, uncles, cousins, and siblings escort you around the farm & treat you like visiting relatives.

HARVEST FESTIVAL

Stroudsburg - Quiet Valley Living Historical Farm. Tractor pulls, antique steam engines, parades, food (made with steam), threshing, baling, cider and apple butter making, hayrides, children's activities, petting zoo & fall crafts. Admission. (second weekend in October

OLD TIME CHRISTMAS FARM

Stroudsburg - Quiet Valley Living Historical Farm. Tours of decorated, historical buildings. Refreshments and musical entertainment. Tours led by lantern lights. Admission. (first two weekends in December)

DELAWARE STATE FOREST

Swiftwater - *HC 1, Box 95A 18370. Phone: (570) 895-4000. www.dcnr.state.pa.us/forestry/stateforests/delaware/*

Messing Nature Center leads to Trails, Horse Trails, ATV Trails (35 miles), Fishing, Cross-Country Skiing.

MAPLE SUGARING

Swiftwater - Delaware State Forest. Actual tapping of trees. Syrup making. Demonstrations of coopering and sugaring off in a realistic sugar camp. Pancakes and syrup served. Messing Nature Center area.

CAMELBACK LODGE & AQUATOPIA WATER PARK & CAMELBACK SKI AREA

Tannersville - *PO Box 168 (I -80, Exit 299) 18372. Phone: (570) 629-1661. www. camelbeach.com or http://skicamelback.com/. Hours: Waterpark open Daily at 10:00am (Summers). Weekends only (early Fall and late Spring). Skiing (December-March). Admission: Avg. $19.00 (twilight) to $39.00 (general).*

AQUATOPIA WATERPARK: the largest indoor waterpark in the Northeast has several never-before-seen attractions, such as the Venus SlydeTrap, a 608-foot-long, fully-enclosed family rafting experience with a record-breaking sphere and open 'manta' wall ride. The Great Kanagawa Wavepool features a snowcap-topped mountain, complete with a real Sno-Cat that uses thousands of LED light and sound effects to create the illusion of an avalanche plummeting into the pool. Bombora FlowRider lets guests ride the waves alone or with a partner. The Lost River is a vast departure from a typical lazy river, enthralling guests with an adventure river ride through the jungle into a mysterious temple to find clues before emerging into daylight and a 60-foot waterfall. New experiences include Venus SlydeTrap, a combo family raft ride; Kartrite's Quest, a next generation aqua play structure; and Storm Chaser, the longest uphill indoor water coaster in North America. The expansion also has an arcade, a 3200 foot long Alpine Slide, bumper boats, go-carts, mini-golf, chairlift rides, and assorted eateries including everything from pizza to waffles.

CAMELBACK SKI AREA: including 36 ski trails; the biggest snowtubing park in the U.S.A. with 42 lanes and a nightly Galactic LED light show experience. PA Ski & Winter Sports Museum is located here.

CAMELBEACH Pennsylvania's largest outdoor waterpark. 22 Water-slides-The most in the region featuring Kahuna Lagoon wave pool, two kids play zone, the Blue Nile Adventure River, bumper boats, mini golf, swimming pool, scenic chairlift & more.

MOUNTAIN ADVENTURES: Pennsylvania's only Mountain Coaster; North America's longest twin, 4,000 ft. zip-flyers.Treetop Adventure Course, Mountain Segways, Zip lines, Euro bungee & Climbing Wall. Call for package rates as they are not typically shown online.

OCTOBERFEST

Tannersville - Camelback. German music, dance, foods & cultural exhibits. "Um-pah-pah" bands & cloggers. Pumpkin painting and hayrides. FREE. (late October)

ECKLEY MINERS' VILLAGE

Weatherly - 2 Eckley Main Street (I-80 West to Exit 40 - SR940 West - then follow signs) 18255. Phone: (570) 636-2070. www.eckleyminers.org. Hours: Monday-Saturday 9:00am-5:00pm, Sunday Noon-5:00pm. Closed State Holidays except summer holidays. Admission: $4.00 adult, $3.50 senior (65+), $2.00 child (6-12). Tours: Guided tours available for small extra charge (recommended) in the summertime only. Note: Great supplement to a nearby tour of a coal mine.

What is a Patch Town? A patch was a cluster of a few dozen company houses along a crooked, unpaved street built within the shadow of black silt ponds and strip mining pits. See an actual town (only slightly restored) just as it appeared in a movie (in the 1970s). Retired miners, miner's widows, and children still live here. Watch a 15 minute video at the Visitor's Center first, then walk by audio displays of a typical miner's day or week (including church on Sunday). School-aged kids will want to take the tour which includes going inside a house (1870s - 1890s - notice all of the updates!), a company store, and a doctor's office. Just imagine having to be a young boy then, helping to support the family by being a "breaker boy" in the smoky, dangerous mill.

PATCH TOWN DAYS

Weatherly - Eckley Miners' Village. Family-oriented living history festival featuring street fair, coal mining and dance troupes, wagon rides, huge craft show with period demos, children's activities, and ethnic food. Admission. (third weekend of June)

HICKORY RUN STATE PARK

White Haven - RD 1, Box 81 (PA Route 534, I-80 exit 274) 18661. Phone: (717) 443-0400. www.dcnr.state.pa.us/stateparks/findapark/hickoryrun/. Admission: to PA State Parks is FREE however swimming, marina and camping/lodging fees apply, with reservation or entrance.

The Boulder Field, a striking boulder-strewn area, is a National Natural Landmark. This large park has over 40 miles of hiking trails, three natural areas and miles of trout streams. Every trail in the park can be hiked. Hiking-only trails have yellow blazes. Blue-blazed trails allow cross-country skiing and orange-blazed trails allow snowmobiling. While at the park, learn about lumbering history at the Visitors Center, observe wildlife or see Hawk Falls. A sand beach is open from late May to mid- September, 8:00am to sunset. Beach & Swimming, Sledding, and numerous Campsites.

JACOBSBURG ENVIRONMENTAL EDUCATION PARK

Wind Gap - *835 Jacobsburg Road (PA 33) 18091. Phone: (610) 746-2801. www.dcnr.state.pa.us/stateparks/findapark/jacobsburg/. Hours: The center office is open 8:00am-4:00pm, Monday through Friday. The center's main parking area on Belfast Road is open from sunrise to sunset, daily. Note: Heritage programming includes displays/demonstrations of early gunmaking at the Pennsylvania Longrifle Heritage Museum.*

Environmental Education Center offers many programs. Once the site where the famous Henry Rifle was made, the Jacobsburg National Historic District lies almost entirely within the park. Heritage programming includes displays and demonstrations of early gunmaking at the Pennsylvania Longrifle Heritage Museum, currently in the Henry Homestead. Henrys Woods offers scenic hikes and the rest of the center grounds have multi-use trails. Horseback Riding and Mountain Biking are most popular here.

AMERICAN FUR TRADE RENDEZVOUS

Wind Gap - Jacobsburg Environmental Education Park. Annual pre-1840s era living history encampment at Boulton historical gun and iron making community. Complete with knife and tomahawk throwing competitions, blackpowder shooting, primitive fishing and archery, hearth cooking, and all the sights, sounds and smells of real history! Crafts and trade goods available for sale. The Longrifle Museum open and scheduled tours offered of the 1834 John Joseph Henry House Museum both days. Admission fee for adults. (last weekend in October)

LENAPE NATION POW WOW

Wind Gap - Mountain View Park. www.lenape-nation.org. Native American singing and dancing. Arts and crafts. Native food storytelling and much more! Admission. (last weekend in September)

FRANCES SLOCUM STATE PARK

Wyoming - *565 Mt. Olivet Road (exit 170B of I- 81, take Rte. 309 North) 18644. Phone: (717) 696-3525. www.dcnr.state.pa.us/stateparks/findapark/francesslocum/. Admission: to PA State Parks is FREE however swimming/marina/camping/ lodging fees apply.*

The horseshoe-shaped lake provides 165 acres for boating and fishing. An environmental interpretive center located in the day use area features exhibits on American Indians and ecological topics. Deer Trail: yellow blazes, 1.3-mile, 2.5 miles, 3.8 miles This interpretive trail has three loops of varying lengths which allow you take a short walk or an adventure of almost four miles. Pool, Campsites, Boat Rentals, Ice Skating and Sledding.

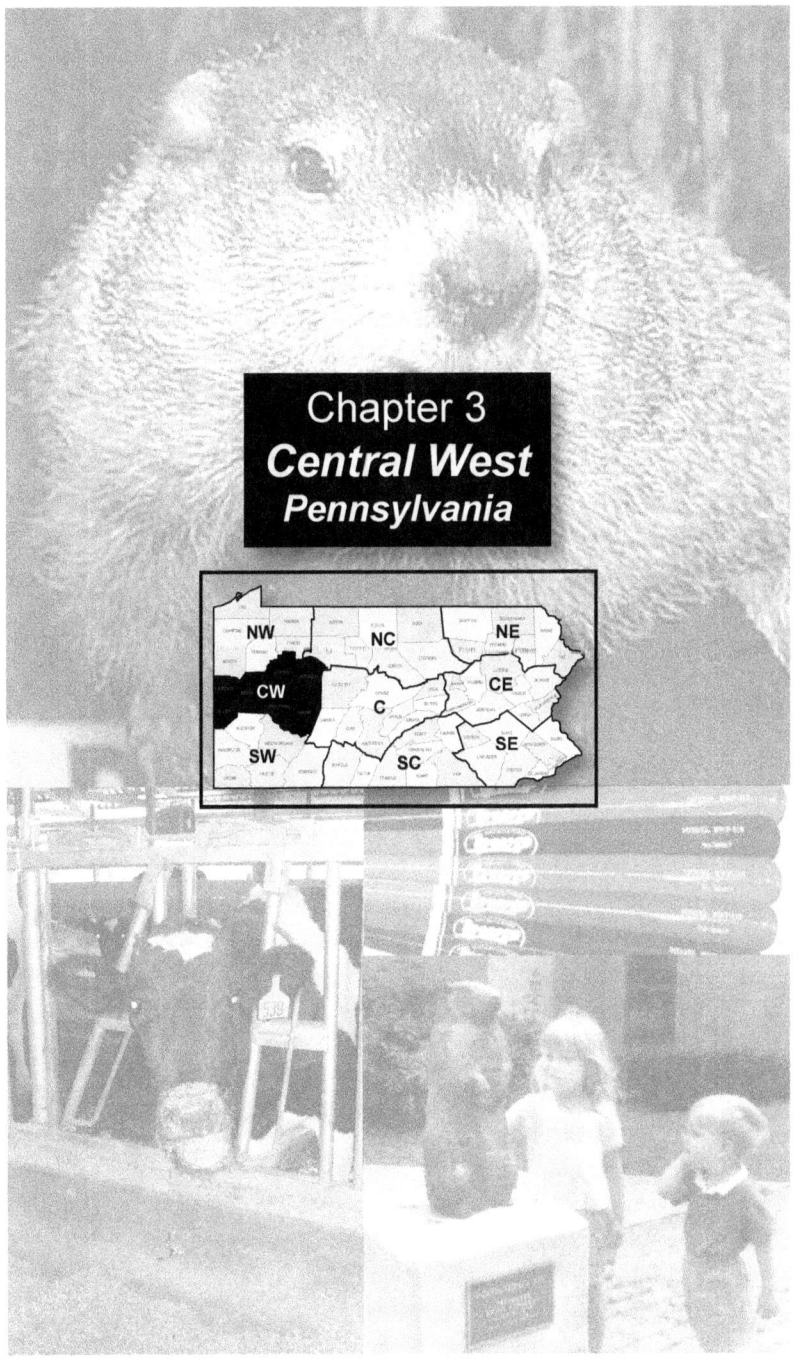

Chapter 3
Central West
Pennsylvania

Butler
- Playthings, Etc. Toy Store
- Butler County Museums
- Schramm's Fall Fest

Cooksburg
- Cook Forest State Park

Cooksburg (Clarington)
- Double Diamond Deer Ranch

Evans City
- Marburger Dairy Farm

Harmony
- Log Cabin Inn

Hookstown
- Raccoon Creek State Park

Indiana
- Jimmy Stewart Museum

Moraine
- Living Treasures Animal Park

New Castle
- Harlansburg Station's Museum Of Transportation
- Fireworks Capital Of America Fireworks Festival
- Cascade Of Lights

Penn Run
- Yellow Creek State Park

Portersville
- McConnell's Mill State Park
- Moraine State Park

Punxsutawney
- Punxsutawney Groundhog Zoo
- Weather Discovery Center
- Groundhog Day

Sigel
- Clear Creek State Park

Slippery Rock
- Jennings Environmental Education Center
- North Country Brewing Company

Valencia
- Harvest Valley Farms Fall Festival

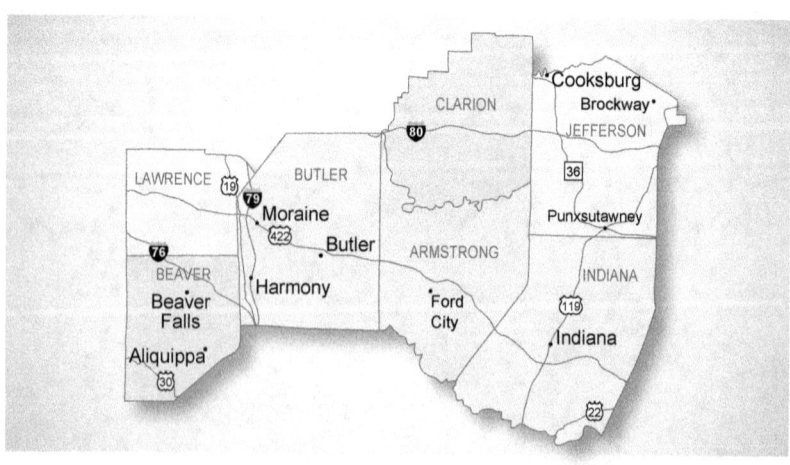

A Quick Tour of our Hand-Picked Favorites Around...

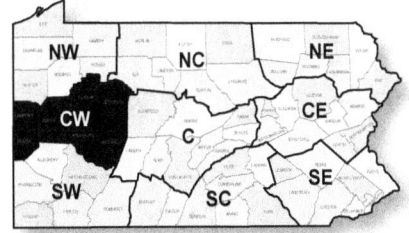

Central West Pennsylvania

This chapter contains many unpretentious towns – one famous little town and others that you may not have heard of. But that's what makes this area so special for families – no frills, just small town folks who allow you to explore their wares and nature in peace.

If the idea of exploring unique shops where you are allowed to touch EVERYTHING is appealing – **Playthings, Etc**. is the place. Don't worry about asking for directions, if you're along Rte. 8, north of Butler, you can't miss the giant silver spaceship building!

Another outdoor adventure can be scheduled at **Marburger Farms** where guests (best to schedule ahead) can come and learn about the giant barn full of Holstein cows and the milking parlor next door. Free milking observation is at 3:00pm each day. In neighboring towns, fresh local products can be found at a handful of Farmers Markets.

On Groundhog Day (February 2), the world looks for "Punxsutawney Phil" each year to peek out of his burrow on Gobbler's Knob and see if his shadow appears. His prediction indicates how much of the winter season is left. Phil and his descendants have been popping out every year since February 2, 1887. He and his family reside at a free **Punxsutawney Groundhog Zoo** in town. But that wasn't enough. These townsfolk realized kids enjoyed Phil so much; why not partner that interest with a **Weather Discovery Center**? Kids and adults alike pass through the door of a 12-foot tall tree stump and into Phil's famous burrow, completely immersing themselves in groundhog culture and science. Did you know this town is the Weather Capital of the World?

State Parks offer recreation and exploration. One park has a 400 ft. deep gorge with giant boulders. Others offer boating and beaches on property near Deer or Animal Parks. Hiking alongside ancient pines, prairies and creek beds is another option.

Sites and attractions are listed in order by City, Zip Code, and Name. Symbols indicated represent:

 Restaurants    Lodging

Butler

PLAYTHINGS, ETC. TOY STORE

Butler - *2483 William Flynn Hwy (7 miles north of Butler on SR 8) 16001. Phone: (724) 285-PLAY. www.playthings-etc.com. Hours: Monday-Saturday 10:00am-8:00pm (closed Sundays).*

If the idea of exploring unique shops where you are allowed to touch EVERYTHING is appealing – Playthings, Etc. is the place. Don't worry about asking for directions, if you're along Rte. 8, north of Butler, you can't miss the giant silver spaceship building! This is the World's Coolest Toy Store inside and out…mostly because, even in a short visit, we played with a plasma car, rubber band guns, an electric train table, pogo sticks (even one that's turbo), a water and sand table, and the largest slot car set we've ever seen. Kids like to play pretend? Let them go wild pushing brightly colored flashing buttons and gears at the space station. Families are encouraged to enjoy a long visit and to try out the many interactive toys inside. Their motto is so cool – "families that pray together and play together will stay together."

BUTLER COUNTY MUSEUMS

Butler - *Downtown 16001. Phone: (724) 283-8116. www.butlerhistory.com. Hours: open to the public Wednesdays, Thursdays and Fridays 11:00am-3:00pm, May through August and for special events. Admission: $5.00 adult, $2.00 youth ages 5-17.*

Country life at 3 different sites: <u>**COOPER CABIN**</u> - (off Rte. 356, Cooper Rd.). The 1810 cabin is still furnished with family heirlooms and memorabilia as well as other period pieces. Out buildings include a spinning house, spring house and tool shed. A self-guided nature trail winds through the more than four acres of land surrounding the cabin. There is also a model oil well and an extensive herb garden. <u>**SENATOR LOWRIE HOUSE**</u> - a summer residence for Butler's only U.S. Senator, Walter Lowrie (1828) at 123 West Diamond St. <u>**LITTLE RED SCHOOLHOUSE**</u> - (1838) living history museum on 200 Jefferson St. which recreates the one-room school experience for visitors and school classes.

CHRISTMAS OPEN HOUSE

Butler - Butler Heritage Center. Tours of decorated, historical buildings. Refreshments and musical entertainment. Admission

SCHRAMM'S FALL FEST

Butler - 291 Crisswell Road. www.schrammfarms.com. Petting zoo, refreshments, pumpkin patch, corn maze, pony or wagon rides. Scarecrows display. Admission. (weekends in October)

COOK FOREST STATE PARK

Cooksburg - *River Road - PO Box 120 (I-80 exit 78, PA 36 north) 16217. Phone: (814) 744-8407. www.dcnr.state.pa.us/stateparks/findapark/cookforest/ Admission: FREE however swimming, marina and camping/lodging fees apply.*

Virgin white pine and hemlock timber stands nick-named the "Black Forest". Highlights are the Forest Cathedral, Log Cabin Inn Visitor Center, Sawmill Craft Center and Theater, the Fire Tower and Seneca Point Overlook. Log Cabin Inn: Cook Forest's environmental learning center is a large log building built in 1934 by the CCC. It is at one end of Longfellow Trail and contains a variety of displays, taxidermy animals and logging tools from early lumbering days. Pool, Horseback Riding, Campsites, Rustic Cabins, Boating, Fishing, Cross-Country Skiing, Sledding and Snowmobiling. Several private canoe rentals are in the Cooksburg area.

DOUBLE DIAMOND DEER RANCH

Cooksburg (Clarington) - *12211 Route 36 (I-80, Brookville exit north on SR36, South of Cook Forest) 15828. https://www.facebook.com/double.diamond.deer. ranch/. Phone: (814) 752-6334. Hours: Daily 10:00am-Dusk (Memorial Day - Halloween). Weekends only (May & November). Admission: $8.00+ (age 5+). Note: A Buck Barn with stuffed animals is also on the property. Playground included: features a real fire truck, a police cruiser, a limo, A Big Rig, a tractor and slides.*

Photograph or watch white tail deer in natural habitats. Covered walkways, scenic trails, and a Museum & gift shop. In the summer months you can see the newborn fawns, plus the regular cast of characters including Tweety, an all white deer with blue eyes. Come see how tiny they are. Kids can help bottle feed the fawns at 2 and 6 p.m. That's also treat time for the adult deer who get apples and carrots." Bottle times" and "Treat Times" are scheduled in June, July and August. The deer do not drop their antlers until February, March and April. The last buck always sheds his antlers around April 15th.

MARBURGER DAIRY FARM

Evans City - *1506 Mars-Evans City Road (I-79 exit 83 east on Rte. 528. South on Rte 68 to Rte 309) 16033. Phone: (724) 538-4800. www.marburgerdairy. com. Tours: Group tours are scheduled ahead of time-usually afternoon milking time.*

Another outdoor adventure can be scheduled at Marburger Farms where guests (best to schedule ahead) can come and learn about the giant barn full of Holstein cows and the milking parlor next door. Free milking observation is at 3:00pm each day. The Marburger farm uses a 12 cow milking parlor; which means that they can milk 12 cows at a time. This farm milks over 150 cows which are fed by the surrounding fields of corn and hay. Be sure to wear your old clothes as you are on a real working farm! Off all the varieties of beverages they package, which is the most popular? Buttermilk. Want some recipes, go to the Recipes icon. We highly recommend their Buttermilk Waffles.

> **Did You Know?**
> A cow that eats only grass can make about 50 glasses of milk a day, but a cow that eats grass, corn, and hay can make about 100 glasses.

LOG CABIN INN

Harmony - 430 Perry Highway (just 5 minutes north of Zelienople on Rt. 19) 16037. Phone: (724) 452-4155. www.springfields.com/log-cabin-inn/. The Log Cabin Inn is just north of the hustle and bustle of Cranberry. Rural and rustic, it is built around a 160 year old cabin. The original dining room area floor is tilted and the logs are huge. Casual Dress. Relaxing atmosphere. Showing all Steeler football games and a great outdoor (heated) deck overlooking the 'Backwoods'. All American fare with children's menu complete with coloring and crayons. Daily, Lunch & Dinner. _____ 🍽️

Hookstown

RACCOON CREEK STATE PARK

Hookstown - *RD 1, Box 900 (3000 SR 18, or enter from US 22 or US 30) 15050. www.dcnr.state.pa.us/stateparks/findapark/raccooncreek/ Phone: (724) 899-2200. Hours: 8:00am-Sunset Admission: to PA State Parks is FREE however swimming, marina and camping/lodging fees apply, with reservation or entrance.*

A centrally located 100-acre lake provides opportunities for outdoor recreation like fishing, boating, and photographing and viewing waterfowl and other wildlife. Wild Flower Reserve (899-3611, Rte 30.) A 315 acre tract of land with over 500 species of wildflowers and wildlife. Frankfurt Mineral Springs - explore the reported "medicinal" properties of the water. There are many hiking trails scattered throughout the park, some only about one mile in length with moderate hills. The 800-foot, accessible sand/turf beach is open from late-May to mid-September, 8:00am-sunset. Visitor Center, Boat Rentals, Horseback Riding, Sledding, Winter Sports, Campsites, and Modern Cabins.

JIMMY STEWART MUSEUM

Indiana - *835 Philadelphia St (Indiana Public Library - 3rd Floor, corner of 9th) 15701. Phone: (724) 349-6112 or (800) 83-JIMMY. www.jimmy.org. Hours: Monday-Saturday 10:00am-4:00pm, Sunday & Holidays Noon-4:00pm. Closed Christmastime and New Years time. Admission: $9.00 adult, $8.00 senior (62+), military and students, $7.00 child (7-17).*

A legendary actor ("It's a Wonderful Life") who had accomplishments in film, radio and television plus civic and family roles. Displays of his great grandfather's uniform, baby photographs, furniture from the family hardware store, original movie posters, props and costumes. Watch films that are shown in a small 1930s vintage movie theatre most weekends.

FESTIVAL OF LIGHTS

Indiana - "It's A Wonderful Life". Blue Spruce Park. Jimmy Stewart's home town. See "Blue the Spruce Ness Monster". Sleigh and pony rides. Drive-thru. Admission. (Evenings-late November through New Year's Day)

LIVING TREASURES ANIMAL PARK

Moraine - *US422 16101. Phone: (724) 924-9571. www.ltanimalpark.com. Hours: Daily 9:00am-8:00pm (Summer). Daily 10:00am-6:00pm (April and May, September, October). Admission: $15.00 adult, $12.00 senior (62+), child (3-12).*

Perfect for the whole family, this large petty zoo features animals from around the world, including timber wolves, lambs, kangaroos, sheep, camels, llamas, pot belly pigs, yaks, zebras, monkeys, bears, turkeys, alligators, snakes and deer. Watch kangaroos, tigers and wolves and ride the miniature horses. Kids love the petting area (babies, reindeer, and camels) and feeding areas (bears, otters, monkeys, goats, sheep, alligators! giraffe! and llamas). Cups of animal feed are available in the gift shop or at coin-operated food dispensers throughout the park. They have a walk-through aviary too. Spring means babies at Living Treasures - even mini donkeys.

New Castle

HARLANSBURG STATION'S MUSEUM OF TRANSPORTATION

New Castle - *West Pittsburgh Road, 424 Old Rt. 19 (US19 & SR108) 16101. Phone: (724) 652-9002. www.harlansburgstation.com. Hours: Tuesday-Saturday 10:00am-5:00pm, Sunday Noon-5:00pm. Weekends Only (March, April, May, September, October, November, December) Admission: $4.00-$5.00.*

This is a story on the creation of one man's dream, his own personal museum that he now shares with the public. Olde time railroad station with display of real Pennsylvania railroad cars outside and memorabilia displayed inside the cars. Meet the mascot conductor and see lots of railroad uniforms. In the station are trains, cars, planes, trucks, and trolleys. The scale train layout depicts four scenes of Western Pennsylvania.

FIREWORKS FESTIVAL

New Castle - Downtown area. http://visitlawrencecounty.com/local-attractions/ featured-attractions/annual-fireworks-festival/ Children's activities, street dancing, musical entertainment, "Ducky Derby", Ice Cream Social, plus a Fireworks Spectacular. No Admission. (second or third Saturday of July).

CASCADE OF LIGHTS

New Castle - Cascade Park. www.newcastlepa.org/Events/events.html. Glistening lights. Visit with Santa. Hot chocolate. Freshly baked cookies. Toy/gift shops. Weekend entertainment. Admission. (Evenings - late November through New Year's Day)

YELLOW CREEK STATE PARK

Penn Run - *170 Route 259 Highway (PA 422 or PA 259) 15765. Phone: (724) 357-7913. www.dcnr.state.pa.us/stateparks/findapark/yellowcreek/. Admission: FREE however swimming, marina and camping/lodging fees apply.*

Yellow Creek State Park is in Indiana County along one of the first "highways" in the state, the Kittanning Path. This trail was used by the Delaware and Shawnee nations and by early settlers. Today, US 422 roughly follows the old Kittanning Path, and provides the main access to the park from Indiana and Ebensburg. The park is named for Yellow and Little Yellow creeks, which create the lake. The creeks have lots of yellow clay in the banks and bottoms. Laurel Run Trail is a 0.5-mile loop which starts at the park office. This easy hike is especially beautiful in the spring when wildflowers abound. Ridgetop

Trail is a challenging 2-mile trail. It begins in the beach/day-use area and winds through a variety of habitats. Damsite Trail is a 2.5-mile trail that offers a view of the Yellow Creek dam. Yurts: These four Mongolian-style tents are round, on a wooden deck and sleep five people in single bunks and double/single bunks. Yurts have a cooking stove, refrigerator, countertop, table, chairs, electric heat and outlets, fire ring and picnic table. Restrooms are nearby. The 800-foot beach is open from late-May to mid-September, 8:00am to sunset. Visitor Center, Boat Rentals, Sledding, Fishing, and Trails.

Portersville

MCCONNELL'S MILL STATE PARK

Portersville - RD 2, Box 16 (near the intersection of PA 19 and U.S. 422) 16051. www.dcnr.state.pa.us/stateparks/findapark/mcconnellsmill/. Phone: (724) 368-8091. Admission: FREE but swimming, marina and camping/lodging fees apply.

A 400 ft. deep gorge with giant boulders and unique eco-system. Slippery Rock Creek flows through the gorge. The steep-sided gorge contains numerous rocky outcrops, boulders, old growth forest, waterfalls and rare plants. Cleland Rock Vista is a great place to view the gorge. You can tour the restored rolling gristmill or the covered bridge. There is also scenic hiking, whitewater boating and two rock climbing and rappelling areas. Historical Center, sledding, boating, fishing, swimming, biking, camping, skiing, and snowmobiling. The park is open sunrise to sunset, daily.

HERITAGE FESTIVAL

Portersville - McConnell's Mill State Park. The festival celebrates the operational era of the Old Mill (1852-1928). Visitors can witness artisans and craftspeople making art and try old time games and crafts. Other activities include mill tours, corn grinding demonstrations, musical entertainment, a Civil War encampment and food vendors. (last full weekend in September)

MORAINE STATE PARK

Portersville - 225 Pleasant Valley Road (bisected by PA Route 422 running east/ west and PA 528 running north/south) 16051. Phone: (724) 368-8811. www.dcnr. state.pa.us/stateparks/findapark/moraine/. Admission: to PA State Parks is FREE however swimming, marina and camping/lodging fees apply.

Moraine State Park is the third largest park in Pennsylvania so you know they'll have plenty to do for the outdoorsy type. There are 10 boat launches around Lake Arthur and sailing is very popular for races and regattas.

At the Crescent Bay Area, sailboats, rowboats, paddleboats, canoes, kayaks, motorboats and pontoon boats may be rented in the summer. Guests who want to be passengers vs. participants can take a pleasant ride around Lake Arthur by sightseeing pontoon boat during warm weather season (www. morainepreservationfund.com, $5.00-$7.00 sightseeing cruises). On tour, you'll learn about the osprey and other wildlife that linger around the water's edge. The park has a nice beach open summers and many hiking and biking trails that meet the needs of a family just wanting a short ride or walk. Look for the nesting Bald Eagles? Of special interest is the Frank Preston Conservation Area and a 7-mile paved bike trail that winds around the north shore of the lake. Also on premises: Visitor Center, Horseback Riding, Mountain Biking, Modern Cabins, and Winter Sports.

Punxsutawney

PUNXSUTAWNEY GROUNDHOG ZOO

Punxsutawney - *300 East Mahoning Street, off Barclay Sq.@ Library (I-80 to exit 97, US119) 15767. Phone: (800) 752-PHIL. www. groundhog.org. Hours: Zoo: (Dawn to Dusk). Admission: FREE Note: All around the town, colorful, whimsical, 6-foot tall fiberglass Phantastic Phils! adorn the public spaces of the Weather Capital of the World. Each of the large fiberglass groundhogs is an individual work of art created by artists from across the state and the country. FREEBIES: Printable Puzzles, games and activities are found here: www.groundhog.org/index.php?id=66.*

On Groundhog Day (February 2), the world looks for "Punxsutawney Phil" each year to peek out of his burrow on Gobbler's Knob and see if his shadow appears. His prediction indicates how much of the winter season is left. The legend was brought to this country by German immigrants. Phil and his descendants have been popping out every year since February 2, 1887. He and his family reside at this zoo. Look for the awning marked, "Phil's Burrow".

We suggest you watch the movie "Groundhog Day" starring Bill Murray prior to your visit to get into the spirit of things! Phil gets almost as much mail as Santa Claus and on Groundhog Day up to 35,000 people come to see him each year! (they have pictures to prove it). It's worth a trip anytime of the year to meet a live groundhog up close ... your family may be surprised how they can change their shape to fit around the landscape.

WEATHER DISCOVERY CENTER

Punxsutawney - *201 North Findley Street (one block off the main street in Punxsutawney) 15767. Phone: (814) 938-1000. www.weatherdiscovery.org. Hours: Thursday-Sunday 11:00am-3:00pm. Open summer Wednesdays. Admission: $8.00 per person.*

The Weather Discovery Center excites and educates visitors about the old and new ways of predicting and studying weather. Kids and adults alike pass through the door of a 12-foot tall tree stump and into Phil's famous burrow, completely immersing themselves in groundhog culture and science. Have you ever seen a tornado from the safety of inside? Tried your hand at being a TV meteorologist? Make

> **DID YOU KNOW?**
> Punxsutawney is the "Weather Capital of the World".

a "Perfect Storm" with your friends--it's electrifying! "Twist & Shout" your way right into a tornado! Through interactive, hands-on exhibits, visitors learn about tornadoes, thunderstorms, meteorology, winds, weather folklore and more. A theater shows weather videos for the extreme weather fans in all of us, and a weather-themed gift shop is in the building.

GROUNDHOG DAY

Punxsutawney - Downtown. (800) 752-PHIL. www.groundhog.org. Join thousands of Phil's faithful followers for his annual prediction. Fun for everyone. What many people don't know is Groundhog Day is just the culmination of an entire weekend of family-friendly activities - most of which are completely free of charge. For instance, kids can explore the science behind meteorology and even try their hand at forecasting (just like Phil) at the Weather Discovery Center. There's the Groundhog Zoo, where kids can meet Phil before his big day. All weekend, there's storytellers, facepainting, ice carving, and more. Hours vary. (morning of February 2)

CLEAR CREEK STATE PARK

Sigel - *RR 1, Box 82 (1-80 to exit 73) 15860. Phone: (814) 752-2368. www.dcnr. state.pa.us/stateparks/findapark/clearcreek/. Admission: to PA State Parks is FREE however swimming, marina and camping/lodging fees apply.*

Set along the Clarion River, Clear Creek is a cozy getaway and a canoeist's paradise. Whether you bring your own canoe or rent one, a popular activity is the 11-mile trip from Clear Creek to Cook Forest State Park.

Rustic log and stone cabins are nestled among ancient pines and hemlocks, making this park the place to spend a secluded, rustic vacation. For a unique experience, try yurts: The two round, Mongolian-style tents are on wooden decks and sleep four people in bunk beds. Yurts have a cooking stove, refrigerator, countertop, table, chairs, electric heat and outlets, fire ring, picnic table and are adjacent to a water pump. The park also has a Beach, Visitor Center, Historical Center, Boat Rentals, Sledding, Campsites, Fishing, Winter Sports, and Trails.

Slippery Rock

JENNINGS ENVIRONMENTAL EDUC CTR

Slippery Rock - *2951 Prospect Road 16057. www.dcnr.state.pa.us/stateparks/ findapark/jennings/. Phone: (724) 794-6011. Hours: Daily, Dawn - Dusk. Educational Center Monday-Friday 8:00am-4:00pm. Admission: FREE. Note: Hiking trails. Picnic areas. Maple Sugaring (tapping trees, syrup making, pancakes!) each mid-March.*

This park's main attraction are the surviving remnants of a Midwest Prairie. A unique attraction at the center is its relict prairie, which includes the spectacular and well-known prairie flower, the blazing star. The relict prairie ecosystem is rare in Pennsylvania. In late July, blooms of blazing star (wild prairie flowers) along with other assorted wildflowers of all varieties are full peak color. Due to the glacial activity, the ground is mostly clay and only supports growth of thin grasses and plants. Community programs present various environmental topics in an informative and entertaining way through slide presentations, trail walks and public workshops.

NORTH COUNTRY BREWING COMPANY

Slippery Rock - 141 S Main St (I-79 exit 105 - three miles east) 16057. Phone: (724) 794-2337. http://northcountrybrewing.com. Like root beer or cream soda? Homemade sodas (and in-house brews) all honor the area with local names everyone recognizes as it flows 10 feet and into your mug. Try some at North Country Brewing Company restaurant in the quaint little college town of Slippery Rock. Sunday's are great for family get togethers. Hardly anything on the menu is prepared the way you're used to so come here hungry (big portions) and adventuresome. We'd recommend an entree prepared with their brews. If you like meat - boy do they have it - especially burgers - and with some homemade sauces or sides. Seafood and pasta available, too. Best time to come with the kiddos? Lunch or Sundays. Note: after dark, the place is very crowded with more of a social scene. Open daily for lunch and/or dinner. The owner is so "go green" he told us he composts all his scrap produce (leftovers from plates), has a grass roof, uses biodegradable straws, recycled wood for tables, and moved to a farm where he'll raise beef cattle and chickens to serve as entrees!

HARVEST VALLEY FARMS FALL FESTIVAL

Valencia - 125 Ida Lane (off Rte 8). www.harvestvalleyfarms.com. Petting zoo, refreshments, pumpkin patch, corn maze, pony or wagon rides. Entertainment on weekends. FREE. (weekends, end of September thru October)

Chapter 4
North Central
Pennsylvania

Austin
- Sinnemahoning State Park
- Elk State Forest/Visitor Ctr

Cross Fork
- Ole Bull State Park

Emporium
- Bucktail State Park
- Sizerville State Park

Galeton
- Cherry Springs State Park
- Lyman Run State Park

Galeton (Coudersport)
- Pennsylvania Lumber Museum

Hughesville
- Crystal Lake Ski Center

Hyner
- Hyner Run State Park

Johnsonburg
- Bendigo State Park

Millerton
- Draper's Super Bee Apiaries

Morris
- Ski Sawmill Mountain Resort

Renovo
- Kettle Creek State Park

Wellsboro
- Hills Creek State Park
- Leonard Harrison State Park

Williamsport
- Hiawatha Riverboat Tours
- Lycoming County Museum - Taber Museum
- Reptiland, Clyde Peeling's
- Little Pine State Park

Williamsport, South
- Little League Museum

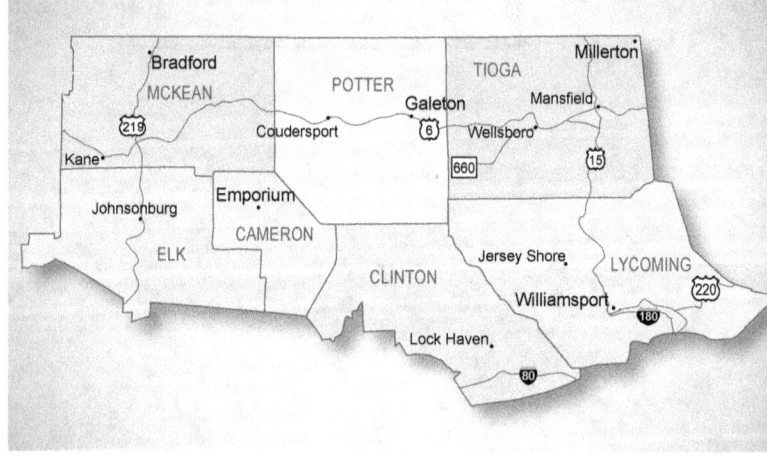

A Quick Tour of our Hand-Picked
Favorites Around...

North Central
Pennsylvania

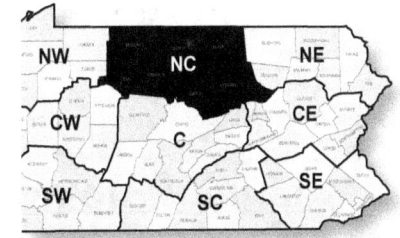

Here, you can wish upon a star in Cherry Springs State Park, Pennsylvania's first dark sky preserve, and hike or bike the Pine Creek Gorge, Pennsylvania's Grand Canyon. Camping is also popular here; many state and national parks offer wilderness buffs the opportunity to get back to nature and even do some whitewater rafting. Imagine more than two million acres of public lands set aside for your enjoyment offering unlimited recreational opportunities.

The "Grand Canyon" of Pennsylvania begins just south of Ansonia, along U.S. Route 6 and continues south for about 47 miles. At **Leonard Harrison** and **Colton Point State Parks**, the depth of the canyon is about 800 feet and these park locations have the most spectacular scenic overlooks. Well worth the drive off the beaten path for the scenic views! If your children are able, we suggest hiking one of the trails up or down the gorge. If not, the Overlook Trail is a short .6-mile loop taking you to Otter View, a vista looking south with good photo ops.

This area is all natural and several family-run nature and animal parks have sprung up. **Draper's Super Bee Apiaries** is one "sweet spot." Every visit warrants a view of the observation hive (don't worry, it's enclosed in safety glass). On tour, you'll learn about different products produced from beehives. Hopefully, you'll be able to get to a bee site, help extract some honey, and then take a taste test.

In Williamsport your family can visit with reptiles or take a Hiawatha Trolley or Paddleboat tour past lumber baron mansions. Of course, the main attraction in town is the **Little League Museum**. The birthplace of Little League is host to the world championship (nationally televised-last weekend in August). From its humble beginnings in 1939 through today and its 3 million participants in over 90 countries, the museum is a tribute to Little League Baseball. Learn about the legends, swing the bat or test your arms pitching.

Did you know Pennsylvania once had a prosperous lumber heritage? The **Pennsylvania Lumber Museum** displays 3000+ objects including old-fashioned logging tools and a logging locomotive. The best part of the visit is the short walk to the preserved remains of, a once very busy, logging camp.

Sites and attractions are listed in order by City, Zip Code, and Name. Symbols indicated represent: 🍽 Restaurants   🛏 Lodging

SINNEMAHONING STATE PARK

Austin - *8288 First Fork Road (junction of PA 872 and US 6 or PA 120) 16720. https://www.dcnr.pa.gov/StateParks/FindAPark/SinnemahoningStatePark/Pages/ default.aspx. Phone: (814) 647-8401. Admission: to PA State Parks is FREE however swimming, marina and camping/lodging fees apply, with reservation or entrance.*

The diverse habitat supports the American eagle, black bear and white-tailed deer. Interpretive pontoon boat rides on George B. Stevenson Reservoir are available during the summer to allow a closer look at lake wildlife. Boating, Fishing, some Trails, Modern Campsites, and one Modern Cabin.

ELK STATE FOREST/ELK COUNTRY VISITORS CENTER

Austin - *PO Box 367 (on US 6) 16915.* www.experienceelkcountry.com

ELK STATE FOREST: Principally in Elk and Cameron Counties, the 200,000 acres of forest land are open to hunting, fishing and general recreation. Within Elk State Forest is a portion of the Quehanna Wild Area, which is south of Sinnemahoning. The Quehanna Trail System provides access for primitive-type forest recreation limited to day use activities and backpack hiking.

ELK COUNTRY VISITORS CENTER. Situated on 245 acres within the heart of Pennsylvania's elk range and within the Elk State Forest, the Elk Country Visitor Center opened in 2010 as the premier elk watching and conservation education facility in the eastern United States. The Center offers state-of-art interpretive and interactive exhibits that inform and educate the public about elk and wildlife conservation.

OLE BULL STATE PARK

Cross Fork - *Box 9 (PA Route 144) 17729. Phone: (814) 435-5000. https:// www.dcnr.pa.gov/StateParks/FindAPark/OleBullStatePark/Pages/default.aspx. Admission: FREE but swimming, marina and camping/lodging fees apply.*

The park area is referred to as the Black Forest of Pennsylvania. Its dense tree cover and mountainous terrain attracts thousands of campers along Kettle Creek. Ole Bull Trail leads to the historic foundation remains of Ole Bull's "home site" and a panoramic view of the park area. The Beaver Dam Nature Trail provides an introduction to the habitats along Kettle Creek. This 0.75-mile trail starts at the concrete fordway and has a flat trail surface. The 85-mile Susquehannock Trail System passes through Ole Bull State Park. The beach is in Camping Area 1 across from the picnic area. The 150-foot sandy beach along Kettle Creek is open from late-May to mid-September, 8:00am to sunset. Modern Cabin rental, Fishing, Trails, and Cross-Country Skiing.

BUCKTAIL STATE PARK

**Emporium - RD 1, Box 1-A (Route 120) 15834. Phone: (814) 486-3365. https://
www.dcnr.pa.gov/StateParks/FindAPark/BucktailStateParkNaturalArea/Pages/
default.aspx. Admission: to PA State Parks is FREE however swimming, marina
and camping/lodging fees apply.**

Hemmed in by mountains, this state park scenic drive follows PA Route 120 as it winds from Lock Haven to Emporium along the West Branch of the Susquchanna River and the Sinnemahoning Creek. It stretches through a narrow valley which has for years been called the Bucktail Trail, named after the famous American Civil War regiment of Woodsmen, the Bucktails or Bucktail Rangers. This is the old Sinnemahoning Trail used by American Indians on their way to and from the eastern continental divide between the Susquehanna and Allegheny rivers. Aside from the three towns named above, the valley is mostly forested land with an occasional small village or isolated farm. The scenic drive has no recreational facilities. In June, the mountain laurel is in bloom and in early October the fall colors are breathtaking. Boating permitted, Fishing, and some Trails.

SIZERVILLE STATE PARK

**Emporium - RD 1, Box 238-A (PA Route 155) 15834. Phone: (814) 486-5605. https://
www.dcnr.pa.gov/StateParks/FindAPark/SizervilleStatePark/Pages/default.aspx
Admission: to PA State Parks is FREE however swimming, marina and camping/
lodging fees apply.**

The Bottomlands, Campground and North Slope trails take the visitor through a variety of lowland habitats and are relatively easy to walk making them ideal for hikers of any age. The Sizerville Nature Trail is a three-mile loop that nearly everyone can enjoy. It has educational stopping points. Maps are available in the park office.

Nady Hollow Trail is a 1.5-mile loop that ascends a 1,900-foot mountain. The "Cutback" section takes the hiker halfway up the mountain and then, gradually runs down along the mountainside. Due to the slope of this trail, it is more challenging. Sizerville State Park is also a trailhead for the Bucktail Path Trail, which is part of an extensive trail system throughout the northern tier region of central Pennsylvania. Within the park, you will find beautiful white pines, hemlocks, spring wild flowers, a butterfly garden and flaming fall foliage in early October. Pool, Visitor Center, and Campsites.

Galeton

CHERRY SPRINGS STATE PARK

Galeton - *RD 1, Box 136 (PA Route 44 - Potter County) 16922. Phone: (814) 435-5010. https://www.dcnr.pa.gov/StateParks/FindAPark/CherrySpringsStatePark/Pages/default.aspx. Admission: to PA State Parks is FREE however swimming/marina, camping/lodging fees apply.*

Cherry Springs State Park is nearly as remote and wild today as it was two centuries ago, a haven for campers who like to rough it and who can appreciate one of the finest scenic drives in Pennsylvania. Its dark skies make it a haven for astronomers. The Susquehanna Trail passes nearby and offers 85 miles of backpacking and hiking. Public Stargazing Saturdays.

CHERRY SPRINGS WOODSMAN SHOW

Galeton - Cherry Springs State Park. www.woodsmenshow.com. Lumberjack competition and horse pulling contest. Entertainment, displays, food. No Admission. (first weekend of August)

LYMAN RUN STATE PARK

Galeton - *545 Lyman Run Road 16922. Phone: (814) 435-5010. https://www.dcnr.pa.gov/StateParks/FindAPark/LymanRunStatePark/Pages/default.aspx. Admission: to PA State Parks is FREE however swimming, marina and camping/lodging fees apply.*

Lyman Run State Park has been carved from the Susquehannock State Forest. The shaded picnic area is popular for picnicking and hiking, and the lake is a fishing hot spot. Beach, Campsites, Fishing, Trails.

Hiking is available on many trails in the **SUSQUEHANNOCK STATE FOREST**, though the main trail is the Susquehannock Trail System, an 85-mile loop through the forested hills and valleys of the region. During the summer months, a 43-mile-ATV trail is available within Susquehannock State Forest. The trail passes through Lyman Run State Park, where parking and sanitary facilities are located. 261,784 acres of Fishing, Trails, Winter Sports, and ATV Trails.

PENNSYLVANIA LUMBER MUSEUM

Galeton (Ulysses) - 5660 US 6 West (just west of PA 449) 16948. Phone: (814) 435-2652. www.lumbermuseum.org. Hours: Wednesday-Sunday 9:00am-5:00pm (April-November). Winters Fri-Sun 10am-4pm. Closed state holidays. Admission:

$5.00-$8.00 (age 5+). Note: The museum is set in the heart of the Susquehannock State Forest, where an abundance of State Parks, campgrounds, rental cabins and motels are available for an overnight stay.

Pennsylvania once had a prosperous lumber heritage with its wealth of white pine and hemlock trees. Now on display, are 3000+ objects including old-fashioned logging tools and a logging locomotive. Interactive exhibits in the Visitor Center simulate activities such as swinging an ax, sawing a tree, piloting a log raft and racing locomotives for a hands-on experience with history. The best part of the visit is the short walk to the preserved remains of, a once very busy, logging camp. See the huge sawmill (buzzing logs that have floated down river), mess hall, dormitories, rails, and engines used for transport. The well kept operational facility is extremely interesting and educational. By 1920, why did they blow the final whistle and leave?

Courtesy of Pennsylvania Historical & Museum Commission

BARK PEELER'S CONVENTION

Galeton - Pennsylvania Lumber Museum. Annual woods festival. Events include crafts, music, saw milling, woodhick demonstrations. Contests: birling, fiddling, tobacco spitting, frog jumping. Admission (weekend before or after July 4th)

CRYSTAL LAKE SKI CENTER

Hughesville - 1716 Crystal Lake Rd (off US 220) 17737. Phone: (570) 584-2698. Snow Report: (570) 584-4209. www.crystallakeskicenter.com.

The facilities include an unusual natural setting of 960 acres of mountain woodlands at elevations from 1550 to 2100 feet, several lakes and ponds, dining facilities for up to 200 in a modern, fully winterized dining hall, lodging for up to 180 in the winter months and recreational facilities. Cross-country skiing, ice skating and snowshoeing.

HYNER RUN STATE PARK

Hyner - Box 46 (Hyner Run Road, PA 1014) 17738. Phone: (717) 923-6000. https://www.dcnr.pa.gov/StateParks/FindAPark/HynerRunStatePark/Pages/default.aspx. Admission: to PA State Parks is FREE however swimming, marina and camping/lodging fees apply.

The terrain of the park is level and occupies the small valley created by Hyner Run, with steep mountains on both sides. The park is entirely surrounded by **SPROUL STATE FOREST**. Hyner Run State Park and Hyner View State Park are in the heart of the 276,764-acre Sproul State Forest. There are many miles of scenic state forest roads, foot trails, snowmobile trails and scenic overlooks. The very first purchase of public lands by the Commonwealth is not far from the park on the Young Womans Creek at Bull Run, where a monument commemorates this event. Pool, Campsites, one Modern Cabin, Fishing, Winter Sports, and Trails. Horse Trails, ATV Trails (32 miles). Hang gliding is a popular activity at the park. Hang gliders take off from the scenic vista and sail out over the West Branch of the Susquehanna River.

BENDIGO STATE PARK

Johnsonburg - 533 State Park Road (four miles northeast of Johnsonburg on SR 1004) 15845. https://www.dcnr.pa.gov/StateParks/FindAPark/BendigoStatePark/Pages/default.aspx. Phone: (814) 965-2646. Admission: to PA State Parks is FREE however swimming, marina and camping/lodging fees apply.

Located in a valley on a bank of the East Branch of the Clarion River, a charming streamside picnic area sits amidst a mixture of hardwood trees. A trout stream provides ample opportunities for anglers and the swimming pool is a big hit in summer. Sledding. Kinzua Bridge (very high railroad bridge).

DRAPER'S SUPER BEE APIARIES

a bee...hard at work making honey...

Millerton - 32 Avonlea Lane (SR15 & SR238. Follow signs. Close to NY border) 16936. Phone: (570) 537-2381. www.draperbee.com. Hours: Monday-Friday 8:00am-4:30pm, Saturday 8:00am-1:00pm. Closed winter Saturdays. Admission: FREE. Tours: Vary per day. Can accommodate any group but they prefer a call in advance for larger groups. Note: Gift shop with honey products and bee keeping equipment for sale.

Every visit warrants a view of the observation hive (don't worry, it's enclosed in safety glass). On tour, you'll learn about different products produced from bee hives. Hopefully, you'll be able to get to a bee site, help extract some honey, and then take a taste test. TIDBITS - Wildflower honey has the most nutrients (why?); the Queen Bee lays 2000 eggs per day (the larva are what bears really love!). Speaking of bears, can you guess how they keep the "locals" away from their outdoor hives? Learn why honey is liquefied in a "hot room" and not boiled. Learn how to identify the difference between worker bees, male drones, and the Queen. An extremely family-oriented, educational, and helpful (health-wise) tour given by people who care deeply about what they do. Well worth the trip into the "Endless Mountains".

SKI SAWMILL MOUNTAIN RESORT

Morris - *383 Oregon Hill Rd (Rte. 220 to Rte. 287) 16938. Phone: (570) 353-7521. Snow Report: (800) 532-SNOW. www.skisawmill.com.*

They have 12 slopes and 3 lifts. Peak elevation is 2,215 feet and base elevation is 1,770 feet - giving a vertical drop of 515 feet. There is also a terrain park adjacent to the double chairlift. Beginner area and tubing area. New in summer/ fall season for groups will be: Paintball Rentals, Mountain Bike Rentals, and Canoe Trips down the pine creek. Also ask about hay rides, bonfires, archery classes and more off-peak season.

KETTLE CREEK STATE PARK

Renovo - *Box 96 (SR 4001) 17764. Phone: (717) 923-6004. https://www.dcnr.pa.gov/ StateParks/FindAPark/KettleCreekStatePark/Pages/default.aspx Admission: to PA State Parks is FREE but swimming, marina and camping/lodging fees apply.*

A 250-foot sandy beach area is open from late-May to mid-September, 8am to sunset. Horseback, Sledding, Campsites, Fishing, Trails, Winter Sports.

HILLS CREEK STATE PARK

Wellsboro - *RD 2, Box 328 (US Route 6 or PA Route 287) 16901. Phone: (717) 724-4246. https://www.dcnr.pa.gov/StateParks/FindAPark/HillsCreekStatePark/Pages/ default.aspx Admission: to PA State Parks is FREE however swimming, marina and camping/lodging fees apply, with reservation or entrance.*

Osprey, loon and waterfowl visit the lake that boasts a variety of warm water fish species. A sand beach is open from late-May to mid-September, 8:00am-to sunset. Lake Side Trail - 1.5-mile - This trail begins at the entrance to the camping area and follows the lake shore in a westerly direction for about one mile, finally arriving at the Beaver Hut Boating Area. A beaver house plus many signs of beaver activity may be seen in this area. Camping, camping cottages, modern cabins, yurts, and picnicking. Visitor Center and Boat Rentals.

LEONARD HARRISON STATE PARK

Wellsboro - *RR 6, Box 199 (take PA Route 660 west from Wellsboro for 10 miles) 16901. Phone: (717) 724-3061. https://www.dcnr.pa.gov/StateParks/FindAPark/ LeonardHarrisonStatePark/Pages/default.aspx Admission: FREE however swimming, marina and camping/lodging fees apply. Note: The environmental interpretive center, at the main overlook entrance, is open during the summer season through the fall foliage season. A video and educational displays interpret the area and its wildlife. Water, soda and juice vending machines are available from late April to late October.*

The "Grand Canyon" of Pennsylvania begins just south of Ansonia, along U.S. Route 6 and continues south for about 47 miles. At Leonard Harrison and Colton Point State Parks, the depth of the canyon is about 800 feet and these park locations have the most spectacular scenic overlooks. Well worth the drive off the beaten path for the scenic views! If your children are able, we suggest hiking one of the trails up or down the gorge. If not, the Overlook Trail is a short .6 mile loop taking you to Otter View, a vista looking south with good photo ops. There is no bridge across Pine Creek at the bottom. A beautiful vista is one-half mile down the Turkey Path Trail. Shortly after the vista, there is a scenic waterfall along the path on Little Four-Mile Run. The Turkey Path Trail, including steps, observation decks and hand rails. The Pine Creek Trail runs through the bottom of the gorge and provides great bicycling. Bring along quarters (for viewers) or binoculars to get detailed views. Rustic camping and Canoe/Raft liveries threaded throughout the park system.

Williamsport

HIAWATHA RIVERBOAT TOURS

Williamsport - *Susquehanna State Park (Docked at Arch Street - US220 to Reach Road Exit - Follow signs) 17701. https://www.facebook.com/hiawatha. paddlewheelriverboat/ Phone: (570) 326-2500. Hours: Tuesday-Sunday, 1:00, 2:30, and 4:00pm. (Summer). Weekends Only in May, Sept & October. Admission: $8.50 adult, $8.00 senior (60+), $4.50 child (3-12). Online coupon. Tours: 1 hour*

An old-fashioned paddlewheel boat cruises along the river as your narrator tells tales of the river when "lumber was king". Snacks and gifts are available on board. Tuesday night is "Family Night" during the summer (reduced family rates) and feature a "make your own ice cream sundae."

LYCOMING CTY TABER MUSEUM

Williamsport - *858 West 4th Street 17701. www.tabermuseum.org. Phone: (570) 326-3326. Hours: Tuesday-Friday 9:30am-4:00pm, Saturday 11:00am-4:00pm, Sunday 1:00-4:00pm. Closed Sundays (November-April). Admission: $9.50 adult, $7.50 senior, $6.00 child (3-12).*

Over 12,000 square feet of exhibits include the history of lumbering, The LaRue Shempp model train exhibit, an American Indian gallery, and period rooms. This unique model train exhibition, one of the finest in the U.S., also features two working layouts for visitors to operate and enjoy. Peek through the windows of a re-created general store to see some of the things people needed, wanted, or thought were extravagant. Visit a one-room school to view a collection of inkwells, slates, and books that illustrate children's education at the turn of the 19th & 20th centuries. See a blacksmith shop and a working gristmill. A changing art gallery is on the premises, also.

REPTILAND, CLYDE PEELING'S

Williamsport (Allenwood) - *18628 US 15 (I-80 exit 210B head north 6 miles) 17810. Phone: (570) 538-1869 or (800) REPTILAND. www.reptiland.com. Hours: Daily 9:00am-6:00pm (Summer). Daily 10:00am-5:00 or 6:00pm (September-May). Admission: $20.00 adult, $16.00 child (3-11) Shows: Every 90 minutes beginning at 10:30. Note: Enjoy a healthy selection of hot and cold sandwiches and salads at Crocodile Creek Café*

A visit to Reptiland explodes common myths and inspires scientific curiosity. The indoor exhibit complex allows comfortable viewing of more than 40 species in recreated natural habitats.

During summer months, Cobras, alligators, pythons, vipers are all slithering around in a tropical garden setting. Visitors experience daily feedings and touch a variety of reptile skins to feel the difference between turtles, snakes and crocodiles. You even get to touch a real snake! Meet "Big Boy" the alligator or poison dart frogs. Shows reveals the close-up world of reptiles and there's often live demos.

LITTLE PINE STATE PARK

Williamsport (Waterville) - *Box 100 (four miles north of PA 44 at Waterville and eight miles south of PA 287) 17776. https://www.dcnr.pa.gov/StateParks/ FindAPark/LittlePineStatePark/Pages/default.aspx. Phone: (570) 753-6000. Admission: to PA State Parks is FREE however swimming, marina and camping/ lodging fees apply, with reservation or entrance.*

Little Pine State Park is located in one of the most beautiful sections of the **TIADAGNTON STATE FOREST** in the Appalachian Mountains. A sand beach with grass turf is open from late-May to mid-September, 8:00am to sunset. Boat Rentals, Sledding, Campsites, Camping Cottages, Yurts, Fishing, 14 miles of Trails, and Winter Sports.

LITTLE LEAGUE MUSEUM

Williamsport, South - *525 Montgomery Pike, US 15 17702. www.littleleague.org/learn/museum.htm. Phone: (570) 326-1921. Hours: Thursday-Monday 9:00am-4:00pm. Admission: $8.00 adult, $5.00 senior (62+), $4.00 child (4-16). Note: The museum is next to the Little League International Headquarters and overlooking the Howard J. Lamade Little League World Series Stadium.*

The birthplace of Little League is host to the world championship (nationally televised-last weekend in August). From its humble beginnings in 1939 through today and its 3 million participants in over 90 countries, the museum is a tribute to Little League Baseball. Learn about the legends, swing the bat or test your arms. Actually "Play Ball" in the batting and pitching areas, and then watch your form on instant replay. Experience the running track, push-button quiz panels, and the opportunity to do your own play-by-play commentary on a World Series game. Learn about nutrition that will help you play your best. Watch videotaped highlights of the most exciting moments of the Little League World Series. Uniforms, balls, gloves, bats, etc from different baseball eras shows how much the sport has grown. And, if you've never seen how a ball, bat and glove are made - they have a display on the process of making them.

Chapter 5
North East
Pennsylvania

Beach Lake
- Carousel Water And Fun Park

Bushkill
- Bushkill Falls

Dalton
- Lackawanna State Park

Estella
- Endless Mountains Winterfest/ Sled Dog Races

Forksville
- World's End State Park

Hamlin (Lake Ariel)
- Claws And Paws Animal Park

Hawley
- Lake Wallenpaupack

Milford
- Grey Towers Historic Site
- Waterwheel Café

Poconos (Bushkill)
- Delaware Water Gap Area
- Pocono Indian Museum

Poconos (Greentown)
- Promised Land State Park

Poconos (Long Pond)
- Pocono Raceway

Scranton
- Electric City Trolley Museum
- Lackawanna Coal Mine
- Steamtown Nat'l Historical Site
- Pennsylvania Anthracite Heritage Museum
- Sno Mountain Ski Area
- Houdini Tour & Magic Show
- Everhart Museum
- La Festa Italiana

Scranton (Moosic)
- Scranton/Wilkes-Barre Yankees

Tobyhanna
- Tobyhanna State Park

Towanda
- French Azilum Historic Site

Troy
- Mt. Pisgah State Park

Union Dale
- Elk Mountain Ski Area

Wilkes-Barre
- Wilkes-Barre/Scranton Penguins Hockey

A Quick Tour of our Hand-Picked Favorites Around...

North East Pennsylvania

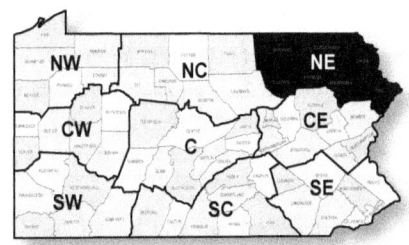

A Northeastern Pocono Mountains family vacation is a wonderful location for families to reconnect in an escape environment not like home. Among the family attractions include a NASCAR raceway or go-carting at one of the family fun parks.

For a more laid back family experience, sightseeing on horseback or taking a ride on America's first locomotive on the Stourbridge line may be fun. **Steamtown** is a land of wonderment for young conductors at heart. It looks like the site popped out of a Thomas Train movie – especially the roundhouse. This fully restored roundhouse and turntable are incredible to watch. As the Baldwin #26 enters the yard, it stops on the turntable, advances to the correct "house" where it sleeps for the night.

The Northeast Pennsylvania Mountains Region is chock-full of wildlife, so if you love communing with cuddly critters, this is the place for you! For 40 miles the Middle Delaware River passes between forested mountains with barely a house in sight. Then the river cuts through the mountain ridge to form the famed **"Delaware Water Gap."** Also in the Bushkill area is the "Niagara of Pennsylvania" – **Bushkill Falls** with its eight waterfalls and Native American village home. Trails and bridges lace the area and the trails are manageable for young families on a scavenger hunt for scenic "bests."

Stretching over miles along the Delaware River, you'll find extremely scenic roads and trails to wander along. This area takes you up around Hamlin and beyond to the forests and nature centers that some of Pennsylvania's wildest residents call home – in nature or in a delightful interactive animal park called **Claws and Paws**.

Sites and attractions are listed in order by City, Zip Code, and Name. Symbols indicated represent: 🍽 Restaurants   🛏 Lodging

CAROUSEL WATER AND FUN PARK

Beach Lake - *1018 Beach Lake Hwy (Rte 6 East to Honesdale, then Rte 652 East) 18405. Phone: (570) 729-7532. www.carousel-park.com. Hours: Daily 1:00pm-9:00pm (late spring to late summer). Waterslides close at 5:00pm. Admission: Free Parking, Free Admission. Pay one price ticket ($14.00-$22.00) or pay per activity ($2.50-$5.00).*

Water slides (regular and juvenile), Go-karts, bumper boats, water slides, kiddie-kars and mini-golf all included in our pay-one price ticket. Also available: hardball and softball batting range, arcade and snack bar.

BUSHKILL FALLS

Bushkill - *Bushkill Falls Road (I-80 to Exit 309 - SR209 North) 18324. Phone: (888) 628-7454 or (570) 588-6682. www.visitbushkillfalls.com. Hours: 9:00am - 5:00-7:00pm (April-November). Basically closes before dusk sets in. Due to weather conditions, some trails may be restricted partly or in full. Admission: $17.00 adult, $16.00 senior (62+), $10.00 child (4-10). Additional $3.00 for adults on weekends/holidays. Mini golf, gemstone mining, trail guide and adventure maps, fishing and*

paddleboats are additional small fee. Note: Check out the Pennsylvania Wildlife Exhibit, fish Twin Lakes, visit a variety of gift shops, stop at the Fudge Kitchen for delectable sweets in the Wagon Wheel Pavilion, take a paddle-boat ride, or enjoy a round of miniature golf. Additional activities run $3-$5.00.

"The Niagara of Pennsylvania," has eight waterfalls. The main falls include Upper Canyon (craggy glen), Bridle Veil Falls (long, misty), Laurel Glen (mountain laurel wildflowers), Pennell Falls and Main Falls (over 100 foot cliff). Trails and bridges lace the area. Visitors may take part in a new Map Adventure while they hike. An official trail map that is especially detailed and accurate has been developed. The map includes 20 "control points" that can be found on the trails. When five, ten, or twenty locations have been found and verified with a unique punch, the hiker becomes eligible for a monthly prize drawing. Waterfalls are just the beginning of your visit to Bushkill Falls. Step into a Native America long-house and experience the Lenni Lanape Native

Americans longhouse exhibit where kids can walk into an Indian home with "beds" - pretty neat! Plan to spend at least one-half day here.

LACKAWANNA STATE PARK

Dalton - *RD 1, Box 230 (I-81 exit 60, travel 3 miles west on PA Route 524) 18414. Phone: (570) 945-3239. https://www.dcnr.pa.gov/StateParks/FindAPark/ LackawannaStatePark/Pages/default.aspx Admission: to PA State Parks is FREE however swimming, marina and camping/lodging fees apply, with reservation or entrance.*

Includes Salt Spring - a 36 acre natural area with old-growth hemlocks, streams and 3 waterfalls. Also Archbold Pothole - world's largest geological pothole - 38 ft. deep, 42 ft. wide. There is a campground, organized group tenting sites and a pool. Boaters and anglers enjoy the 198-acre Lackawanna Lake, and Kennedy Creek. This park is a favorite of canoeists, hikers, nature enthusiasts and campers. A series of looping trails wander through the campground and day use areas of the park, and additional loops explore forests, fields, lakeshore areas and woodland streams. Biking, skiing, and snowmobiling.

ENDLESS MOUNTAINS WINTERFEST SLED DOG RACES

Estella - Camp Brule. Phone: (570) 836-5431. Sled dog teams compete for cash prizes. Mid-distance and sprint races. Food, displays. Admission. (Last weekend in January or first weekend in February)

WORLD'S END STATE PARK

Forksville - *PO Box 62 (PA Route 42 from 1-80, then to Rte. 184) 18616. Phone: (570) 924-3287. https://www.dcnr.pa.gov/StateParks/FindAPark/WorldsEndStatePark/ Pages/default.aspx. Admission: to PA State Parks is FREE however swimming, marina and camping/lodging fees apply, with reservation or entrance.*

Virtually in a class by itself, this wild, rugged and rustic area seems almost untamed. Camping, rustic cabins and hiking on the Loyalsock Trail attracts many visitors. Be prepared for rocky pathways. Use proper hiking footwear. The scenery is spectacular, especially the June mountain laurel and Fall foliage. Canyon Vista, reached via Mineral Spring and Cold Run Roads, has outstanding views. Beach, Horseback Riding, Visitor's Center, Fishing, Boating, Horse Trails, and Winter Sports.

World's End State Park is adjacent to the **LOYALSOCK STATE FOREST** and offers hiking, hunting fishing and other outdoor recreation. 570-387-4255.

CLAWS AND PAWS ANIMAL PARK

Hamlin (Lake Ariel) - *1475 Ledgedale Road (SR590 East - then follow signs) 18436. Phone: (570) 698-6154. www.clawsnpaws.com. Hours: Daily 10:00am-6:00pm (May- mid- October). Admission: $22.50 adult, $21.50 senior (65+), $19.50 military, $17.50 child (2-11). Note: Snack bar. Gift shop. Picnic Area. Large walk-in petting zoo. Dino dig, lorikeet and giraffe feeding, and Turtle Town interactive.*

When was the last time you saw a parrot ride a bike or you got to pet an alligator? This "zoo in the woods" in the Pocono Mountains region offers unique hands on activities for the entire family. "Get Close to the Animals" is their theme...and you will! Many cages have glass front enclosures - so animals can walk right up to your face and you're still protected. During posted times, you can feed giraffes using a long stick or hand-feed fruits and vegetables to Lory Parrots (colorful, small, tame parrots). The animals are comfortable with visitors and they're not bashful about getting close to get a good nibble from your snack-filled hands. During the summer months they have unique Performing Parrot shows and Wildlife Encounter shows. Claws n' Paws features more than 120 unique species of animals, including a white tiger, black panther, and African lion, as well as educational programs and demonstrations throughout the day.

LAKE WALLENPAUPACK

Hawley - *US 6 18428. https://www.poconomountains.com/plan-your-vacation/explore-our-area/lake-wallenpaupack/ Phone: (570) 226-3191*

Located in the Poconos, it's the third largest lake in the state, offering a diversity of water recreation activities.

- RITZ COMPANY PLAYHOUSE - (570) 226-9752. www.ritzplayhouse. com. 512 Keystone Street.

- BOAT TOURS - US6, Gresham Landing. www.wallenpaupackboattour. com. (June - October). Sit back and relax on a patio boat. Enjoy a cruise on picturesque Lake Wallenpaupack as your tour guide describes the area and the history behind this charming region. Daily scenic tours for 50 minutes. Tour boats run daily from 11am to 6pm on weekends from May-October and daily from June 15 through Labor Day. Adm: $14-$19.00.

- TRIPLE "W" RIDING STABLE RANCH - Beechmont Drive - off Owego Turnpike. (570) 226-2670 or www.triplewridingstable.net. Horse ranch and western riding trips from one hour to overnight camping ($25 - 100+). Overnight accommodations at Double "W" Bed and Breakfast.

Milford

GREY TOWERS NATIONAL HISTORIC SITE

Milford - *151 Grey Towers Drive (84 East to Exit 46, Milford. Bear right off ramp onto Highway 6 East) 18337. Phone: (570) 296-9630. https://www.fs.usda.gov/ greytowers Tours: Tours of the mansion and surrounding gardens are conducted Thursday-Monday at 11:00am and 2:00pm from Memorial Day wkend - October 31. Fees are: $8.00 adult, $7.00 senior, $5.00 youth (12-17). Under 12 are FREE.*

Grey Towers is the ancestral home of Gifford Pinchot, first chief of the US Forest Service and twice Governor of Pennsylvania. House and garden tours are offered every day from Memorial Day weekend through October 31. A guided tour of the mansion and grounds is an interesting and unique way to learn about how one family shaped and influenced our conservation ideals and values, while experiencing what life might have been like at Grey Towers in the early 20th century. The one hr. guided tour takes the visitor through three first-floor rooms of the mansion and several garden areas. Other Grey Towers activities include short hiking trails, on-site programs, and conservation education programs for all ages.

CHRISTMAS OPEN HOUSE

Milford - Grey Towers National Historic Site. Tours of decorated, historical buildings. Refreshments and musical entertainment. Admission.

WATERWHEEL CAFÉ

Milford - 150 Water Street (off US6 - follow signs) 18337. www.waterwheelcafe. com. Phone: (570) 296-2383. Hours: Daily 8:00am-5:00pm (May-October). Other times of year, by season. Weekend (Thursday-Sunday) evening dinner served by reservation. An early 1800s water-powered gristmill still operates and you can watch the giant water wheel turn which drives a series of shafts, gears, and pulleys. Through the glass walls of the café, you can see the stones and grain milling equipment at work. Water rushes over the three-story high waterwheel, driving a series of shafts, gears, pulleys and belts that power the stones and grain milling equipment. A self-guided tour enables you to understand this whole fascinating process. Sit down and enjoy whole grain pancakes, muffins, and scones or multi-grain bread sandwiches. _____ 🍽️

Poconos Area

DELAWARE WATER GAP NATIONAL RECREATION AREA

Poconos (Bushkill) - *(I-80 to US209 north along the Delaware River) 18324. Phone: (570) 588-2451. www.nps.gov/dewa. Admission: Park Entrance no fee. Only for guarded beaches & falls and boat ramp access (April-October). Generally $10.00 per vehicle. Educators: The Many Faces of Delaware Water Gap program curriculum outline is found here: www.nps.gov/dewa/forteachers/ curriculummaterials.htm.*

For 40 miles the Middle Delaware River passes between low forested mountains with barely a house in sight. Then the river cuts through the mountain ridge to form the famed "Water Gap." Stretching over miles along the Delaware River, you'll find extremely scenic roads and trails to wander along. Great canoeing & rafting (some short - kid friendly), fishing, skiing, and snowmobiling. (For updated information call 1-800-POCONOS or www.800poconos.com).

*   <u>DINGMAN'S FALLS</u> - A flat boardwalk trail, accessible to wheelchair-users, leads through a hemlock ravine to the base of Dingmans Falls (1/2 mile round-trip, no climb.) From the base of the falls, a steep climb of 240 steps reaches the top of the falls. Rangers give guided walks to the falls on summer weekends at 2:00 p.m. Dingmans Falls is on Johnny Bee Road, which is just south of the traffic light on Route 209 in Dingmans Ferry PA (milepost 13). www.nps.gov/dewa/planyourvisit/dingmans-falls.htm.

*   <u>BUSHKILL VISITOR'S CENTER</u> - Daily 9:00am-5:00pm (summer). Weekends only in late spring and early autumn.

*   <u>RAYMONDSKILL FALLS</u> - A 1/4-mile round-trip hike leads through a hemlock ravine to the Upper Falls. (70 ft. climb) The Middle Falls are a 1/2-mile round-trip, using steep, uneven stairs (150 ft. climb.) Raymondskill Creek at the bottom of the ravine is a 1 mile round-trip with a steep ascent on the return (200 ft. climb.) Directions: Raymondskill Road is a sharp left turn, if northbound on Route 209, just north of milepost 18.

Both Visitor's Centers offer "ranger picked must sees" during each season. They also have a Junior Ranger program which includes a kid's self-guided exploring booklet. During the summer, rangers present programs just for kids, as well as family campfire programs and guided walks suitable for children.

POCONO INDIAN MUSEUM

Poconos (East Stroudsburg) - *5905 Milford Road (SR209 North off I-80 exit 209) 18302. Phone: (570) 588-9338. https://www.facebook.com/PoconoIndianMuseum/ Hours: Daily 10:00am-5:30pm. Extended summer hours. Admission: $7.00 adult, $3.50 child (age 6-16). Free arrowhead with each child admission.*

The museum recreates the life of the Delaware Indians from B.C. to the contact period with Europeans to post American Revolution. You will be given an audio device which will guide you step by step through the museum in great detail. See their lifestyle through homes (some made of bark - and you thought they only lived in tee-pees!), weapons, and kitchen pottery. Most of these items were unearthed in the Delaware Water Gap. Boys like the "150 year old scalp" and buying an authentic "peace pipe".

PROMISED LAND STATE PARK

Poconos (Greentown) - *RD 1, Box 96 (PA Route 390) 18426. Phone: (717) 676-3428. https://www.dcnr.pa.gov/StateParks/FindAPark/PromisedLandStatePark/Pages/default.aspx Admission: to PA State Parks is FREE however swimming, marina and camping/lodging fees apply. Boat Rentals, Rustic Cabins, Fishing, and Winter Sports.*

Promised Land lies in the heart of the Poconos. Two lakes, campgrounds, many hiking trails and beautiful scenery make the park popular in all seasons. There are about 50 miles of hiking trails in Promised Land State Park and the surrounding state forest, providing access to many natural scenic places. Hike Bruce Lake Road to a natural glacial lake, or see the little waterfalls along Little Falls Trail, or walk a loop around Conservation Island. A seasonal museum explores CCC contributions and area wildlife. There are two sand beaches that are open from late-May to mid-September, 8:00am to sunset.

POCONO RACEWAY

Poconos (Long Pond) - *184 Sterling Road 18344. Phone: (800) RACEWAY. www.poconoraceway.com.*

Pocono Raceway has long been recognized as one of NASCAR's most competitive raceways. Pocono's unique 2.5 mile track features three turns, each with its own degree of banking. Home of the tricky triangle. NASCAR 2.5 Mile super speedway - NASCAR racing, mid-June and early August.

Scranton

ELECTRIC CITY TROLLEY MUSEUM

Scranton - *300 Cliff Street (on the grounds of the Steamtown National Historic Site, I-81 exit 185) 18503. Phone: (570) 963-6590. www.ectma.org/museum.html. Hours: The trolley museum is open daily 9:00am-4:00pm, except Christmas, New Years and Thanksgiving Day. Special excursions for holidays. Admission: Average $5.00-7.00 museum fee. $8.00-$10.00 fee for trolley ride. Combo rates are $10.00-$12.00. Tours: During the operating season (May-October), trips are scheduled four days a week at 10:30am, 12:00 Noon, 1:30pm and 3:00pm, Thursday thru Sunday.*

A late 19th century mill building serves as the museum. Trolleys are exposed for viewing and rides. Interactive displays, where visitors will actually generate electricity and learn how this energy form is harnessed to serve transportation needs. The Electric City, a hands-on interactive kids exhibit, puts children in the operator's seat of a recreated open-style trolley car as they view a model trolley in operation on a suspended track.

- TROLLEY EXCURSIONS: The scenic route follows a portion of the former Lackawanna & Wyoming Valley Railroad right-of-way as it parallels Roaring Brook and makes stops at the Historic Iron Furnaces and continues through the Crown Avenue Tunnel. At 4747 feet long, the tunnel is one of the longest interurban tunnels ever built.

LACKAWANNA COAL MINE

Scranton - *McDade Park (I-81, Exit 57B or 51 – follow signs) 18503. Phone: (570) 963-MINE or (800) 238-7245 https://coalminetournepa.com/. Hours: Daily 10:00am–4:30pm (April–November). Closed Easter and Thanksgiving. Admission: $10.00 adult, $9.50 senior (65+), $7.50 child (3-12). Company Store – souvenir coal jewelry and such. Food service. Constant 55 degrees F. below so bring along a jacket. McDade Park has excellent areas for picnics and play.*

"Go down in history" where you descend (by railcar) 300 feet below the ground to see how men "hand harvested" coal. Actual miners are your guides as they share personal stories about the hard life, the work, and the dangers of digging for "black diamonds". A walking tour of three veins of mine floor is started by watching a movie on mining history. After descending (on a steep grade) in a mine car, the rest of the tour is on foot. Can you imagine working 10 hours a day in near pitch darkness? The tour guides and staff are super friendly here.

STEAMTOWN NATIONAL HISTORICAL SITE

Scranton - *350 Cliff Street (I-81, exit 185 - toward downtown) 18503. Phone: (570) 340-5200. www.nps.gov/stea. Hours: Daily 10:00am-4:00pm. Reduced winter hours. Closed New Years Day, Thanksgiving Day, and Christmas Day. Admission: FREE. The Park includes access to the railroad yard, History Museum, Theater, Technology Museum, Roundhouse and all walking tours and theater programs. Shuttles: Scranton Limited Train Rides, seasonally (April-October - $6.00 per person). Educators: Their excellent online downloadable Student Activity Guides are age appropriate and include Teaching info plus games and short stories: www.nps.gov/stea/forteachers/index.htm.*

The National Steamtown Historic Site preserves the steam railroading era so visitors can relive that time period as the fire-breathing behemoths lumber back to life. "This is just like Thomas the Train" squealed our kids as we all saw the roundhouse come to life! This fully restored roundhouse and turntable are incredible to watch. As the Baldwin #26 enters the yard, it stops on the

The roundhouse...watch it come to life!

turntable and advances to the correct numbered house where it will "sleep" or receive maintenance. While you are out walking around the roundhouse, talk with the crew as they share stories about their jobs and the engines. The conductors love to wave and are good photograph opportunities. The Visitor's Center (mostly oriented for older kids) has both a Technology Center and History Museum of American Steam Railroading. The theater at Steamtown shows an 18-minute film called Steel and Steam. This short film follows one man's career on the railroad, and illustrates the massive changes railroads underwent in a fairly short time during the early 20th century. Join a Park Ranger or a Volunteer for a walking tour through a portion of the former locomotive shops to see and learn what it takes to keep steam-era railroad equipment operational. On select weekends, the Chilidren's Discovery Center is open to storytelling activities.

The Union Pacific #4012 "Big Boy" - over a million pounds of hardworking iron!

PENNSYLVANIA ANTHRACITE HERITAGE MUSEUM

Scranton - *22 Bald Mountain Road (I-81 - Exit 57B or Exit 51 - Follow signs to McDade Park) 18504. www.anthracitemuseum.org. Phone: (570) 963-4804 or (570) 963-4845. Hours: Friday-Sunday 10:00am-5:00pm (Closed holidays - except summer holidays). Closed January and February. Admission: $5.00 to $7.00 (ages 3+).. Educators: Lesson plans are found here: http://explorepahistory. com/story.php?storyId=11*

Explore the culture created by life and work in the coal towns. Their collections include highlights of the mines, canals, railroads, mills, and factories. Scenes also peak into family's homes and neighborhoods with a scene in the kitchen and a seat at the local Church. This was really hard work! To see a close-up of the mills producing iron "T" rails for America's railroads, stop over to the park setting of Scranton Iron Furnaces.

MONTAGE MOUNTAIN SKI RESORT

Scranton - *1000 Montage Mountain Road 18505. Phone: (570) 969-7669. Snow Report: (800) GOT-SNOW. www.montagemountainresorts.com.*

Montage Mountain offers day and night skiing and a professionally staffed ski school. Last season, Montage Mountain became one of only five Zip Rider attractions currently operating in the U.S. The mile-long Zip Rider zip line cable ride offers a completely hands-off adventure down the terrain of the resort at speeds reaching 50 mph. Longest Run: 1+ miles; 21 Slopes & Trails. Ice skating and snow tubing, too. Summer...a waterpark with a snow theme - wavepool, lazy river, alpine run waterslide, a racer luge, and polar bear pond kiddie area. Summer rates $25-$30. Food Court and Lodge on premises.

HOUDINI TOUR & MAGIC SHOW

Scranton - *1433 North Main Avenue (I-81 to exit 190, left two miles) 18508. Phone: (570) 342-5555. http://houdini.org/. Hours: Weekends 1:00-4:00pm (Memorial Day – June), Daily (July, August – Labor Day Weekend). Open Holiday Weekends throughout the year. Reservations best for weekends. Admission: $2.95-$39.95 per person (discounted if make reservations). Tours: Guided tours plus the show offered several times each afternoon. Note: Gift/Magic Shop. Admission includes video presentation and live magic shows (check website or call for exact times of shows). Very enthusiastic magicians answer questions and perform illusions before your eyes.*

The world's only exhibit devoted entirely to Houdini. It helps to know the magic word if you want to get into the Famous Houdini Museum (Houdini

Lives!). Houdini and his brother Hardeen toured through this area often. The show is perfect for all ages featuring noted professional magicians and live animals, as well as a fun guided tour of the collection in the 100-year-old historic building and see rare film footage of Houdini doing escapes. Nationally known magicians re-create these shows daily using Houdini-style equipment and live doves, a rabbit and two poodles. They float an audience member up in the air, pass a hoop around them and float them back down. Wander around and see Houdini's favorite trick props and photographs.

EVERHART MUSEUM

Scranton - *1901 Mulberry Street (Mulberry and Arthur Avenue, Nay Aug Park) 18510. Phone: (570) 346-7186. http://everhart-museum.org. Hours: Generally, Daily Noon-5:00 pm, except Closed Monday-Wednesday. PLEASE check online FOR HOURS as they change each season. Closed major holidays & January. Admission: $5.00 adult, $3.00 senior, child (6-12). Educators: This website has quizzes just for kids: www.everhart-museum.org/Education/Kids/Kids.htm*

Housing exhibits of American Folk, Native American, Oriental and primitive art. They also have fun exhibits for kids in dinosaur hall and the bees and bird collections. Children's store.

LA FESTA ITALIANA

Scranton - Courthouse Square. www.lafestaitaliana.org. Italian style festival features delicious ethnic food, crafts and live entertainment to suit young and old. Great fun for the whole family. FREE. (Labor Day weekend)

SCRANTON/WILKES-BARRE RAILRIDERS

Scranton (Moosic) - *PNC Field, 235 Montage Mountain Rd. 18507. Phone: (570) 969-2255. www.swbrailriders.com. Admission: Single game tickets run $10.00-$14.00.*

Wear your best pinstripes to catch a game by the 2008 Governor's Cup Champions and AAA affiliate of the New York Yankees. With stunning batting performances and strikeouts from major league players on rehab, there's no wonder why this team gathers an annual average attendance of 400,000 fans. Local families love to come by on Domino's Family Dinner nights - great value or on a promo night for t-shirt giveaways, live entertainment and fireworks.

TOBYHANNA STATE PARK

Tobyhanna - *PO Box 387 (accessible from I- 84 via PA Routes 507, 191 and 423) 18466. Phone: (570) 894-8336. www.dcnr.state.pa.us/stateparks/findapark/ tobyhanna/ Admission: to PA State Parks is FREE however swimming, marina and camping/lodging fees apply, with reservation or entrance.*

The 5,440-acre park includes the 170-acre Tobyhanna Lake. Tobyhanna is derived from an American Indian word meaning "a stream whose banks are fringed with alder." Beach, Boat Rentals, Campsites. Also in this location are Big Pocono and Gouldsboro State Parks. Trails and Winter Sports are on rugged terrain.

FRENCH AZILUM HISTORIC SITE

Towanda - *469 Queens Rd (Rte. 6 take SR 187 south. off SR187 - follow signs) 18848. Phone: (570) 265-3376. www.thefrenchazilum.com. Hours: Friday-Monday 11:00am-4:00 pm. (late May thru late October). Admission: $3.00-5.00 (age 12+). Note: Picnic pavilion. Nature trails.*

Few sites in Pennsylvania address another country's historic events like this one does. Founded in 1793, 50 log cabins were created as a refuge for French nobility fleeing the Revolution. After Napoleon's pardon, most left the area. Although no structures from the original town survive, an original foundation has been left exposed for public viewing. A reconstructed and relocated log cabin, circa 1790, serves as a small museum with artifacts pertaining to the settlement. Nearby is the 1836 LaPorte House containing period furnishings. Warm weather archeological digs occur frequently. Stand around and ask what they're finding.

MT. PISGAH STATE PARK

Troy - *RD 3, Box 362 (2 miles north of US Route 6) 16947. Phone: (570) 297-2734. www.dcnr.state.pa.us/stateparks/findapark/mtpisgah/ Admission: to PA State Parks is FREE however swimming, marina and camping/lodging fees apply, with reservation or entrance.*

At the base of Mt. Pisgah and set along Mill Creek. A dam on Mill Creek forms Stephen Foster Lake, named after the famous composer and onetime local resident. The 75-acre lake provides fishing, boating and skating. Adjacent to the park are Mt. Pisgah County Park. Also Pool, Visitor Center, Trails, and Winter Sports.

MAPLE SUGARING

Troy - Mt. Pisgah State Park. Actual tapping of trees. Syrup making. Demonstrations of coopering and sugaring off in a realistic sugar camp. Pancakes and syrup served. (last weekend in April)

ELK MOUNTAIN SKI AREA

Union Dale - *RR 2, Box 3328 (I-81 exit 206) 18470. Phone: (570) 679-4400. Snow Report: (800) 233-4131. www.elkskier.com.*

Elk Mountain was one of the first commercial ski areas to open in Pennsylvania in 1959. Today, Elk has seven lifts and 27 slopes, including some of the most challenging terrain in the region. The resort also has its own distinctive character; the resort regularly plants Norway Spruce and red and white pines. Since the mid-1980s, more than 13,000 trees have been planted. Skiing and Snowboarding. Longest Run: 1.75 miles; 27 Slopes & Trails.

FALL FESTIVAL

Union Dale - Elk Mountain. Petting zoo, refreshments, pumpkin patch, corn maze, pony or wagon rides. Scenic chair lift rides, entertainment. (second weekend in October)

WILKES-BARRE/SCRANTON PENGUINS HOCKEY

Wilkes-Barre - *Ice Rink at Coal Street 18702. www.wbspenguins.com. Phone: (570) 208-PENS.*

Kids Club activities, section and skate. AHL Hockey (October-early April). Join their Kids Club or come on promo nights for bobbleheads and such.

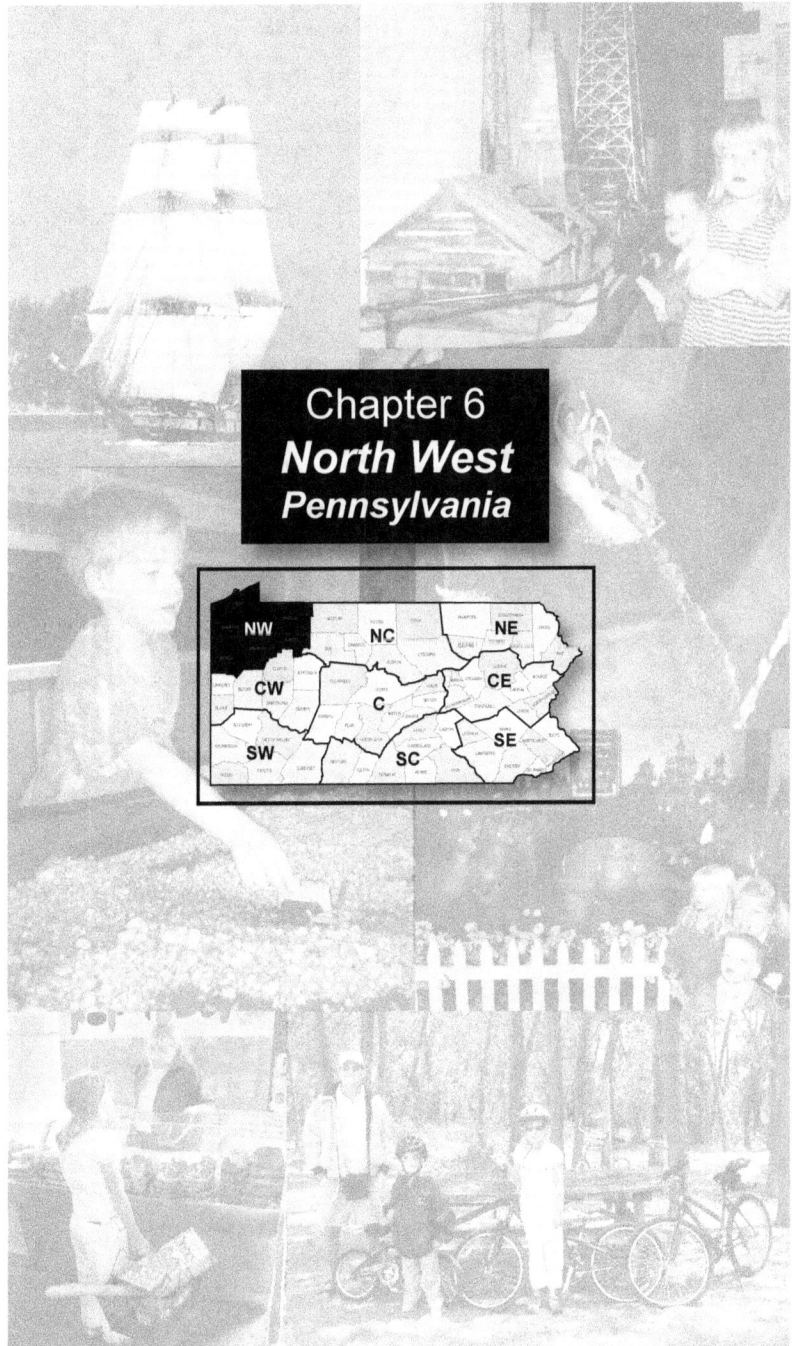

Chapter 6
North West
Pennsylvania

General
- Maple Sugaring Taste Weekend

Clarendon
- Chapman State Park

Clarion
- Clear Creek State Forest

Conneaut Lake
- Conneaut Lake Park

Edinboro
- Wooden Nickel Buffalo Farm
- Edinboro Highland Games

Erie
- Bicentennial Observation Tower
- Erie County Historical Museum
- Erie Otters Hockey
- Erie Sea Wolves Baseball
- Presque Isle Scenic Boat Tours
- Presque Isle State Park
- Waldameer Park & Water World
- Erie Maritime Museum / U.S. Brig Niagara
- Experience Children's Museum
- Firefighter's Historical Museum
- Erie Zoo
- Splash Lagoon

Franklin
- DeBence Antique Music Museum

Greenville
- Greenville Canal Museum
- Greenville Railroad Park

Grove City
- Wendell August Forge

Hermitage
- Philadelphia Candies

Jamestown
- Pymatuning Deer Park
- Pymatuning State Park

North Warren
- Cornplanter State Forest

Oil City
- Oil Creek State Park

Sandy Lake
- Goddard State Park, Maurice K.

Sharon
- Daffin's Candies

Titusville
- Drake Well Museum
- Oil Creek & Titusville Railroad

Warren
- Kinzua Dam/ Big Bend Visitor's Center

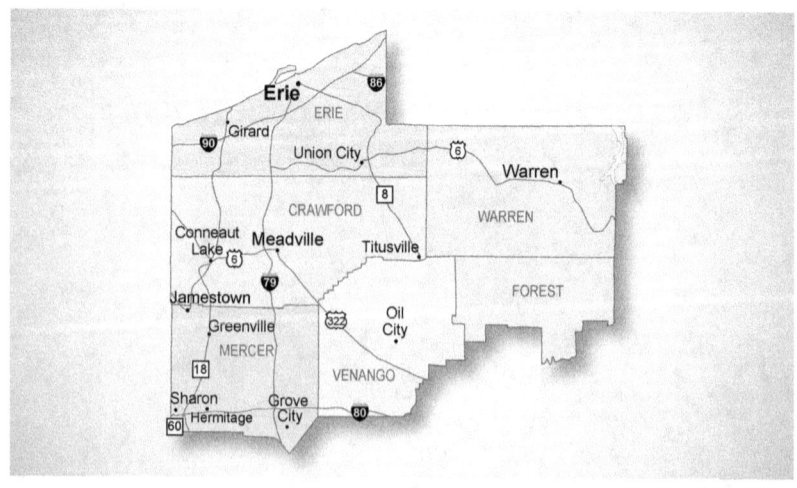

A Quick Tour of our Hand-Picked
Favorites Around...

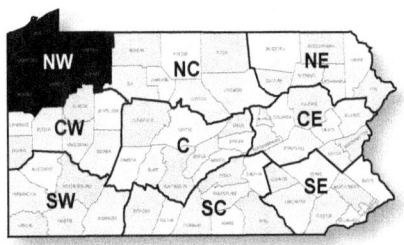

North West Pennsylvania

Northwest Pennsylvania is the center of ingenuity. Here you'll find some old-fashioned amusement parks, an indoor waterpark (**Splash Lagoon**) where we love the tall, tall slides, industrial Erie, family-friendly state parks, the discovery of oil, and some fun factory tours.

Presque Isle State Park is a wonder with seven miles of sandy beaches (one of the top 100 swimming holes) and it has the only surf beach in the Commonwealth. On a nice day, many locals and visitors head to Presque Isle for boating, fishing, nature walks or biking. The park is so clean, the beaches multi-purpose paths allow easy transport around most of the 14 miles of the isle. It's really one of the best state parks for families we've found.

The **United States Brig Niagara**, restored and moored on Erie's bayfront, is the only ship of her type, which is still in existence from the War of 1812. The Niagara is the tallest "tall ship" on the Great Lakes and you can board it! Once aboard, see over 200 oars, steered with a tiller instead of a wheel, sleeping quarters, and rows of cannons. Inside the **Erie Maritime Museum** is another ship to tour and pretend you're a sailor on the treacherous Lake Erie.

Erie Zoo has monkey and otter habitats that are especially fun to watch and they even have one area with gorilla that get so close to the clear wall you feel they're trying to communicate with you. There are some deer parks and loads of ducks near Pymatuning State Park.

If you like factory tours, this area has got one that hammers metal (**Wendell August Forge**) and others that produce some yummy and funny chocolates. **Philadelphia Candies** has covered most every sweet thing in chocolate and **Daffins** has a display of some chocolate animals that are hundreds of pounds each!

Finally, Titusville is the home of the discovery of oil and the birthplace of the petroleum industry. **Drake Well Museum** and the **Oil Creek & Titusville Railroad** are really interesting to tour. Inside the museum there are many push button exhibits and squeeze and sniff oil samples from all over the world. Outside, they occasionally demonstrate how they fired the hole. See the first oil fields in the world as they tell a story of the oil rush boom days in the valley from a railcar scheduled train ride located near the museum.

Sites and attractions are listed in order by City, Zip Code, and Name. Symbols indicated represent: 🍽 Restaurants   🛏 Lodging

MAPLE SUGARING ANNUAL TASTE & TOUR WEEKEND

General - https://pamaple.org. You're invited to spend the weekend exploring the heart of the Pennsylvania Maple Producer. Each of these sugaring operations are unique in their own way. Demonstrations all day both days, and the little sugarhouse is packed with people. A local Boy Scout troop camps at the site that weekend and demonstrates how Indians and early settlers made sugar and syrup. There's free maple hot chocolate and samples of other maple goodies. Hot dogs boiled in maple water are for sale at a nominal price. (Yummy with maple mustard, too!) The warming tent has hay bales for seating as well as a kids table with crayons and maple scene pictures for coloring. The sugarhouse is off the road about 3/4 of a mile, so you can either walk or take a haywagon drawn by a tractor or teams of draft horses. All quite picturesque. FREE. Note: Hurry Hill site in Edinboro: The owner has produced a video for teachers on /Miracles on Maple Hill, a children's storybook that won a Newberry Award which would be excellent for homeschoolers / educators in connection with the book. That video runs on a loop in a warming tent near the sugarhouse and the stand where a large variety of maple products are sold. (mid-March weekend)

CHAPMAN STATE PARK

Clarendon - *RD 2 Box 1610 (off US Route 6) 16829. Phone: (814) 723-0250. https://www.dcnr.pa.gov/StateParks/FindAPark/ChapmanStatePark/Pages/default.aspx Admission: to PA State Parks is FREE however swimming, marina and camping/lodging fees apply, with reservation or entrance.*

Chapman sits on the banks of the West Branch of Tionesta Creek. Among its many recreational offerings, the park boasts a 68-acre lake that provides swimming at a beach and warm and cold water fishing. A sand beach is open from late-May to mid-September, 8 a.m. to sunset. Boat Rentals, Campsites, Fishing, Trails, and Winter Sports.

CLEAR CREEK STATE FOREST

Clarion - *158 South Second Avenue 16214. Phone: (814) 226-1901. www.dcnr. state.pa.us/forestry/stateforests/clearcreek/index.htm*

Points of interest within the State Forest are the Clear Creek State Park with overnight camping facilities, swimming, fishing, hiking trails, and day-use areas; Bear Town Rocks, a vista with an excellent view accessible by trail or automobile; and Hays Lot Fire Tower with a panoramic view of great distances. Early June tour the laurel fields located on Spring Creek Road.

CONNEAUT LAKE PARK

Conneaut Lake - *12382 Center St (I-79, exit 147B west on Rte. 322, follow signs to PA 618) 16316. Phone: (814) 382-5115. www.newconneautlakepark. com. Hours: Saturdays 1:00 to 10:00pm, Sundays 1:00-6:00pm. (Memorial Day weekend-Labor Day weekend). Most summer Thursdays and Fridays open 4:00-10:00pm. Admission: FREE, pay for each ride or day pass. Miniature Golf, rides, waterpark. Single Tickets are $5.00 and Day Passes are $10.00.*

Old-fashioned 100 year old park with rides, water attractions, kiddie land, restaurant, Camperland and beach/boardwalk. Conneaut Lake Park has dozens of old-fashioned rides, including the famous Blue Streak Wooden Roller Coaster (1938). Splash City Water Park, too.

PUMPKIN FESTIVAL

Conneaut Lake - Conneaut Lake Park. Pumpkin painting and carving, pie-eating contests. Pumpkin patch (wagon rides out there). Refreshments. (second weekend)

Edinboro

WOODEN NICKEL BUFFALO FARM

Edinboro - *5970 Koman Road (I-79 to exit 166 - go east - follow signs) 16412. Phone: (814) 734-BUFF. www.woodennickelbuffalo.com. Hours: Daily 11:00am-5:00pm (late Aug-October). Weekends only rest of year. Admission: $5.00 per person ($40.00 per tour, minimum charge). Reservations required. Before leaving, every person in the group receives one newsletter and a Wooden Nickel as a souvenir. Note: Wooden Nickel Restaurant serves Bison burgers and sides.*

This 150-acre farm is home to more than 50 wild buffalo and offers visitors the opportunity to learn more about these wild animals as well as the health benefits of bison meat. The owners loved the meat when they first tried it and decided to breed and sell buffalo products. The tour includes a talk on Bison as you view them in the pastures.

The buffalo herds roam the farm pastures freely, and guests have the opportunity to watch cows tending to their young or witness the challenges between bulls in the herd. You will learn about their history and relationship with Native Americans, see the handling facilities, and view authentic Native American art and Bison products in the Gift Shop. American Indian folklore and festival in late July. Feel a real buffalo hide or admire cute baby bison.

CORN MAZE

Edinboro - Wooden Nickel Buffalo Farm. Have fun wandering around the miles of the 6-acre maze to find game sheet stations. Admission. (weekends in September, daily in October).

EDINBORO HIGHLAND GAMES & SCOTTISH FESTIVAL

Edinboro - Edinboro University. https://edinboro.edu/events/highland-games/index.php. Highland dance, pipe band competition, music, sheep-herding, medieval camp, kids games & crafts. FREE. (late July weekend)

Erie

BICENTENNIAL OBSERVATION TOWER

Erie - Dobbins Landing   16501. https://www.porterie.org/bicentennialtower/ Phone: (814) 455-6055.   Hours: Open at 10:00am - closing varies seasonally between 6:00-9:00pm (April-October). November - March (open Saturday & Sunday only) 12PM - 4PM. Admission: $2.00-$6.00 (age 7+). Free admission on first Tuesday of the month.

Enjoy an aerial view of the city and Presque Isle Bay. The 187-ft tower features two observation decks, and markers of Erie's harbor history and geography. 210 stairs to the observation deck (or, yes, there is an elevator!). If you climb the stairs, follow the 16 stations that highlight various landmarks. Souvenirs and food available in tower lobby.

HAGAN HISTORY CENTER

Erie - 356 W 6th St (I-79 to Bayfront Parkway) 16501. Phone: (814) 454-1813. https://www.eriehistory.org/. Hours: Tuesday-Saturday 11am-5pm, Sunday Noon-5pm. Admission: $10 adult, $7.50 senior, $5.00 student/veteran. Educators: go to this website link: www.eriecountyhistory.org/education/teacher-resources/ for some really interesting historical links to U.S. History - even one on toys.

Local history, architecture and industry. The two-building complex contains the Museum of Erie County History, which features Voices, an interactive exhibit offering selective views of Erie County's rich heritage from pre-settlement to present day, the Maritime Hall, an exhibit presenting the region's ongoing maritime legacy, and the Kids Korner children's area filled with captivating educational, fun activities. The Watson-Curtze Mansion houses the Regional History Museum, which is located on the second & third floors while the first floor interprets Victorian furniture & decor.

ERIE OTTERS HOCKEY

Erie - 809 French Street (office) (Louis J. Tullio Civic Center) 16501. Phone: (814) 452-4857 (Box Office) or 455-7779 (office). www.ottershockey.com. Admission: $12.00-$20.00

Canadian Hockey League (players between the age of 16-20). The Otters play a 68-game regular season schedule (34 home, 34 away), plus playoffs.

ERIE SEA WOLVES BASEBALL

Erie - 110 East 10th Street (office) (UPMC Ballpark) 16501. Phone: (814) 456-1300. www.seawolves.com. Admission: $7.00-$11.00

The Erie Seawolves are the Class AA Affiliate of the Detroit Tigers. You can visit UPMC Park and see future MLB stars as alumni include Justin Verlander, Aramis Ramirez, and more than 100 others. Fireworks, giveaways, on-field stunts, kids' zones and more make the game on the field just one aspect of the excitement. Check out the deals on Friends & Family Nights.

PRESQUE ISLE SCENIC BOAT TOURS

Erie - (Departing from Perry Monument on Presque Isle State Park) 16505. Phone: 814-836-0201 or toll free 800-988-5780. www.piboattours.com. Admission: Rates are adults: $18.00 and $10.00 child (5-12). Cruise schedules and prices are subject to change. Any trip may be cancelled due to severe weather, mechanical difficulties, or fewer reservations than required. Tours: Tour departures vary seasonally: Mid-May through Mid-June and after Labor day through September 30; are Saturdays and Sundays. The summer season of mid-June through Labor day; are 7 days per week and sunset cruises which depart 1 hour prior to sunset.

Experience the scenic beauty of the Peninsula and Erie waterfront while viewing three historic lighthouses on the 65-foot great lakes vessel, "Lady Kate." The 14-mile, 90-minute tour ventures out onto the open waters of Lake Erie. You will view Presque Isle's shores, Erie's skyline, lighthouses, ships, the beaches, Gull Point Nature Preserve, wildlife and numerous other sights. Live narration takes place on each tour by knowledgeable guides that identify and describe points of interest.

PRESQUE ISLE STATE PARK

Erie - *301 Peninsula Drive (Lake Erie, reached by PA Route 832 or by boat) 16505. Phone: (814) 833-7424. https://www.dcnr.pa.gov/StateParks/FindAPark/ PresqueIsleStatePark/Pages/default.aspx. Admission: FREE however swimming,*

marina and camping/lodging fees apply. Camping, skiing, & snowmobiling.

Seven miles of sandy beaches (Top 100 swimming holes) and it has the only surf beach in the Commonwealth. Because of the many unique habitats, Presque Isle contains a greater number of the state's endangered, threatened and rare species than any other area of comparable size in Pennsylvania. On a nice day, many locals and visitors head to Presque Isle for boating, fishing, nature walks or biking. The park is so clean, the beaches well-maintained, and the paved multi-purpose paths allow easy transport around most of the 14 miles of the isle. We especially recommend biking 5 miles of the trails, stopping every now and then to enjoy a beverage or dip in the water along the beaches. The Multi-purpose National Recreation Trail makes a 13.5-mile paved circuit of the park. This ADA accessible trail is popular with bicyclists, in-line skaters and joggers. Stop in their nature center first to discuss your plans with a ranger…they were most helpful!

A boat rental concession is located in the Grave Yard Pond area and provides a variety of powered and non-powered craft. Beaching of boats along Presque Isle shoreline is permitted except at the Gull Point Natural Area between April and November, and within 100 feet of designated swimming areas.

PRESQUE ISLE LIGHTHOUSE, which dates to 1872 is at Lighthouse Beach, on the north shore of the Park. Daily 10am-5pm summers. $8.00 to climb the tower. $3.00 to tour the house. https://www.presqueislelighthouse.org/

The gateway to Presque Isle is the <u>TOM RIDGE ENVIRONMENTAL CENTER</u> (TREC - www.trecpi.org). TREC is dedicated to teaching visitors about Presque Isle and the many different forms of life that inhabit this unique peninsula. TREC also serves as a center for research, contributing to conservation efforts and promoting environmental awareness, helping to preserve the unparalleled beauty of Presque Isle. There is free admission to the interactive exhibits and the 75-foot observation tower. In addition to the 'Big Green Screen' movies and the changeable exhibit area, there are special activities like scavenger hunts, family night at the movies, and music concerts.

For updates & travel games visit: **www.KidsLoveTravel.com**

WALDAMEER PARK AND WATER WORLD

Erie - *220 Peninsula Drive (Close to entrance of Presque Isle State Park) 16505. Phone: (814) 838-3591. www.waldameer.com. Hours: Tuesday-Sunday (Mid-May - Labor Day) Admission: WaterWorld only $23-$29 wristband. Combo unlimited wristband to entire park ranging from $31.50 - $41.50. There is no admission fee to enter the amusement park. ALL Parking is FREE! Individual ride tickets also available for everyone. (Due to ride restrictions, we recommend the use of individual ride tickets, not wrist band, for children under two years old.) Everyone must pay to enter Water World. Note: Restaurants. Tubes and life jackets are free. Smoke free. Bring own towel.*

Five incredible body slides, Three fabulous double tube slides, The Wild River single tube slide, A daring free fall slide, a speed slide, A refreshing Endless River innertube ride, A heated relaxing pool, Three tad pool areas with five great kiddie slides, and Beautiful parks. Thunder River log flume ride plus many more classic amusement rides in Waldameer Park. They have a coaster called Ravine Flyer II, also. Puppet shows and concerts, too! Although the park has grown, this park has kept its low key approach to fun and family. Because they offer free admission into the park, parents or grandparents that are not interested in riding can go along (and hold loose items!) at no charge. If you're a rider, the lines aren't usually that long.

ERIE MARITIME MUSEUM / U.S. BRIG NIAGARA

Erie - *150 East Front Street (I-79 North to Bayfront Parkway) 16507. Phone: (814) 452-BRIG. www. flagshipniagara.org   Hours: Monday-Saturday 9:00am-5:00pm, Sunday Noon-5:00pm. Closed Sundays in October. Closed Sunday-Wednesday (November-March) Admission: $10.00 adult, $8.00 senior (65+), $5.00 youth (3-11). Note: Shipwright gift shop. First-person costumed interpreters are featured on weekends and for special events.*

Berthed within yards of the museum, Niagara is visible from the building's bay side picture window. Tour the flagship "Niagara" (when in

Courtesy of Pennsylvania Historical & Museum Commission

port) built to fight in the War of 1812 - the Battle of Lake Erie - Commodore Perry's ship. Once aboard, see over 200 oars, steered with a tiller instead of a wheel, sleeping quarters, and rows of cannons. Do you know the difference between a Brig (2 sails) and a ship (3 sails)?

Students can experience aspects of the life of a sailor in Perry's fleet. Maybe drill on the carronade, set the sail, and learn to tie basic knots as part of the museum experience. Inside, the centerpiece exhibits of the museum are a former steam-powered electricity generating station and a reconstruction of the mid-ship section of the Lawrence. The replicated Lawrence, Commodore Oliver Hazard Perry's first flagship during the Battle of Lake Erie, comes complete with mast, spars and rigging to foster hands-on learning in the ways of sail handling. Probably the most powerful display is the adjoining section of the Lawrence replica that has been blasted with live ammunition from the current Niagara's own carronades. This "live fire" exhibit of the Lawrence recreates the horrific carnage inflicted upon both ships and men during the Battle of Lake Erie and throughout the Age of Fighting Sail. Why can't cannons fire all at once on one side of the ship?

EXPERIENCE CHILDREN'S MUSEUM

Erie - 420 French Street (Discovery Square) (I-79 North to Bay Front Highway) 16507. Phone: (814) 453-3743. www.eriechildrensmuseum.org. Hours: Wednesday-Saturday 10:00am-5:00pm, Sunday 1:00-5:00pm. Closed Tuesday during school year. Admission: $9.00 general (ages 2+) Note: Aimed at 2-8 year old children. The Much More Store gift shop.

For a smaller museum, we were impressed how they use their space in this old building. A few of our favorites: People At Work where kids move vehicles and stones to change the way a stream flows; Discovery Corner outdoor classroom; and their Market was the most colorful, realistic and well-stocked we've ever seen...check out the meat and seafood market items! The first floor is full of science - from giant bubble creations to energy, light, and motion. Check out Radar Rooster weather, a Bedrock Cave, or the Circles and Cycles (pollution - unregulated and innumerable, and its effects on the Lake Erie watershed). Children are challenged to create a safe community. The second floor is the "The Healer Within" and has career dress up areas, Rookie Reporter newsroom, the Corner Store, Senses, Safety, Construction, and your heartbeat. Visit with Lake Erie fish and learn about where our water comes from! Aerodynamics is a colorful assortment of plastic balls that actual pop, chute and slide around the space.

FIREFIGHTER'S HISTORICAL MUSEUM

Erie - 428 Chestnut Street (I-79 to Route 5) 16507. Phone: (814) 456-5969. firefightershistoricalmuseum.org. Hours: Saturday 11:00am-4:00pm, Sunday 1:00-4:00pm (June-August). Saturday - Sunday 1:00-4:00pm (September, October). Admission: $1.00-$4.00 (students+)

The #4 Erie Firehouse has 1300+ items on display including antique equipment, uniforms, badges, helmets, masks, fire extinguishers, hand pumps and horse drawn carts. They have the only display of an 1889 horse drawn fire engine and an understandable demonstration of the relay system in fire call boxes.

ERIE ZOO

Erie - 423 West 38th Street (I-90 to exit 27) 16508. www.eriezoo.org. Phone: (814) 864-4091. Hours: Daily 10:00am-5:00pm (March through November). Admission: $11.00 adult, $9.00 senior (62+), $7.00 child (2-12). Slightly reduced admission in the winter. Note: Train & Carousel rides ($1.50 -$2.00 extra)

The Erie Zoo is home to over 500 animals, representing more than 100 species, from around the world. Winding walkways take visitors through the beautifully landscaped grounds. The Zoo features everything from lowland gorillas to African waterbirds with special events and activities for the entire family. Go on an African safari of sorts to see cheetahs and rhinos at the Zoo's Kiboka Outpost, meet red pandas and orangutans in the Wild Asia exhibit, or meet the Zoo's newest resident, Norton the polar bear. The Children's Zoo features special educational programs, feed & petting area and even an indoor wildlife carousel. Monkey and otter's habitats are especially fun to watch and they even have one area with traditional lions, and tigers and bears. Various gardens include the Butterfly gardens, the Greenhouse, and the great gardens at Kiboka Outpost where the rhinos roam. The animals are so-o-o close and the settings (indoor/outdoor) were well done and easy to manage. Our favorites were the gorillas and orangutans that are so endearing to watch and communicate with!

ZOOLUMINATION

Erie - Erie Zoo. Glistening lights. Visit with Santa. Hot chocolate. Freshly baked cookies. Toy/gift shops. Weekend entertainment. Admission. Walk-thru.(mid-to-late December)

SPLASH LAGOON

...it looks like a giant "MouseTrap" game...what fun!

Erie - 8091 Peach Street (I-90 exit 24, Rte. 19 south) 16509. Phone: (866) 3-SPLASH. www.splashlagoon.com. Hours: Generally 9:00am-10:00pm. Closed some weekdays during school year. Admission: Waterpark passes are $40.00-$65.00 each. More on holiday weekends. Note: 4 hotels are part of the indoor waterpark resort and are directly connected to Splash Lagoon (range $150-$300, include 4-6 waterpark passes and complimentary breakfast).

Splash passes are valid from Noon on the day of arrival until Close of the day of departure. Bring your own towels.

An indoor waterpark resort with a: Tree House packed with interactive water fun, 48-Ft Tall Tipping Bucket regularly dumps 1,000 gallons of water, 4 twisting & turning 4-story high Body Slides, A Swirling Body Coaster with speeds of over 40 MPH, Swirling Tube Coaster for 1 or 2 riders, Two 25 Person whirlpools, Laaaazy River, Activity Pool featuring 8 water basketball hoops, Dancing Water Play Area, Little People Activity Pool with zero depth entry, 6,000 Sq. Ft. Arcade, Lazer Tag Arena, and Food Court. Clean, fresh (check out all the filters they use...both air and water) and full of something for every child and adult to ride and lounge in. Compared to other indoor waterparks, we especially liked that every ride had a different "twist" and they even have some of the new rides we affectionately call "toilet bowls"...chute down a tube, then swirl around a bowl and drop out the middle. None of the rides are strenuous and plenty of staff are on hand to gently escort you to another area or help you out of your raft. On busy days (esp. rainy day Saturdays), be prepared for long lines up the dozens of steps to the big rides (watch out for your neighbors raft bumping).

We recommend going online and reserving one of the Splash Lagoon overnight stay packages because you get two day waterpark passes and hotel accommodations in large rooms with complimentary continental breakfast (real value for the money). You'll want to break up your day(s) at the waterpark every two hours or so with a rest - naps and several light meals at local eateries (our favorite, Quaker Steak & Lube) are recommended.

DEBENCE ANTIQUE MUSIC MUSEUM

Franklin - *1261 Liberty Street, Route 8 (Downtown, off I-80 to exit 29) 16323. Phone: (814) 432-5668 or (888) 547-2377. www.debencemusicworld.com. Hours: Tuesday-Saturday 11:00am-4:00pm, Sunday 12:30-4:00pm (April - October). Admission: $8.00 adult, $7.00 senior (60+), $5 students, $3.00 child (3-14).*

"To See and Hear Museum". 100+ antique, automated music machines from the gay 90's - roaring 20's. See and hear demonstrations of nickelodeons, Swiss & German music boxes, waltzes and polkas, merry-go-round band organs, calliopes, player pianos, and a variety of antique organs. We were most fascinated by the nickelodeons that had glass panel inserts showing the musical instrument "guts". This was the first time we have ever seen a violin or accordion playing as an accompaniment. Bring the grandparents along for this visit.

Greenville

GREENVILLE CANAL MUSEUM

Greenville - *60 Alan Avenue (Lock 22 - Alan Avenue, near Riverside Park) 16125. Phone: (724) 588-7540. www.greenvillecanalmuseum.org. Hours: Saturday-Sunday 1:00-5:00pm (summer). Admission: Small admission for students+.*

History of Erie Extension Canal - artifacts like tools and photographs. The Erie Extension Canal played a vital role as the first efficient transportation into northwestern Pennsylvania for settlers and commerce. Great Lakes iron ore was shipped on the canal, which was combined with coal at iron and steel mills. Small settlements along the canal grew, forming new towns. See a full size replica of an 1840s canal boat - Rufus Reed, and view a working model of a canal lock.

GREENVILLE RAILROAD PARK MUSEUM

Greenville - *314 Main Street - Rte. 358 16125. Phone: (724) 588-4009. http://members.tripod.com/~greenville/rrpark.html. Hours: Generally, Weekends 1:00-5:00pm (Summer). Call ahead if driving distance to museum.*

Climb aboard the largest switch engine - #604 - used in the steel industry. Plenty of railroad cars - hopper cars, cabooses, and a 1914 Empire auto touring car. World's first parachute invented by local Stefan Banie in 1914. Stationmasters quarters, dispatch office and displays of railroad uniforms.

WENDELL AUGUST FORGE

Grove City (Mercer) - *2074 Leesburg-Grove City Rd (I-79, exit 31- follow signs-(Route 208, one mile east of outlet mall) 16137. Phone: (800) WAF-GIFT. www.wendellaugust.com. Hours: Monday-Saturday 10:00am-5:00pm, Sunday 11:00am-5:00pm (except several days surrounding holidays). Admission: FREE Note: Children can create their own work of metal art for just $2.00 per child. Old time Nickelodeon, W.A. Parrot (who talks and does impressions), LGB train on a surrounding track up above and a 225 gallon ocean reef tank. These keep the kids amused while adults shop.*

Because of fire early 2010, the original Forge building burned but they have relocated near the Outlet Mall and are still hand-crafting pieces. Real workshop

..."edging" the metalwork

tours are unavailable at this time but instead they have set up a neat simulated workshop area for guests, including a history center. A self-guided tour of the simulated production workshop is fascinating to watch as metal is taken through an eleven step process. The gift metal is hammered over a pre-designed template with random hand, or machine-operated hammer motions. At one point, you'll get a chance to pick up a hammer that is used - they weigh up to 3 pounds. You'll understand why a craftsman thought to automate the hammering process - tired, tired hands! Once the impression is set, the item is forged (put in a log fire) to produce smoke marks that bring out the detail of the design. The item is cooled and cleaned and finished by thinning the edges. Each piece is marked with a sign particular to the craftsman. This is a wonderful place to show children the balance between old world craft and new, automated craftsmanship.

PHILADELPHIA CANDIES

Hermitage - *1546 East State Street (off SR18 North) 16148. Phone: (724) 981-6341. www.philadelphiacandies.com. Hours: Daily 9:00am-4:00pm (lunch between 12:00-1:00pm). Admission: FREE. Tours: Pre-arranged, 15-20 minutes around floor. Note: annual "Chocolate Factory Tour" from 9:00am - 4:00pm, Saturday, two weeks before Easter, showing the public where and how all the delicious candy is made for shipment to its own stores as well as other fine stores throughout the country. You will be able to see skilled candy makers creating milk chocolate bunnies, specialty baskets, and delicious chocolates. The 7,000-pound chocolate tank, chocolate enrobers, a chocolate bunny depositor, and a lollipop machine will be labeled and operating for the self-guided tour.*

Have you ever tried chocolate covered cookies, potato chips, marshmallows or orange peels? Free samples are abundant at the factory store and you can get a peek at whatever chocolate concoction they're sweetening that day. Here are some "fun" numbers for you: 30,000 square foot facility, 80 year old family business, 7000 pounds of chocolate are melted at one time, sugar comes in 50 pounds bags, and corn syrup is delivered in 55 gallon drums!

Jamestown

PYMATUNING DEER PARK

Jamestown - *Route 58, 804 East Jamestown Road (off US 322, 3 Miles South of Pymatuning Dam) 16134. Phone: (724) 932-3200. www.pymatuningdeerpark.com. Hours: Monday - Friday 10:00am-5:00pm, Saturday, Sunday, Holidays 10:00am-6:00pm (Summer). Weekends only in May, September (weather permitting). Admission: Average $8.00-$10.00 per person. Animal Food $2.00 per package. Note: Train and pony rides additional $3.00.*

While strolling through the wooded setting under a canopy of trees, visitors encounter both domestic and exotic animals including Siberian Tigers, African Lions, Camels, Black Bears, assorted Primates and of course, several species of deer. Some animals you pet and some you don't! The "Kiddie Zoo" welcomes young and old alike to get up-close and personal with featured baby animals and a variety of domestic farm animals. Petting and feeding in the Kiddie Zoo is a highlight for most park visitors. Cracker-crunching deer, bucket-pulling monkeys, and biscuit-begging black bears make for endless feeding adventures throughout the entire park.

PYMATUNING STATE PARK

Jamestown - *Box 425 (accessible by U.S. Route 6, U.S. Route 322, PA Route 18, PA Route 285, and PA Route 58) 16134. Phone: (724) 932-3141. https://www. dcnr.pa.gov/StateParks/FindAPark/PymatuningStatePark/Pages/default.aspx Admission: FREE however swimming, marina and camping/lodging fees apply.*

Flood control reservoir along the Ohio border. The spillway is perhaps one of the best known locations because the fish being fed are so plentiful that the "ducks walk on the fishes' backs" to compete for the food fed by the visitors. The largest body of water in the state. More people visit Pymatuning than almost any other PA state park. But the biggest thing about Pymatuning is the fun you can have boating, fishing, swimming, camping and enjoying other recreational opportunities. There are trails near Tuttle and Jamestown campgrounds, and the abandoned railroad grade on the Spillway is a flat, wide trail.

In addition to the state park facilities, the PA Fish and Boat Commission operates a fish hatchery and the PA Game Commission has wildlife viewing areas. Wildlife Museum - state's largest colony of nesting eagles. Beach, Boat Rentals, Sledding, Campsites, Modern Cabins, Fishing, and Trails.

PIONEER AND ARTS FESTIVAL

Jamestown - Pymatuning State Park. Displays, demonstrations, arts and crafts, Indian dancers, frontier activities, encampment, historical program, tour of the Gatehouse, food and live entertainment. No Admission. (last weekend in July)

CORNPLANTER STATE FOREST

North Warren - *323 N. State Street 16365. Phone: (814) 723-0262. www.dcnr. state.pa.us/forestry/stateforests/cornplanter/index.htm*

1,256 acres named for Chief Cornplanter, a famous Indian Chief of the Seneca tribe. Highlights include Hunter Run Demonstration Area and Lasure Trail. This is a combined interpretive area with about 1-1/2 miles of self guided foot trails. It is heavily used by the surrounding schools for environmental education. There are seven miles of cross-country ski trails for the winter sports enthusiast. The trail is located 4 miles N. of Tionesta off SR 36. ATV Trails.

OIL CREEK STATE PARK

Oil City - *RD 1, Box 207 (the main entrance to the park is off of PA Route 8) 16301. Phone: (814) 676-5915. www.dcnr.state.pa.us/stateparks/findapark/oilcreek/ Admission: FREE however swimming, marina and camping/lodging fees apply.*

The site of the world's first commercial oil well, this park tells the story of the early petroleum industry by interpreting oil boom towns, oil wells and early transportation. Many sites can be seen while traveling the 9.5-mile paved bicycle trail through the scenic Oil Creek Gorge, or on an excursion train.

Displays and programs are at Petroleum Centre, the focal point of the early oil boom. "A Contrast in Time" slideshow takes you on a six-minute journey through time. The noise of pumping wells and shouting men in the 1860s contrasts with the rustling leaves in a gentle breeze in present  day Oil Creek. The train station is open Noon-5:00pm Saturdays and Sundays (June-October). Visit the Train Station Visitor Center for historical displays, an exciting diorama and an interactive computer information center. A train still chugs through the valley and stops at the Train Station in Petroleum Centre, just as it did over 100 years ago! Hike the "wickedest hollow east of the Mississippi." Choose from one to four trails including: Wetlands Trail (one mile); Geology Trail (one mile); Oil History Trail (0.25 mile); Forestry Trail (0.25 mile). Also: Boat Rentals, Sledding, Fishing, and Cross-Country Skiing.

GODDARD STATE PARK, MAURICE K.

Sandy Lake - *684 Lake Wilhelm Road (I-79 exit 34, west on Rte. 358) 16145. Phone: (724) 253-4833. www.dcnr.state.pa.us/stateparks/findapark/mauricekgoddard/ Admission: FREE however swimming, marina and camping/lodging fees apply.*

The 1,860-acre Lake Wilhelm is an angler's paradise. The large lake, abundant wetlands, old fields and mature forests provide a diversity of habitats which attract wildlife in all seasons. Boat Rentals, Sledding, Trails, & Winter Sports.

PIONEER FROLIC

Sandy Lake - Goddard State Park. Every June the Friends of Goddard (FROG) co-sponsor the Pioneer Frolic which is two days of festivities that examine what historical rural Pennsylvania life was like along the Sandy Creek during the 1750s to 1840s. Crafters, artisans, and demonstrators display there wares and skills which can include a blacksmith, pioneer toys, spinner, food, entertainment and an encampment.

DAFFIN'S CANDIES

Sharon - *496 East State Street (Factory - 7 Spearman Avenue, SR60 in nearby Farrell) 16146. Phone: (724) 342-2892. www.daffins.com. Hours: Monday-Saturday 10:00am-6:00pm, Sunday 11:00am-5:00pm. Admission: FREE. Tours: Monday - Friday 9:00am-3:00pm (mid September through mid April). By reservations. 15+ people (add-ons to other groups accepted). 45 minutes long. Note: Tours in the fall and winter are best - more activity preparing for Christmas and Easter Holidays. The Chocolate Kingdom is available to view whenever the store is open.*

Daffin's Candies has earned a national reputation for its delectable sweet and semi-sweet milk chocolate candy with nearly 100 years of experience and three generations of chocolate makers. Start in the Chocolate Kingdom inside the World's Largest Candy Store. The Kingdom is inhabited by a 400-pound chocolate turtle, a 125-pound chocolate reindeer and 75-pound chocolate frog. Chocolate castles, a train, a village, and a Ferris Wheel bring this whimsical land to life. As the tour continues, you'll learn how cocoa beans are removed from pods, mashed into paste, and finally processed into the chocolate forms we all know and love.

Daffin's still hosts its annual event known as Swizzle Stick Day on the Sunday before Palm Sunday. The facility holds plant tours that day, drawing nearly 8,000 people during the four-hour session. Patrons also get a free sample of a swizzle stick dipped in fresh candy filling with fresh chocolate dipped on top.

Regular factory tours are also available year-round. At the Factory, the group will see a short video tape of Daffin's and the History of chocolates. The seven foot Rabbit and other artistic chocolate items are also on display at the factory. Then, the group will take a tour thru the factory and see how some chocolates are made. At the end of the tour, each person will receive a candy sample.

Titusville

DRAKE WELL MUSEUM

Lots of fun pushin' the buttons

Titusville - *East Bloss Street, 205 Museum Lane (I-80 to exit 3, off SR8 North) 16354. Phone: (814) 827-2797. www.drakewell.org. Hours: Wednesday-Sunday 10:00am-4:00pm (April-October). Friday-Sunday (November-March). Admission: $10.00 adult, $8.00 senior (65+), $5.00 child (3-11). Note: Head over to Pithole City (off SR227 between Pleasantville and Plummer) Visitor's Center (June-Labor Day). Within the park is a bike trail and tourist train ride depot. Blacksmith demos occasional Saturdays each month. Look at Calendar of Events. Educators: before you visit, ask when they are offering a Nitro Show to student groups and ask to tag along. Their education dept. has lesson plan materials they can send you.*

The birthplace of the petroleum industry. Edward Drake drilled the first oil well in 1859 through layers of sandstone. Start your visit with a video about the challenges Drake and his driller, "Uncle" Billy Smith faced to succeed. The museum's indoor and outdoor exhibits explain the progress of the oil industry. Operating oil field machinery, historic buildings, and scale models demonstrate primitive and modern drilling processes. Many exhibits have "push buttons" and "cutaways" of the machinery in action (the kids will really like pushing the small button to make all the working parts move). And, they can "squeeze and sniff" oil samples from all over the world, make plastic, send telegraph messages, and find unusual items made from oil in the museum lobby. Some will surprise you (ex. Tape, aspirin). Be sure to purchase a souvenir vial of real crude Pennsylvania oil in the Museum Store and eat your ice cream on the patio.

OIL CREEK & TITUSVILLE RAILROAD

Titusville - *409 South Perry Street (I-80 exit Route 8 north to Perry Street Station) 16354. Phone: (814) 676-1733. http://octrr.org/. Hours: Weekend departures at 1:00pm (June-October). Selected weekday runs in July, August and October. Admission: $20.00 adult, $18.00 senior (60+), $14.00 child (2-12). Tours: 2 1/2 hour narrated trip by guide and audio recording. Note: Railroad memorabilia displays, souvenir area, and snack shop. Caboose Motel right across the street. The Motel features 21 caboose units.*

See the first oil fields in the world tell a story of the oil rush boom days in the valley (similar to the gold rush). Stop by Rynd Farm and Drake Well Park. Ride in restored 1930s passenger cars. One car is the only working railway Post Office car - have your postcard to grandma hand-stamp cancelled while on board.

EASTER BUNNY TRAIN RIDES

Titusville - Oil Creek & Titusville Railroad. Candy treats with the Easter Bunny riding along. Admission. (Weekend before Easter)

SANTA TRAINS

Titusville - Oil Creek & Titusville Railroad. Sing songs and eat treats as you ride the train with Santa aboard. Admission. (second weekend in December)

Warren

KINZUA DAM/ BIG BEND VISITOR'S CENTER

Warren - *1205 Kinzua Road - Route 59 (I-79 to Route 6 east to Route 59 east) 16365. Phone: (814) 726-0661. www.lrp.usace.army.mil/Missions/Recreation/ Lakes/KinzuaDamAlleghenyReservoir.aspx Hours: Daily 10:00am-4:00pm (Summer). Weekends (September, October). Admission: FREE.*

A flood control dam has created a vast waterway known as the Allegheny Reservoir (within Allegheny National Forest). Center features exhibits which explain the purpose of the dam and power plant.

In the summer, there are numerous activities ranging from swimming, boating and water-skiing, to camping, fishing and sightseeing. During the autumn, the Kinzua countryside produces colorful displays of fall foliage with miles of hiking trails and country roads from which to enjoy the brilliant fall scenery. Winter doesn't signal an end to the enjoyment of the outdoors. Hikers turn to cross-country skiing, fishermen continue their sport on the ice and snowmobiles speed along the

many trails and forest roads. The blossoming of the woodland wildflowers signals the arrival of spring in Kinzua Country; and with it, the arrival of trout fishermen, canoeists and nature enthusiasts.

BIG BEND OVERLOOK VISITOR CENTER - The U.S. Army Corps

A railcar post office?

of Engineers maintains a nice visitor center and picnic area just downstream of the Kinzua Dam. The visitor's center, which is open daily from Memorial Day weekend through Labor Day, and weekends in September and October, contains exhibits, displays and brochures which illustrate the purpose of the Kinzu Dam, and highlight recreational and sightseeing opportunities in the area. Several overlooks provide great views of the Kinzua Dam and Allegheny Reservoir.

Chapter 7
South Central
Pennsylvania

Bedford
- Fort Bedford Museum
- Old Bedford Village

Bedford (Schellsburg)
- Gravity Hill

Carlisle
- Kings Gap State Park
- Army Heritage Trail&Museum

Carroll Valley
- Liberty Mountain Ski Area

Fayetteville
- Caledonia State Park

Fort Loudon
- Cowan's Gap State Park

Gardners
- Pine Grove Furnace State Park

Gettysburg
- American Civil War Museum
- Battlefield Bus Tours
- Eisenhower Nat'l Historic Site
- Explore & More Children's Museum
- Gettysburg History Center
- Gettysburg Nat'l Military Park
- Jennie Wade House & Olde Town
- Land Of Little Horses
- Lincoln Train Museum
- Lincoln's Lost Treasure - Downtown Adventure
- Battle Of Gettysburg

Gettysburg (Biglerville)
- National Apple Museum

Halifax
- Lake Tobias Wildlife Park

Hanover
- Codorus State Park
- Utz Potato Chips
- Snyders Of Hanover

Harrisburg
- Fort Hunter Mansion & Park
- Pennsylvania State Capitol Building

- Whitaker Center For Science And The Arts
- Pennsylvania National Fire Museum
- National Civil War Museum
- City Island
- Pride Of The Susquehanna Riverboat Tour
- Harrisburg Senators Baseball
- State Museum Of Pennsylvania
- Wildwood Lake Sanctuary
- Pennsylvania Farm Show

Hershey
- Antique Automobile Club Of America Museum
- Hershey Bears Hockey
- Hershey Gardens
- Hershey Lodge
- Hershey Story - The Museum On Chocolate Avenue
- Hershey Trolley Works
- Hersheypark
- Hershey's Chocolate World Visitors Center
- Zoo America North American Wildlife Park

Hummelstown
- Indian Echo Caverns

Imler
- Blue Knob State Park

Lewisberry
- Gifford Pinchot State Park
- Ski Roundtop

Mercersburg
- Whitetail Ski Resort And Mountain Biking Center

Middletown
- Middletown And Hummelstown Railroad

New Park
- Maize Quest Fun Park

Newport
- Little Buffalo State Park

For updates & travel games visit: **www.KidsLoveTravel.com**

Newville
- Colonel Denning State Park

Orrtanna
- Mr. Ed's Elephant Museum

Schellsburg
- Shawnee State Park

Thomasville
- Martin's Potato Chips

York
- Harley-Davidson Motorcycle Museum Tour

York (cont.)
- Agricultural & Industrial

Museums
- York County Heritage Museums
- York Little Theatre
- York County Fire Museum
- Christmas Magic - A Festival Of Lights

York (Hellam)
- Shoe House

Zionsville
- Stahl's Pottery Festival

Travel Journal & Notes:

A Quick Tour of our Hand-Picked
Favorites Around...

South Central
Pennsylvania

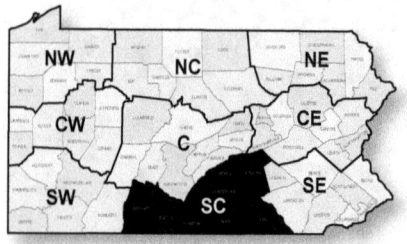

Take a roadtrip honoring our Civil War past in the beautiful South Central PA region. The Road to Gettysburg tells the story of the cost and sacrifice of the Commonwealth, for the common good. This memorable journey will take you beyond the battlefields. Your family can also experience firsthand the people, places, and events that shaped our Civil War heritage. The area is also well-known for its yummy farm and factory tours.

Your road to Gettysburg begins in the capital city, Harrisburg. The painful and proud history of the American Civil War is recounted here at the **National Civil War Museum**. Who wants to see Dinosaur bones? Who wouldn't! Then come to **The State Museum of Pennsylvania** next on your itinerary and plunge through the pages of Pennsylvania history. Lots of hands-on activities for the little explorers are in the Curiosity Connection. Take a late lunch or give the family a mid-day snack at the one of the yummy pizza joints downtown. Round two can begin with a production at the Popcorn Hat Players inside Strawberry Square or head over to Harrisburg's City Island for a host of activities. **Whitaker Center for Science and the Arts** sparks the imagination and encourages thought provoking conversations with your family as you try all of the hands-on exhibits in the Harsco Science Center.

Hershey Harrisburg is great for stimulating little ones senses when it comes to experiencing the outdoors or darting indoors on rainy days. No matter what season, this region is a wonderland to behold and traverse through. Play along the Susquehanna River, relax at a state park or be really brave and try a new thrill ride at **Hershey Park**! Many of the attractions surrounding the amusement park enrich the trip – whether it's a trolley tour of town or experimenting in the Chocolate Lab or being treated to chocolates on your pillow each night at Hershey Lodge.

Once in York, there's a historic site nearly everywhere. One of its museums, the **Agriculture and Industry Museum**, houses a collection of York County-built automobiles, an authentic Conestoga Wagon, and a 1937 Aeronca K airplane. Part of the fun is trying to figure out what each piece of machinery did. It's like a quirky game to meander through the museum maze of "junk." Nearby are many snack food tours in the Hanover area.

Enjoy a living history re-enactment of the war at the American Civil War Museum. At the **Gettysburg National Military Park Museum and Visitors Center**, experience one of the largest Civil War collections brought to life with interactive exhibits. They've added more flare and engagement to the site allowing kids to enjoy history from simple, colorful displays. Later, take a simulated ride to Gettysburg on the **Lincoln Train**.

Many who visit the Gettysburg area may miss the chance to escape the historical district and venture out into the countryside. The **National Apple Museum** is nearby and offers a cute, homespun museum plus periodic tours of the apple orchards. Why are the trees so small? Kids get involved right from the beginning (they eat an apple snack with juice). As you sip on your juice, watch a film about apple varieties, picking, and production. They show footage of actual apple product factory production lines located in town.

Another enchanting part of the Gettysburg countryside is off US 30 west to the **Land of Little Horses**. As you enter you'll be greeted by adorable small horses (most only a few feet tall) that seem to be just the right size for kids to enjoy. Take in a horse show or costume parade.

Sites and attractions are listed in order by City, Zip Code, and Name. Symbols indicated represent:

 Restaurants    Lodging

Bedford

FORT BEDFORD MUSEUM

Bedford - *110 Fort Bedford Drive (I-76, exit 11, SR320 - Pitt Street - Downtown) 15522. Phone: (814) 623-8891 or (800) 259-4284. www.fortbedfordmuseum. org. Hours: Wednesday-Sunday 11:00am-5:00pm (mid-May thru mid-October). Saturday-Sunday 10am-4pm (Nov-May). Admission: Generally $5.00-$7.00*

The French and Indian War fort site - "The Fort in the Forest". A blockhouse structure that houses the large scale model of the original fort along with Native American household artifacts. From flint rock rifles to hand tools to clothing – each help you explore pioneer and frontier days in western Pennsylvania. In order to secure the water and secure the banks of the stream, a gallery with loopholes extended from the central bastion on its north front down to the water's edge. A ladder-like arrangement of steps led down the river's bluff-like south bank. This enclosed gallery was a real military curiosity. The fort controlled the river gap and served a British stockade against the French for years.

OLD BEDFORD VILLAGE

Bedford - *220 Sawblade Road (1/2 mile south of PA Turnpike (I-70/76), exit 11-Route 220) 15522. oldbedfordvillage.com. Phone: (814) 623-1156. Hours: Daily (except Wednesday) 9:00am-5:00pm (Memorial Day-Labor Day). Thursday-Sunday (September/October). Admission: $10.00 adult, $9.00 senior, $5.00 student (age 6-18). Tours: Self-guided. Guided tours are available with advance notice. Note: Dress for walking on the natural roadways. Pendergrass Tavern. Many warm weather re-enactment weekends.*

Craftsmen are in action as you relive the past walking through 40 log homes and shops (see them making brooms, baskets, bread, pottery). There are seasonal productions such as "Welcome to Early America" - a recreated world of the 1790s Pioneer America or summer theatre musical, comedies or mysteries (814-623-7555 for reservations). In 1794, President George Washington led federal troops with his battle headquarters here in Bedford. After the troops left, the colonial industry flourished with blacksmiths, attorneys, a doctor, distillers, innkeepers, soldiers, millers, and farmers setting up shop in the village. In all, over 14 period skills are represented at the Village, and many of the products made on site can be found at the Village Craft Shop. And don't miss the opportunity to learn one of the many crafts available through Old Bedford Village's educational programs.

PUMPKIN FESTIVAL

PUMPKIN FESTIVAL

Bedford - Old Bedford Village. Pumpkin painting and carving, pie-eating contests. Pumpkin patch (wagon rides out there). Refreshments. (third weekend in October)

CHRISTMAS OPEN HOUSE

Bedford - Old Bedford Village. Tours of decorated, historical buildings. Refreshments and musical entertainment. Re-enactors. Admission. (1st & 2nd weekend in December)

GRAVITY HILL

Bedford (Schellsburg) - *Bethel Hollow Road 15522. . www.gravityhill.com.*

Tucked away in the "less traveled" area of Bedford County is a marvel. Often talked about, but seldom found, Gravity Hill is a phenomenon. Cars roll uphill, water flows the wrong way ... it's a place where gravity has gone haywire. Some people like to take water or various other non-flammable, bio-degradeable liquids and pour them onto the road. The liquids will flow uphill. There are directions on the website about finding Gravity Hill with a minimum of wrong turns. Daylight hours suggested.

KINGS GAP STATE PARK

Carlisle - *500 Kings Gap Road 17013. https://www.dcnr.pa.gov/StateParks/ FindAPark/KingsGapEnvironmentalEducationCenter/Pages/default.aspx Phone: (717) 486-5031. Admission: to PA State Parks is FREE however swimming, marina and camping/lodging fees apply.*

Kings Gap offers a panoramic view of the Cumberland Valley. Sixteen miles of hiking trails interconnect three main areas and are open year-round. Kings Gap offers environmental education programs from the pre-school environmental awareness program to environmental problem solving programs.

US ARMY HERITAGE MUSEUM

Carlisle - *950 Soldiers Drive (Pa Turnpike exit 226 to Rt 11 South) 17013. www. armyheritage.org Phone: (717) 245-3972. Hours: Monday-Saturday 10am-5pm & Sunday Noon-4pm. Admission: FREE*

HERITAGE TRAIL: The Army Heritage Trail; a mile long interactive outdoor trail with macro exhibit components spanning from the French and Indian War period to Current Operations. Examples include a replica of Redoubt #10 from the Battle of Yorktown, Winter Civil War Cabins; WWI trench, WWII Barracks, and HESCO Bastion barrier checkpoint, along with several pieces of military equipment.

MUSEUM: Plan your visit to "The Solider Experience" interactive exhibit featuring a parachute landing simulation, marksmanship practice and instructions from a digital drill sergeant on how to salute, stand at attention and turn and more.

LIBERTY MOUNTAIN SKI AREA

Carroll Valley - *78 Country Club Trail (Rte. 30 to Rte. 116, Liberty Mountain Resort is 8 miles on the left) 17320. Phone: (717) 642-8282. https://www. libertymountainresort.com/*

Nestled near the scenic Catoctin Mountains on 275 beautiful acres, with more than 100 acres of skiing, snowboarding and snow tubing trails. Just eight miles southwest of historic Gettysburg. Skiing, Snowboarding and Snow Tubing. Longest Run: 5300 ft.; 16 Slopes & Trails. Snow Monsters Kids club.

CALEDONIA STATE PARK

Fayetteville - *40 Rocky Mountain Rd (US Route 30) 17222. Phone: (717) 352-2161. https://www.dcnr.pa.gov/StateParks/FindAPark/CaledoniaStatePark/Pages/default.aspx. Admission: to PA State Parks is FREE however swimming, marina and camping/lodging fees apply.*

Known locally as South Mountain, Caledonia located on the northern-most section of the Blue Ridge Mountains fifteen miles west of Gettysburg via Route 30. The Appalachian Trail passes through the central portion of the park. It is a great place for family outings: The park features a large, ADA accessible swimming pool with a small snack bar. The pool is open 11:00am-7:00pm from Memorial Day weekend to Labor Day, unless posted otherwise. Visitor Center, Campsites, Fishing, Trails, and Cross-Country Skiing. Mr. Ed's Elephant Museum (a collection of 6000 elephants) is open daily just 2 miles east of the park on Rte. 30.

COWAN'S GAP STATE PARK

Fort Loudon - *(PA 75 North to Richmond Furnace, follow signs) 17224. Phone: (717) 485-3948. https://www.dcnr.pa.gov/StateParks/FindAPark/CowansGapStatePark/Pages/default.aspx Admission: to PA State Parks is FREE however swimming, marina and camping/lodging fees apply, with reservation or entrance.*

Logging Road Trail: 1.7-mile, easy hiking. This old logging road can be walked from one end of the park to the other and is a good trail to use to make loop hikes with other trails on the side of Cove Mountain. Lakeside Trail: 1.5-mile, easy hiking. This very pleasant, nearly level, scenic trail encompasses Cowans Gap Lake. This is the most popular trail in the park. Beach, Visitor

Center, Boat Rentals, Campsites, Rustic Cabins, and Winter Activities. Buchanan's Birthplace State Historical Park nearby. Environmental Education and Interpretation (April-November). Check out the landslide exhibit on Knobsville Road Trail.

PINE GROVE FURNACE STATE PARK

Gardners - *1100 Pine Grove Road (PA Route 233 & 34) 17324. Phone: (717) 486-7174. https://www.dcnr.pa.gov/StateParks/FindAPark/PineGroveFurnaceStatePark/Pages/default.aspx Admission: to PA State Parks is FREE however swimming, marina and camping/lodging fees apply, with reservation or entrance.*

This park was once the site of the Pine Grove Furnace Iron Works that dates from 1764. Historical buildings include the ironmaster's mansion, a gristmill, an inn and several residences. The self-guiding historical trail leads you through the remains of the iron works. The Appalachian Trail passes through the park. Two beaches are open from May 1 to September 30, 8:00am to sunset. Visitor Center, Boat Rentals, Campsites, Kite-flying Area. Fishing, short Hiking Trails, and Cross-Country Skiing.

APPALACHIAN TRAIL MUSEUM

From Memorial Day through Labor Day the Museum is open every day from noon to 4:00 PM, and in the spring and fall during the same hours but only on weekends. Admission is free. www.atmuseum.org.

Located about two miles from the midpoint of the Appalachian Trail, the Museum is halfway between Maine and Georgia. Appropriately, the Museum is housed in a building that is itself a historical artifact, a structure built more than two hundred years ago as a grist mill. It stands across the road from the Pine Grove general store, a site famed in hiker lore. It is here that thru-hikers traditionally stop to celebrate reaching the midpoint by eating—or attempting to eat—a half gallon of ice cream in one sitting.

Current exhibits include a trail shelter that was built by hiker legend Earl Shaffer. The shelter, which has been replaced with a more modern one, was painstakingly disassembled at its former site on Peters Mountain in Pennsylvania and reassembled in the new Museum. In addition, there are artifacts that belonged to other hiking pioneers such as Grandma Gatewood, Gene Espy, and Ed Garvey. In the Museum computers display the more than 12,000 photos that have been taken of thru-hikers as they reached Harpers Ferry on their journeys either north or south. There is also a children's discovery area and hiker welcoming areas both inside and outside.

Gettysburg

AMERICAN CIVIL WAR MUSEUM

Gettysburg - *297 Steinwehr Avenue (US15 - Business Route) 17325. Phone: (717) 334-6245. www.gettysburgmuseum.com. Hours: Daily 9:00am-5:00pm (March-December). Admission: $9.00 adult, $7.00 child (6-12). Note: Several weekends throughout the year, the Gettysburg Heritage Center hosts complimentary Living History Encampments. Visitors are welcomed to actively learn by strolling through the camp, viewing drills and demonstrations, and engaging in conversation with historians. Freebies: scavenger hunt: https://www.gettysburgmuseum.com/uploads/2/6/5/5/26550332/new_scavenger_hunt.pdf*

More than 200 life-size wax figures in 30 different scenes re-create crucial moments but also describe the cause and effects of the conflict called the Battle at Gettysburg. Besides strategic planning and battle scenes, voices from history blend with scenes and words to recreate the past. Jennie Wade bakes bread before being fatally shot in her sister's kitchen. John Brown, bound in ropes, walks to the gallows. Slaves using the Underground Railroad try to escape to freedom. And Abraham Lincoln sits in the theatre on that fateful day. At the end of the tour, you'll enter the Battleroom Auditorium where the battle is re-enacted (with wax figures and lighting). It's an easy explanation of the three days of battle (not too technical for kids). Lincoln arrives and gives his address at the end.

BATTLEFIELD BUS TOURS

Gettysburg - *778 Baltimore Street 17325. www.gettysburgbattlefieldtours.com. Phone: (717) 334-6296. Hours: Daily 9:00am-9:00pm (Summer), 9:00am-7:00pm (Spring & Fall), 9:00am- 5:00pm (rest of year). Weather permitting. Admission: $38 adult, $23 child (6-12). Tickets can be ordered or purchased at area hotels. Tours: 23 mile tour of "The Battle of Gettysburg". 2 hour narration audiotape tours leave several times daily, depending on season. Reserve timed tickets online.*

A Hollywood cast of actors, technicians, and special effects recreate the Battle of Gettysburg as you tour the Battlefield from the famous Double Decker buses (seasonal, warm months). Battlefield Guide bus tours offer the visitor a truly unique perspective into the struggles of the three days' battle. And you re-live it all under the skies of Gettysburg most famous landmarks: Little Round Top, Devil's Den, Wheatfield, Peach Orchard, Pickett's Charge, and High Water Mark. Enclosed bus for other cold, rainy season tours. Note: a family's only concern may be the length of the tour - too long for squirmy toddlers and hyper young kids. Better to buy the audio drive tour and go on your own.

EISENHOWER NATIONAL HISTORIC SITE

Gettysburg - *1195 Baltimore Pike (adjacent to Gettysburg Battlefield) 17325. www.nps.gov/eise. Admission: FREE. Tours: Shuttle buses leave the Battlefield Visitors Center several times daily 9:30am-3:30pm.*

During his Presidency, President and Mrs. Eisenhower used the farm as a weekend retreat, a refuge in time of illness, and a comfortable meeting place for world leaders. From 1961 to 1969, it was the Eisenhower's home during a vigorous and active retirement. Today the farm is maintained as it was during the Eisenhower years and the President's home retains nearly all its original furnishings. You are invited to tour the home and grounds, and take a walk to the cattle barns and skeet range. It's surprising how much you can learn about a President by checking out his house and snooping through his stuff!

EXPLORE & MORE CHILDREN'S MUSEUM

Gettysburg - *20 East High Street (near the circle) 17325. Phone: (717) 337-9151. www.exploreandmore.com. Hours: Wednesday-Friday 10am-4pm, Saturday 10am-5pm, Sunday 10:30am-3:30pm. Admission: $13.00 adult (age 1+). Note: Toy store.*

Located in an historic home, they have seven rooms where children can create a work of art, play house the way people lived around the time of the Civil War, make a bubble large enough to stand inside of, or experiment with mixing colors (make color explosions in milk!) and waterworks. Children can make puppets and then perform a show with them. More pretend play in the Construction Zone area (receiving, conveyor, shipping, recycling – clean up) or the Black Light Dress Up Room (wild!). We especially liked the 1860s Room and all the dress up clothes and play items to play Civil War era "house". At this place, you can even play with an overhead projector, just like a teacher. Best for kids ages 3 to 8. Give your children a break from the battlefield nearby!

GETTYSBURG HISTORY CENTER

Gettysburg - *241 Steinwehr Ave 17325. www.gettysburgdiorama.com. Phone: (717) 334-6408. Hours: Daily 9:00am-8:00pm. Extended weekend and summer evening hours. Admission: $6.00-$9.00 (age 6+).*

The Gettysburg Diorama is the largest military scale model in the United States. The fully narrated diorama features more than 20,000 hand-painted soldiers, horses, cannons as well as Gettysburg buildings that became famous during the battle. Learn what role your home state played in the Battle. See the armies' arrival, battle lines forming, and the advances and retreats of armies.

The hills, roads and fields are accurate to scale and provide an overview of all three days of battle with an exciting sound and light show.

GETTYSBURG NATIONAL MILITARY PARK

Gettysburg - *1195 Baltimore Pike (follow signs off US 15) 17325. Phone: (717) 334-1124 Park or (717) 338-9114 Eisenhower Site. www.nps.gov/gett. Hours: Daily 8:00am-5:00pm. Open until 6:00pm (April-September). The park is open at 6:00am each day and closes after dark. Closed Thanksgiving, Christmas and New Years. Admission: VISITOR CENTER/BATTLEFIELD - FREE. MUSEUM: $12.75 adult, $10.75 youth (ages 6-12). Add $3-$6.00 for film and cyclorama. Tickets can be purchased on site or online at www.gettysburgfoundation.org. Tours: Park grounds and roads - Self guided tours 6:00am - 10:00pm. Educators: Find curriculum: www.nps.gov/gett/learn/ education/curriculummaterials.htm*

The Battle of Gettysburg was a turning point in the Civil War, the Union victory in the summer of 1863 that ended General Robert E. Lee's second and most ambitious invasion of the North. It was the war's bloodiest battle with 51,000 casualties. It also provided President Abraham Lincoln with the setting for his most famous address.

Visitors to Gettysburg National Military Park should begin at the Museum and Visitor Center where the park offers information, a vast museum about Gettysburg and the Civil War, the fully restored Gettysburg Cyclorama and the film "A New Birth of Freedom", narrated by Morgan Freeman, a central feature in the new center that orients visitors to the significance of Gettysburg. The center provides information on the numerous ways to tour the battlefield park. The center also has an expansive bookstore and a refreshment saloon, which offers snacks, sandwiches and drinks.

When visitors tour Gettysburg, they don't have to picture the battle in their minds. The recent restoration of this National Park and the new Cyclorama bring the Civil War to life in dramatic ways. If you haven't visited the park in a while, it is a must see for families. Here is the site of the major Civil War battle and Abraham Lincoln's Gettysburg Address:

- BATTLEFIELD - The most important major blow to the Confederate Army and the most casualties (51,000) on the first few days of early July 1863. See key places: Cemetery Hill and Ridge, Culp's Hill, Little Round Top, and Observation Tower. (We suggest the audio tape tour for kids).

- <u>NOVEMBER 19, 1863, CEMETERY</u> - President Lincoln dedicated the National Cemetery on the battlefield and delivered his famous speech "The Gettysburg Address".

- <u>DAVID WILLS HOUSE</u>: 8 Lincoln Square (downtown). The 1863 house includes the restored office where prominent attorney David Wills coordinated post-battle recovery efforts and invited a war-worn President Lincoln to deliver "a few appropriate remarks" when he dedicated the cemetery. Visitors will be able to see the restored second-floor bedroom where the President finished revising the Gettysburg Address on Nov. 18, 1864. **https://www.nps.gov/gett/planyourvisit/david-wills-house.htm**. (Hours: Friday-Sunday 1:00am-5:00pm (Memorial Day thru late November), occassional winter and spring hours. Admission: FREE

- <u>CYCLORAMA</u> - A 30 minute description while standing in the middle of a 360 degree circular wall painting of the battlefield and Pickett's Charge, the climactic moment of the battle (a sight & sound experience). Climb the stairs into the Cyclorama tower (in the new Museum & Visitors Center) and be taken back to July 3, 1863. As the audio narration begins, you hear the story of the charge and lights highlight certain portions of the canvas. Rocks, weapons and bushes in front of the painting bring a sense of depth...putting you in the middle of the battle. 9:00 am - 4:30pm (every 1/2 hour).

- <u>MUSEUM OF THE CIVIL WAR</u> - A large collection of Civil War artifacts,  especially weapons and uniforms. The Camp Life exhibits are the most interesting relating visuals to the life of a soldier.

ANNIVERSARY OF LINCOLN'S GETTYSBURG ADDRESS

Gettysburg - Gettysburg National Military Park. Daytime, Gettysburg National Cemetery. The annual observance of President Abraham Lincoln's famous address with brief memorial services and noted speakers. (one day in the third week in November)

JENNIE WADE HOUSE & OLDE TOWN

Gettysburg - 548 Baltimore Street (Adjacent to Olde Town) 17325. Phone: (717) 334-4100. jenniewadehouse.com Hours: Sunday-Friday 10:00am-4:00pm, Saturday 9:00am-5:00pm. Guided Tour: $12.00-$15.00 (age 6+). Self-guided slightly less. Note: Due to the dramatic nature and story of this tour - parents with children younger than 1st or 2nd grade should probably arrange to be part of a school tour. They only give brief descriptions of the events and not full details.

With minor changes and repairs, the Museum remains much as Jennie must have known it over 140 years ago. Authentically furnished from cellar to attic, the museum is a shrine to Jennie and to life and living during the American Civil War. Jennie Wade was the only civilian killed during the battle of Gettysburg and the situations that led to her death were quite dramatic. While baking bread for the soldiers in her kitchen, a stray bullet hit and killed young 20 year old Jennie. (a realistic hologram of Jennie is seen in the kitchen - and you see the actual bullet hole). A soldier tells you all the details including the fact that her fiancé was killed just days later in battle, but never knew of Jennie's fate!

LAND OF LITTLE HORSES

Gettysburg - 125 Glenwood Drive (3 miles West on US30, then follow signs) 17325. Phone: (717) 334-7259. www.landoflittlehorses.com. Hours: Monday-Saturday 10:00am-5:00pm, Sunday Noon-5:00pm (June-Labor Day). Weekends only (May, September, October).
Admission: $10.99 general (age 3+). Note: Air-conditioned arena. The Gift Horse Shop. Carousel, train tram, petting farm. Put on a "feed bag" at the Hobby Horse Café. Wagon and pony rides available for extra $5.00.

As you enter you'll be greeted by adorable small horses (most only a few feet tall) that seem to be just the right size for kids to enjoy. Many are in separate pens throughout the park, some are in the barn, others are getting ready for the show in the arena. We took in the Barn Show first and loved the chance to see the horses prance around and be gently petted. Especially cute are the mothers with their young. The highlight of this farm is the Performing Animals Show. They get the kids involved by "kissing a pig" (there's a trick involved - 2 kids volunteered and did it!), or helping with the animal tricks. "Something Special" is a daily event at the Land of Little Horses. The event changes every day, and can be anything from Miniature Horse costume parades (where you dress up horses and show them off to the entire park), fun games with prizes for the winners, goat milking & sheep sheering, photo opportunities with the stars of Arena Performances, and much more! They also have cart races, saddle kids, and host weekend chicken races - so cute, pick your favorite animal and cheer it on!

LINCOLN TRAIN MUSEUM

Gettysburg - *425 Steinwehr Avenue   17325. www.lincolntrain.com. Phone: (717) 334-5678. Hours: Daily 10:00am-2:00pm, extended to 5pm weekends (April-October). Reduced days & hours each winter. Admission: $7.00-$9.00 (age 6+). Note: Events (in the diorama display) that led up to this historic train ride. Large train collection layout that reproduces the Civil War Era.*

A simulated 1836 train ride with Lincoln and statesmen on a 12 minute trip. See Civil War grounds and overhear conversations that might have occurred on that trip. They project actual footage of a steam train ride as your seat and floorboards move to the straights, curves, and rumbles of the track. Statesmen speak of this time, in the still present war, Mr. President's ill son, and thoughts of re-election. We suggest this stop for young kids (all ages for that matter) because it easily and uniquely illustrates the emotion/history behind the Gettysburg Address. The Lincoln Toy Train collection features over 1000 trains and dioramas illustrating the railroad's role during the Civil War.

BATTLE OF GETTYSBURG

Gettysburg - Yingling Farm (3 miles outside of town). https://www.thepcwa.org/. (717) 338-1525. Reenactments, events at Yingling Farm (site of film) include camps, gallant stands and charges. Interpreters give a really nice narrative of what's happening with each battle. Although it's a three day event, if you only had one day to select, pick the day when they re-enact Pickett's Charge. It's the most well known and elaborately staged of the battles. Food concession are plentiful. If sunny day, wear sunscreen, hats, etc. Admission: $15.00-$30.00 per person. (long week of July 4th)

NATIONAL APPLE MUSEUM

Gettysburg (Biglerville) - *154 West Hanover Street (From Gettysburg, take Rt. 34 north 6 miles to Rt. 394, turn left, go three blocks. Museum on left. Look for big red barn) 17307. Phone: (717) 677-4556. www.nationalapplemuseum.com. Hours: Saturday 10:00am-4:00pm, Sunday 1:00-4:00pm (May-October). Call for special group arrangement during other days and times. Admission: FREE, donations appreciated. Tours: Guided every 2 hours (last one at 3:00pm). Self-guided audio tape tours. Note: Picnic area. Gift shop - everything in there has apples on it!*

Miles and miles of sweet, juicy apples...

What a treat this place is! America's favorite fruit (red delicious, the most popular) is highlighted here. Kids can get involved right from the beginning (eat a snack of apple juice and cookies). As you sip on your juice, they show a film about apple varieties, picking, and production. This film is entertaining (not boring at all) and the kids are thrilled seeing thousands of apples in every scene. Because many apple production facilities don't give tours, you'll get a great video look at how they "produce" apples for applesauce. How do they keep apples unbruised and ripe all year long? Antique equipment displays and old town dioramas are upstairs. The bug displays really appeal to the kids. See the "apple biz" come to life when you drive just up the road through apple orchards. Do you know why orchards love bees, ladybug beetles, and dwarf trees?

APPLE BLOSSOM FESTIVAL

Gettysburg (Biglerville) - South Mountain Fairgrounds. Live entertainment, orchard tours, scenic wagon rides, delicious apple foods, plus! (first full weekend of May)

NATIONAL APPLE HARVEST FESTIVAL

Gettysburg (Biglerville) -South Mountain Fairgrounds. www.appleharvest.com. An Old time festival of apple products, live country music, hundreds of arts and crafters, antique autos and tractors, steam engines, orchard tours and food. Admission. (first and second weekend in October)

LAKE TOBIAS WILDLIFE PARK

Halifax - *760 Tobias Drive (Rt. 322/22 West to Dauphin. Rt. 225 North to Halifax. Four miles on Rt. 225 North to Fisherville) 17032. www.laketobias.com. Phone: (717) 362-9126. Hours: Monday-Friday 10:00am-6:00pm, Saturday & Sunday 10:00am-7:00pm (Summer), Weekends only (May, September, October). Admission: Park admission: $9.00 walk about and/or $8.00 drive thru safariri) (ages 3+). Military FREE. Tours: Last Safari Tour One Hour Before Closing.*

Hundreds of wild and exotic animals - alligators, buffalo, llamas, monkeys and reptile animal shows. Visit with giraffes, too. Specially designed cruisers take you across 150 acres of rolling land where you see herds of wild and exotic animals from around the world. Tour guides travel with you giving expert info on the various species and their habitats. You will be surprised at how close you come to these animals. Also a petting zoo and fishing ponds for "tamer" activity.

For updates & travel games visit: **www.KidsLoveTravel.com**

CODORUS STATE PARK

Hanover - *1066 Blooming Grove Road (PA Route 216) 17331. Phone: (717) 637-2816. https://www.dcnr.pa.gov/StateParks/FindAPark/CodorusStatePark/Pages/default.aspx. Admission: to PA State Parks is FREE however swimming, marina & camping/lodging fees apply.*

The 1,275-acre Lake Marburg is popular with fishermen, boaters and swimmers. Codorus is also an excellent place to observe spring and fall migrations of waterfowl and warblers. The park offers interpretive programs and hikes. Boat rentals are available and a restaurant is convenient to the park. Pool, Visitor Center, Horseback Riding, Sledding, Campsites, Fishing, Trails, Winter Sports. Like Disc Golf? Codorus Disc Golf Course is rated one of the most challenging courses in Pennsylvania.

UTZ POTATO CHIPS

Hanover - *900 High Street (SR94 North & Clearview Streets) 17331. Phone: (717) 637-6644. www.utzsnacks. com. Hours: Monday-Wednesday 10:00am-3:00pm, Thursday 10am-Noon. Admission: FREE Tours: Self-guided (30 minutes) Note: Outlet store. Try a new flavor like Crab or Carolina BBQ.*

Walk along an elevated, glass enclosed observation gallery to observe potato chips in production. View close up TV monitors and listen to the descriptions of each step of the process. This is a modern and very clean facility. We probably got the closest to large conveyors of fried chips here (behind glass of course!). A new experience was watching home-cooked kettle chips being made. As you study family history photographs, enjoy a free bag of chips! We especially liked the "platform bridges" that they had throughout the tour so the "little ones" could see too!

SNYDERS OF HANOVER

Hanover - *1350 York Street 17731. www. snydersofhanover.com/our-story/bakery-tour.html Phone: (800) 233-7125 ext. 8592. Admission: FREE. Tours: Tuesday, Wednesday, Thursday at 10am, 10:30am, 11am, 11:30am & 1pm, 1:30pm & 2pm. (24 hour notice is needed). Ages 5 and up. The tour lasts 30 minutes and participants must be able to climb stairs.*

Snyder's has been known as America's Pretzel Bakery for a century, and today, the company still makes a variety of snack foods, led by its famous hard pretzels. Free guided tours are offered with advance reservations. Meet at the factory storefront (where you'll no doubt be nibbling on samples before touring). Watch a short video covering the company history starting with potato chips made at home in the early 1920s to the 1970s when they established sourdough hard pretzels. After that you'll see the oven room where you can almost taste the pretzels. The guide then finishes up by showing you how potato chips are made from beginning to end. The differences you'll notice on

DID YOU KNOW?

Pennsylvania is the "Snack Food" capital of the US.

this snack food tour are the numerous and extra large baking ovens and highly automated packaging systems. Machines build boxes while another machine fills the bags and yet another machine boxes the bags and then seals the cases shut. Kids love all the automation!

Harrisburg

FORT HUNTER MANSION & PARK

Harrisburg - 5300 North Front Street (from US 81 take exit 66. Take North Front Street 2 miles. 17110. Phone: (717) 599-5751. www.forthunter.org. Hours: Park is open daily from 8:00am to dusk. Admission: $4.00-$7.00. Tours: Mansion tours are Tuesday-Saturday 10:00am-4:30pm, Sundays Noon-4:30pm (May-December). The Mansion is closed Mondays, Holidays and January thru April.

Fort Hunter was part of a chain of forts along the Susquehanna River built by the British in 1756 at the outset of the French and Indian War. Spectacularly situated on a bluff overlooking the Susquehanna River and the Blue Mountain Range, this 40 acre park invites visitors to relax and explore Pennsylvania history. Professionally guided tours of the elegantly restored Mansion look back in time to sophisticated country living in the nineteenth century. Fort Hunter is a 19th century plantation complex hosting nine structures listed on the National Register of Historic Places.

FORT HUNTER DAY

Harrisburg - Fort Hunter Mansion & Park. Autumn festival featuring a visit from Abraham Lincoln, children's crafts and games, exhibits, farm animals, music, craft show, demonstrations, food and more. FREE. (third Sunday in September)

CHRISTMAS AT FORT HUNTER

Harrisburg - Fort Hunter Mansion & Park. Decorated for the season with natural trimmings; guided tours are offered. Toy Train Exhibit. Festival of Trees. Regular admission. (mostly weekends in December but also Mansion tours regular weekday hours)

PENNSYLVANIA STATE CAPITOL BUILDING

Harrisburg - *Third & State Streets 17101. www.pacapitol.com. Phone: (800) TOUR-N-PA. Hours: Monday-Friday 8:30am-4:00pm, Saturday, Sunday, & Holiday 9:00am, 11:00am, 1:00pm, & 3:00pm. Closed major holidays. Admission: FREE Tours: Guided - every 1/2 hour, weekdays (except lunch - 12:00 - 1:00pm). Schedule them: www.pacapitol.com/book-a-tour. Specific times listed for weekends above.*
Guided tours are 30 minutes long and worth the time. Note: Stop at Info Center first for a brochure of self-guided tour. Welcome Center is open weekdays only. Educators: wait until you see all the fun, colorful or coloring worksheets they have under Teachers Tools: www.pacapitol.com/teachers_tools.html

The 272-foot dome will stun everyone as you stand underneath it and look up. Your neck could get sore because you'll be staring a good while. As you pass though bronze and ornately carved wooden doors, you can climb the stairs to the second and fourth floors to view the elegant and handsome Senate and House chambers. The favorite (and most educational) area is the Welcome Center. From the Ben Franklin video in miniature, to Hello History (take a telephone call from famous Pennsylvania leaders and athletes) to the glass window case full of colored balls (representing the number of bills that a state legislator considers in a year - there's a lot!). Other exhibits that encourage learning about laws (for kids and adults) are interactive displays of a "Day in the Life of a Legislator" (try to get your birthday as a holiday), voting (actually sit in a voting desk) and the making of a law (presented through a colorful display - like the game "Mousetrap" full of tracks, pulleys, and chains that follow a funny course). What a wonderful way to teach government!

WHITAKER CENTER FOR SCIENCE AND THE ARTS

Harrisburg - *222 Market Street (Downtown - Diagonal to the State Capitol) 17101. Phone: (717) 214-ARTS. www.whitakercenter.org. Hours: Tuesday-Saturday 9:30am-5:00pm. Sunday 11:30am-5:00pm. Admission: $15.00 adult, $13.00 senior (60+), $10.00 child (age 3+). IMAX additional charge. Combo discounts offered. Note: Center closed Thanksgiving and Christmas Day. Food court attached by walkway. In addition to hands-on exhibits, the Science Center also features Stage Two, a "black box" theater; & Big Science Theatre.*

Their motto is "Question Everything". Nine different themed exhibit areas use performing arts to teach science concepts. How is dancing linked to science and physics? What are backstage secrets of how lighting and special effects contribute to the theater experience? Have you ever "walked through" a kaleidoscope? (you can here!). The younger kids will spend most of their time in the "kids hall" (ages 8 and below) where they too, get to experiment with light and sound! Other exhibits: Culture and Communication (They can look beneath their skin to see what really happens when they smile, and try to echo sounds from languages they've never heard before). Physics which includes Forces and Motion, Simple Machines, Bodies In Motion: The Physics of Human Movement (explores the art of the human body as it moves), and Backstage Science. KidsPlace includes a Midtown Market, Storybook Stage, Waterworks, ArtWorks, and a City Building for construction fanatics. What we like best - they are always focused on making each space engaging and change exhibits - for example, Legos or Tinkertoys traveling spaces.

PENNSYLVANIA NATIONAL FIRE MUSEUM

Harrisburg - *1820 N. Fourth St., downtown 17102. www.pnfm.org. Phone: (717) 232-8915. Hours: Tuesday-Saturday 10:00am-4:00pm, Sunday 1:00-4:00pm. Closed Mondays and Holidays. Admission: $10.00 adult, $7.00 senior and student. Family: $30.00.*

Housed in the 1899 Victorian firehouse Reily Hose Company No. 10, the Pennsylvania National Fire Museum displays the history of the Fire and Emergency Services. Several displays feature hand and horse-drawn equipment from the 1700 and 1800's and motorized apparatus from 1911 through 1947. There is a wide array of firefighter artifacts throughout the museum including firefighters' tools and fancy parade helmets. The museum is staffed by volunteers and they gladly answer kids' questions or will show you a video about firefighting history.

NATIONAL CIVIL WAR MUSEUM

Harrisburg - 1 Lincoln Circle at Reservoir Park (Interstate 83, Take Exit 50 West (Progress Exit & US Route 22 / Walnut Street) 17103. Phone: (717) 260-1861 or (866) BLU-GRAY. www.nationalcivilwarmuseum.org. Hours: Monday-Saturday 10:00am-5:00pm, Sunday Noon-5:00pm. Extended spring/summer hours Sunday mornings and Wednesday evenings. (Closed Thanksgiving, Christmas & New Year's Day). Admission: $15 adult, $14 senior (60+), $13 student, $56 family.

From slavery to camp life, the museum will give your kids a better understanding of our country and its people. Follow video screens of an abolitionist, brothers or a slave. A House Divided features comparisons of the Northern and Southern economies, the John Brown raid on Harpers Ferry, the election of Abraham Lincoln, and a map showing the division of the country. The "We the People" video introduces you to ten Americans – Northerners and Southerners, men and women, white and black, military and civilian – who endured typical hardships and heartache in the four-year conflict. One interesting display is set up like a news conference where visitors can ask LIncoln questions and wait for his answer. Because its emphasis is on the humanness of the conflict, you will see more common artifacts - items found in homes or soldier's pockets. Do you know what a "pain bullet" is?

CITY ISLAND

Harrisburg - Walnut & Market Street Bridges (Susquehanna River) 17104. www. watergolfcityisland.com. Hours: Weekdays 6pm-Dark. Wkends 11am-Dark. Note: accessed by Market Street Bridge and Walnut Street Walking Bridge.

City Island's 63 acres hosts a variety of entertainment, food and activity vendors along with a BallPark that is home to the Harrisburg's Senators baseball club. Once ashore, a miniature train provides a leisurely round-the Island tour of all the sights and attractions. Some of the Island's most popular activities are located on its north end, where the unique Water Golf miniature golf course awaits. Nearby, the distinctive Harbourtown Children's Play area beckons visitors with a scaled-down re-creation of an 1840s canal town. Playhouse-type structures include a pirate ship, lighthouse and stores. This mid-19th Century-themed retail village contains a variety of picnic facilities, gazebos, scenic decks and plenty of places to feed the Island's ever-hungry ducks and geese. Water Golf Rates: $9.00 adult, $8.00 child.

PRIDE OF THE SUSQUEHANNA RIVERBOAT

Harrisburg - *(Docked at City Island) 17104. https://www.hbgriverboat.org/. Phone: (717) 234-6500. Hours: Tuesday-Sunday Noon-3:00pm (June-August) Admission: $11.00 adult, $9.00 senior (59+), $6.00 child (3-12). Wednesday has reduced fares. Tours: Indoor and outdoor seating. 45 minute narrated cruise leaves on the hour summer afternoons. Note: Dinner cruises are $35.00 per person from May-October with reservation.*

This short family boat trip passes under 6 bridges and by the grave of the city's founder, John Harris on an authentic paddlewheel boat. Take your children back to yesteryear, and experience a unique method of transportation that was used over 150 years ago. The boat is docked on City Island, which is situated in the middle of the Susquehanna River. The recorded history talk on the way out tells us that the Susquehannock Indians lived on the islands in the river and fished the waters of the Susquehanna River in the 17th Century.

HARRISBURG SENATORS BASEBALL

Harrisburg - *Metro Bank Park (City Island) 17105. Phone: (717) 231-4444. www.senatorsbaseball.com. Admission: $9.00 -$16.00*

The Harrisburg Senators, AA Class farm team of the Washington Nationals, has been a longtime favorite for baseball fans in Pennsylvania's capital city. The first stage of its $45 million renovation project of Commerce Ball Park features a new LED scoreboard, video boards around the stadium, and expanded picnic areas for families. Come see talented players hit it out of the park in the state's capitol. Meet Rascal, the mascot on Sunday afternoons.

STATE MUSEUM OF PENNSYLVANIA

Harrisburg - *300 North Street (3rd & North Street) (Downtown) 17120. Phone: (717) 787-4980. www.statemuseumpa.org. Hours: Wednesday-Saturday, 9:00am-5:00pm., Sunday 12:00-5:00pm. (Closed holidays except Memorial Day and Labor Day) Admission: $5.00-$7.00 per person (age 1+). FREE military. Note: Planetarium (additional $3.00) shows. Gift shop. FREEBIES: Scavenger Hunt Activity Sheets are here:http://statemuseumpa.org/wp-content/uploads/2015/02/2015-Museum-Scavenger-Hunt.pdf Educators: For Teachers Guides, Student Workbooks: www.ExplorePAhistory.com/teach.php.*

The Official Museum of the Commonwealth features 4 floors of historical exhibits: Geology, Archeology (pretend to dig like the professionals - what types of things are found at a typical site?), Military (Gettysburg, etc.), Industry, The Arts and Technology. Do you know what animal has the most highly developed brain? Do you know the difference between a paleontologist and an archaeologist? Do you know what important document served as an instrument of peace during a time of great turmoil? Do you know what camp near Harrisburg had more soldiers trained and organized into regiments than any other camp during the Civil War? Do you know what kind of wagon early Pennsylvania farmers used to haul their products to market? All of ancient and modern Pennsylvania history in one place.

CURIOSITY CONNECTION - Interactive Computer and dress up for kids age 5 and below. The adventure begins in a Child's Magical Bedroom and continues through secret portals leading to an entire miniature world of Curiosity. Other areas such as The Living Forest, Industry and Transportation Zone, Farm Land, Construction Zone and Art Wall allow children to discover the world around them and express their creativity through interactive play.

WILDWOOD LAKE SANCTUARY

Harrisburg - *100 Wildwood Way (Lucknow Industrial Park, north of Harrisburg Area Comm. College) 17110. Phone: (717) 221-0292. www.wildwoodlake.org. Hours: Dawn to dusk. Nature Center Tuesday-Sunday 10:00am-4:00pm. Admission: FREE general admission , small fee for special programs.*

It's a 212 acre lake with wonderful walkways through marshes, meadows and woodlands. The nature center has great interactive displays for children…they take a card through the exhibit and get stamps at various stations which teach them about the wetlands while creating a picture. There's also a Discovery Room with quick, easy arts and crafts. Bird enthusiasts can watch the birds from the special glass enclosed bird blind that overlooks the lake and offers numerous bird feeders that attracts an abundant number of species that come to eat. The pathways outside are well marked, paved or mulched, and lend themselves to a lot of discovery…turtles on logs, butterflies, etc. Gift shop with exploration toys. Our relatives from Pennsylvania love this place!

PENNSYLVANIA FARM SHOW

Harrisburg - Farm Show Complex. https://www.farmshow.pa.gov/Pages/default.aspx   The largest indoor agricultural event in America. The Farm Show Complex houses 16 acres under roof, spread throughout 7 buildings. Favorite annual events and sights delighted crowds like the 1,000-pound butter sculpture, Sheep to Shawl contest, Farm Show Detectives and Celebrity Cow Milking Contest. Visitors also enjoyed the many new attractions like the Best Burger Showdown, sticky bun contest and Broadway and puppet shows. The famed Food Court lived up to its reputation, offering the best Pennsylvania-produced products. America's Top Rodeo/Livestock Events. FREE, but parking fee of $15.00. (second week of January)

Hershey

ANTIQUE AUTOMOBILE CLUB OF AMERICA

Hershey - 161 Museum Drive (322 East into Hershey and exit onto HERSHEYPARK Drive) Turn left onto Hershey Road (Rte. 39 West) at GIANT Center) 17033. Phone: (717) 566.7100. www.aacamuseum.org. Hours: Daily 9:00am-5:00pm (except major winter holidays). Admission: $10.00-$14.00 (age 4+). Active Military FREE.

What was your first car? Do you have a Dream Car? You may find them at the Museum. At any given time, you can see 85-100 classic cars and trucks on display. The Museum's highly detailed dioramas present carefully restored vintage vehicles in elaborate scenes that bring the history of the automobile to life. From a tiny machine shop in turn-of-the-century New York to the asphalt apron of San Francisco's Golden Gate Bridge. In the activity room, younger visitors can ride a pedal car, do a crayon rubbing of an antique license plate and engage in hands-on projects. At the Photo Stop, kids can dress up in period clothing and have their picture taken sitting in a car.

HERSHEY BEARS HOCKEY

Hershey - 100 West Hershey Park Drive (Giant Arena) 17033. Phone: (717) 534-3911. www.hersheybears.com. Admission: $16.00-$22.00. Family Four Packs w/ food offered at a discount. AHL, Washington Capitals affiliate. Join CoCo the Bears Kids Club.

HERSHEY GARDENS

Hershey - 170 Hotel Road (on the grounds of the Hotel Hershey) 17033. Phone: (717) 534-3492. www.hersheygardens.org. Hours: Daily 9:00am-5:00pm. Extended summer evening hours. Admission: $9.50-$13.50 (age 3+).

This 23-acre botanical gem has over 7,000 roses and seasonal flower displays, 25,000 tulips in the spring, a Japanese garden and an outdoor Butterfly House with 400 butterflies (1st weekend in June - 3rd Saturday in Sept), weather permitting. The Children's Garden provides opportunities for hands-on learning, self-discovery, and fun with water features, hideaways, creatures, surprises, whimsical characters, and more all within nearly 30 themed areas.

HERSHEY LODGE

Hershey - 325 University Drive 17033. Phone: (717) 533-3311. www.hersheylodge. com. A very family-friendly way to stay in the area comfortably. With lodging rates starting in the $199 range, it includes a free shuttle to HersheyPark and other attractions. The packages they offer are the best value, especially if you're *planning to visit several attractions. On site, at the lodge, are tennis courts, basketball courts, miniature golf, gameroom, bocce ball, bike rentals, and their fabulous pools – indoor and outdoor. Kids will like to eat at Lebbie Lebkichers casual buffet or the Bears' Den hockey-themed sports café. Watch the game on a 9'x12' video wall, check out the game room, and order from the Kids Menu (we recommend the Bear Puck Dessert...or anything chocolate!). Great way to enjoy Hershey, PA without a lot of hassle. _____*

HERSHEY STORY - THE MUSEUM ON CHOCOLATE AVENUE

Hershey - *63 West Chocolate Avenue (next to arena) 17033. Phone: (717) 534-3439 or (800) HERSHEY. http://hersheystory.org. Hours: Daily 9:00am-5:00pm. Holidays and peak season hours extended. Arrive early to book your Chocolate Lab Class, as they fill quickly. Classes may only be purchased at the admissions desk on the day of the class. Admission: Chocolate Lab or Museum are each: $15.00 adult, $14.00 senior (62+), $11.00 child (3-12). Or, do both and save a little. Note: Strollers not allowed. Café Zooka light food and beverage. Apprentice Program: After paying museum admission plus $3.00, visitors can become Milton Hershey's apprentice and receive a special booklet that helps them discover the Chocolate King's secrets to success. By answering questions and solving puzzles throughout the Museum Experience, their efforts are rewarded along the way, culminating with a personalized prize at the end. Educators: https:// hersheystory.org/teacher-lesson-plans/ for chocolate lesson plans. We liked Chocolate Graphing.*

KISSTORY - Explore this fun-filled, interactive exhibit that takes a nostalgic look at one of America's most treasured treats. Learn how Mr. Hershey failed as a candy maker in Philadelphia and New York - but became a millionaire manufacturing caramels in Lancaster, Pennsylvania. He sold that business to start a chocolate factory in his birthplace farmland. Go behind the scenes of innovations in chocolate (how do they wrap Hershey Kisses?) as the centerpiece of this area comes to life with a roar and a rumble. Other exhibits explore Hershey, Pennsylvania. They trace its lavish architecture, much of it inspired by Milton and Kitty Hershey's travels abroad and life in the factory. Be transported back in time to 1940s Cuba to Milton Hershey's other "model town," named — you guessed it! — Hershey. There, the Sweet Venture in Sugar exhibit tells the story of Milton Hershey's venture into sugar manufacturing through interactive exhibits, vintage film, photos, and other memorabilia teach you about sugarcane and sugar manufacturing process. Elsewhere, kids can "punch a real time clock" or sit in an original HersheyPark roller coaster car (kind of virtual reality).

<u>CHOCOLATE LAB</u> - Chocolate making is a sweet recipe for learning about art and science! The Chocolate Lab offers participatory classes such as molding, dipping and even making chocolate from scratch. Located on the main floor, it is inspired by Milton Hershey's own candy-making apprenticeship and his flair for experimentation. The Chocolate Lab explores the unique qualities of chocolate through playful, hands-on experiences on a variety of subjects including geography, history, economics and science.

HERSHEY TROLLEY WORKS

Hershey - *(Departs at entrance to Hershey's Chocolate World) 17033. Phone: (717) 533-3000. http://hersheytrolleyworks.com. Hours: Rain or Shine. Same hours as the park. Last tour is 1 hour before closing. Admission: $18.95 adult, $15.95 child (3-12). Tours: Summer Trolley Show: (available Memorial Day – Labor Day). The Christmas Adventure: (only available during Christmas Candylane). Due to limited seating, guests are encouraged to purchased tickets upon arrival to Chocolate World or online. Each token is valid only for a specific time.*

Family adventure through America's sweetest town. Old time songs and visits throughout from famous "characters" plus lots of little-known facts about the town as you pass historic sites. The conductors are entertaining, informative, and loaded with candy! The tour lasts about 45-60 minutes and usually includes either a stop at Founder's Hall, the focal point the Hersheys' legacy, or a stop in downtown Hershey featuring the grand lobby of the Hershey Theater.

HERSHEYPARK

Hershey - *100 W. Hersheypark Drive (Off SR 743 & US 422) 17033. Phone: (800) HERSHEY. www.hersheypa.com. Hours: Daily - opens at 10:00am (summer). Weekends only (May, September). Admission: Range $49.95-$84.95 (Ages 3+). Online discounts.*

Begin by "measuring up" for size. From "Kisses" on up, the rides are rated by candy type. 110 acre theme park with 70 rides and attractions. You'll also find: German Area, English Area, Penn Dutch Area (and food to match), a SeaLion & Dolphin Show, Night Lights Musical Laser Spectacular. 21 kiddie rides and live entertainment at Music Box Theater or the Amphitheatres. Rollercoasters you'll find include: GREAT BEAR inverted looping roller coaster; SooPER DOOPER LOOPER - is a milder form of Great Bear; and COAL CRACKER - an awesome interactive water coaster. Reese's Cupfusion attraction merges the world's love of chocolate and peanut butter with a dark ride experience and multi-level game player technology. Reese's Cupfusion will engage multiple senses during the ride; sight, smell, touch and sound.

As a grand tribute to the boardwalks of the East Coast beaches, The Boardwalk At Hersheypark will captivate you with over 100 fun-in-the-sun experiences. Get ready to rocket through splash-filled hills, open-air Flying Saucer turns, and sweet thrills aboard a four-person in-line raft on the Breakers Edge Water Coaster, then grab a mat to beat the competition as you sail through the curves and tunnels of the longest mat racing slide in the world at the WhitecapSM Racer. Coastline Plunge (with four water slides), the East Coast Waterworks (seven slides), and the largest water-play structure in the world! Then dry off and enjoy the parks 70+ rides and other attractions from the flavors, sounds, and activities of an old-fashioned boardwalk. Just remember not to go swimming on a stomach full of chocolate!

The attractions at Hersheypark are constantly getting upgraded and added to, and new roller coasters appear every few years. The entire park is very clean and the staff, friendly.

CHRISTMAS CANDYLANE

Hershey - Hersheypark. www.hersheypa.com. More than 1,000,000 lights, unique shops, holiday entertainment, great food and rides. Look for Santa and his live reindeer! Admission for rides, park entrance free. Lodging packages. Breakfast with Santa. (mid-November - New Year's weekend)

HERSHEY'S CHOCOLATE WORLD VISITORS CENTER

Hershey - *101 Chocolate World Way 17033. https://www.chocolateworld.com/ home.html. Phone: (800) HERSHEY. Hours: Daily 9:00am-5:00pm (everyday but Christmas). - Extended hours for special events, weekends and peak season. Admission: FREE. Note: Shuttles to other attractions leave from here. 8 unique gift shops. Food court. Chocolate Town Café. Create Your Own Candy Bar. Factory Mystery 4-D Show, an immersive three-dimensional musical featuring the HERSHEY'S Product Characters as they come to life. (movie charges fee).*

A factory tour on an automated tram into the simulated world of chocolate production! Start at the cocoa bean plantation (rainforests and tropic) to dairy farms to making chocolate through the years at Hershey. Actual video footage of a real factory and the wonderful scent of chocolate pervades. It even gets warmer as you pass through the "roaster oven" part of the ride.

Learn why different chocolate manufacturers have different flavors (the secret is where the cocoa beans came from). The updated Chocolate Making Tour Ride is an immersive experience…and it ends with a free sample!

HERSHEY'S Unwrapped: A Chocolate Tasting Journey - family friendly show and zanny tasteologists. With your Official Chocolate Tasting Kit in hand, get ready to see, touch, hear, smell and taste chocolate. Then, head into the chocolate laboratory with Doc Chocolate as he dreams up sweet creations with the audience! $14.95-$17.95.

ZOO AMERICA NORTH AMERICAN WILDLIFE PARK

Hershey - *201 Park Avenue (opposite Hershey Park) 17033. Phone: (717) 534-3860. www.zooamerica.com. Hours: 10:00am-5:00pm. (Open until 8:00pm in the*

summer). ZOOAMERICA is open year-round except Thanksgiving, Christmas and New Year's Day. Admission: $13.00-$15.00 (age 3+).

An eleven acre North American attraction that hosts wildlife from 5 regions (200+ species) including bears, bobcats and lynx. ZooAmerica began as The Hershey Zoo in 1916, when Milton S. Hershey opened his private animal collection to the public. "Desert of Night" area is unique and wonderful. "Visit" with creatures of the night like owls, snakes and bats. ZooAmerica welcomed another new addition, the black-footed ferret, which can be seen in The Great Southwest. Thought to be extinct at one point, these ferrets are one of the most endangered species on this continent. Feisty ferrets are fun to watch. The American crocodile exhibit and interactive Maze learning stations are fun zoo exhibits. Guests can even take advantage of a special falconry demonstration or naturalist educational sessions.

INDIAN ECHO CAVERNS

Hummelstown - *368 Middletown Road (Off I-283 and US 322 at Hummelstown / Middletown Exits) 17036. Phone: (717) 566-8131. www.indianechocaverns. com. Hours: Daily 9:00am-5:00pm (Summer). 10:00am-4:00pm (rest of year). Admission: $22.00 adult, $20.00 senior (62+), $13.00 child (2-11). Online coupon. Tours: 45 minutes, guided Note: Gift shop - Southwestern, Rocks, quirky items. Pan for gems at Gem Mill Junction (open seasonally). Wagon ride to the Petting Barnyard. Playground with Indian Tepee and Conestoga Wagon. Shaded picnic area.*

You'll walk the same paths that the Susquehannock Indians did hundreds of years ago and be entertained with many stories and legends surrounding Indian Echo. Check out the Wilson Room and the Story of William Wilson who lived in the caverns for 19 years - "the Pennsylvania Hermit". The Indian Ballroom is the largest room. There are 3 lakes and a variety of stalactites, stalagmites, and flowstone. As with any caverns, small, squirmy children may not enjoy the tour and get bored easily.

BLUE KNOB STATE PARK

Imler - *RR 1, Box 449 16655. Phone: (814) 276-3576. https://www.dcnr.pa.gov/ StateParks/FindAPark/BlueKnobStatePark/Pages/default.aspx. Admission: to PA State Parks is FREE however swimming, marina and camping/lodging fees apply.*

Blue Knob State Park is named for the majestic dome-shaped mountain. Bob's Creek is great for trout fishing and Blue Knob boasts the second highest peak in the state, which gives great views of up to 42 miles. Off-peak season, ride the ski resort's chairlift for great views. All park trails are open to mountain biking and many are less than two miles long-easy hiking for families. Weather permitting, the swimming pool is open daily from 11:00am-7:00pm from Memorial Day weekend to Labor Day, unless posted otherwise. Horse-back Riding, Down-hill Skiing, Campsites, Fishing, Winter Sports.

Lewisberry

GIFFORD PINCHOT STATE PARK

Lewisberry - *2200 Rosstown Road (Route 177) 17339. Phone: (717) 432-5011. https://www.dcnr.pa.gov/StateParks/FindAPark/GiffordPinchotStatePark/Pages/ default.aspx Admission: to PA State Parks is FREE however swimming, marina and camping/lodging fees apply, with reservation or entrance.*

Pinchot Lake is a great warm water fishery and is popular for sailing. The trails between the campground and the Conewago Day Use Area are for joint-use by hikers, cross-country skiers and bikers. Shorter trails are marked with white, double bar blazes. Most trails interconnect to allow hikers to tailor their outing to meet their individual desires. A large, ADA accessible beach in the Quaker Race Day Use Area is open from late-May to mid-September, 8:00am to sunset. Visitor Center, Boat Rentals, Horseback Riding, Disc Golf course, Sledding, Campsites, Modern Cabins, Yurts, Fishing, and Cross-Country Skiing.

SKI ROUNDTOP

Lewisberry - *925 Roundtop Road 17339. Phone: (717) 432-9631. Snow Report: (717) 432-7000. www.skiroundtop.com.*

Minutes from tourist destinations like Hershey and Gettysburg, Ski Roundtop is a four-season resort with plenty of snow sports to keep visitors busy. Roundtop was one of the first ski resorts in the area to offer tubing, where skiers can shed their skis and slide down a hill in an inner tube. Magic Mountain area is set aside just for kids. With its own Magic Carpet lift, your children can learn in a secure area physically separated from the other slopes. Longest Run: 4100 ft.; 15 Slopes & Trails - Skiing and Snowtubing. Paintball, ropes, mtn treks.

WHITETAIL SKI RESORT AND MOUNTAIN BIKING CENTER

Mercersburg - *13805 Blairs Valley Road 17236. www.skiwhitetail.com. Phone: (717) 328-9400.*

Longest Run: 4900 ft.; 17 Slopes & Trails. Terrain Park: 1 rail, 8 snow features, and a fun box for snow tubing and snow boarding. SnowMonsters kids program.

MIDDLETOWN AND HUMMELSTOWN RAILROAD

Middletown - *136 Brown Street (SR283 to Middletown exit - Race Street Station) 17057. Phone: (717) 944-4435. www.mhrailroad.com. Hours: Memorial Day Weekends - October. July & August - Thursday also. Admission: Regularly scheduled: $20-$25 (age 2+). Tours: Generally departures at Noon & 1:30pm. Check schedule for detailed times. Note: Special event trains- Reservations suggested. New: Little Red Caboose Rides.*

The yard has several rail cars on display. During the ride, the train follows the towpath of the historic Union Canal and alongside the peaceful Swatara. The narrator relates the history of the Canal (completed in 1827) and the location of Canal Lock #33, as well as a century old limekiln and Horse Thief Cave. Passengers will want to have their cameras out while crossing a 35-foot bridge above the Swatara Creek. On the return trip from Indian Echo Cave Platform, you will enjoy a "sing-a-long" of tunes from the railroading days, as well as fun songs for young and old alike. Can you still "Chicken Dance"?

EASTER BUNNY TRAIN RIDES

Middletown - Middletown And Hummelstown Railroad. Candy treats with the Easter Bunny riding along. Live music. Admission. (Easter Weekend and weekend before)

CIVIL WAR REMEMBERED

Middletown - Middletown And Hummelstown Railroad. Reenactment with skirmishes along the tracks and during the ride. Trains leave two times each day. Admission. (last weekend in September)

SANTA EXPRESS OR THE POLAR EXPRESS

Middletown - Middletown And Hummelstown Railroad. Sing songs and eat treats as you ride the train with Santa aboard. Admission. (Saturdays in December)

MAIZE QUEST FUN PARK

New Park - 2885 New Park Road. www.mazefunpark.com. Petting zoo, refreshments, pumpkin patch, corn maze, pony or wagon rides. 10 acres of corn maze with fountains and bridges. Indoor Playground. Admission. (outdoor park open weekends in September and October thru mid-November)

LITTLE BUFFALO STATE PARK

Newport - RD 2, Box 256A (PA Route 34) 17074. Phone: (717) 567-9255. https:// www.dcnr.pa.gov/StateParks/FindAPark/LittleBuffaloStatePark/Pages/default. aspx. Admission: to PA State Parks is FREE however swimming, marina and camping/lodging fees apply.

Explore historical features including a covered bridge, restored grist mill, an old farm house built on the site of a colonial tavern, and a narrow gauge railroad. Programs are offered year-round. Many programs feature Shoaff's Mill. Over 12,000 people visit the mill annually. Today, the Perry County Historical Society operates and maintains a museum and library in the farmhouse (open every Sunday during the summer months). Little Buffalo has approximately 8 miles of hiking trails. Sturdy footwear is recommended because of rocky footing on some of the trails. Pool, Visitor Center, Year-round Education & Interpretation Center, Boat Rentals, Sledding, Fishing, and Trails.

CHRISTMAS WALK

Newport - Little Buffalo State Park. This family oriented activity has become a popular holiday event in the county. Thousands of lights and holiday cutouts dot the East Picnic Area and provide the perfect holiday atmosphere. Santa always makes an appearance. Local 4-H Clubs sell cookies and hot chocolate. Local choirs sing carols many of the nights. (evenings one week mid-December)

COLONEL DENNING STATE PARK

Newville - *1599 Doubling Gap Road (Doubling Gap, North Cumberland County, along PA Route 233) 17241. Phone: (717) 776-5272. https://www.dcnr.pa.gov/ StateParks/FindAPark/ColonelDenningStatePark/Pages/default.aspx Admission: to PA State Parks is FREE but swimming, marina, camping/lodging fees apply.*

The wooded park area nestles at the side of a mountain and has a scenic lake and excellent hiking trails. A hike on a 2.5 mile trail rises to Flat Rock for a beautiful vista of the Cumberland Valley. The one-mile, self-guiding Doubling Gap Trail is a moderate hike. The sand beach is open from late-May to mid-September, 8:00am to sunset. A visitor center, exhibiting plants, animals and minerals found in the park, is open during the summer season. Campsites, Fishing, and Cross-Country Skiing.

MR. ED'S ELEPHANT MUSEUM

Orrtanna - *6019 Chambersburg Road (along Rte. 30, 12 miles outside of Gettysburg) 17353. Phone: (717) 352-3792. www.mistereds.com. Hours: Daily 10:00am-5:00pm. Admission: FREE.*

Forty-two years ago Ed Gotwalt began collecting elephants. Now that collection - 12.000 pachyderms in all - is his livelihood. As you approach the place, you're greeted by Miss Ellie, a 9.5 foot tall white elephant with animated eyes and ears who may wink at you as you walk near. Miss Ellie also talks, blathering about the area, telling a few jokes and then goes back to sleep. Inside, although nothing is labeled, Ed is ready to share the story behind any treasure you ask about. You would not believe the different kinds of elephant collectibles you will find.... from an elephant potty chair to a hair dryer.... there is even an elephant pulling a 24-karat gold circus wagon. The reason most kids love this place - Ed sells peanuts and boasts he has the largest selection of candy in the area - like a room full of Pez candy.

SHAWNEE STATE PARK

Schellsburg - *Box 67 (Ten miles west of historic Bedford along Route 30) 15559. Phone: (814) 733-4218. https://www.dcnr.pa.gov/StateParks/FindAPark/ ShawneeStatePark/Pages/default.aspx Admission: to PA State Parks is FREE however swimming, marina and camping/lodging fees apply.*

Of particular interest is Shawnee's long sand and turf beach that receives ample use between Memorial Day and Labor Day. The lake is popular for boating and fishing. Boat Rentals, Mountain Biking, Sledding, Campsites, Modern Cabins, Trails, and Winter Sports.

MARTIN'S POTATO CHIPS

Thomasville - *5847 Lincoln Highway (US Route 30) 17364. Phone: (717) 792-3565 or (800) 272-4477. www.martinschips.com. Admission: FREE. Tours: Tuesdays @ 9:00, 10:00 and 11:00am. 45 minutes long. Closed-toe shoes required. Cameras permitted.*

Enjoying the benefit of the rich loamy soil, farmers had to find ways to use their excess crops. From the farm kitchen of Harry and Fairy Martin in 1941, a unique potato chip found its way into homes. All potato chips and popcorn are made in their 40,000 sq. ft. Thomasville facility which produces over one million bags each month. Presidents G.W. Bush, Clinton and Obama may have munched on Martin's Potato Chips at 10,000 feet aboard Air Force One. Take the Martin's tour and you'll get a fresher chip than even the president when you sample them hot off the line.

York

HARLEY-DAVIDSON MOTORCYCLE MUSEUM TOUR

York - *1425 Eden Road (on US30 or Exit 21 East of I-83) 17402. Phone: (877) 883-1450. www.harley-davidson.com (click on events icon). Hours: Tour center and gift shop 8:00am-4:00pm Monday thru Friday and some summer Saturdays. Admission: FREE Tours: Tours begin at regular intervals between 9:00a.m.and 2:00p.m. Monday through Friday. Tickets are distributed on a first-come, first-served basis. It is recommended that you arrive early in the day. Modified tours may be conducted due to manufacturing requirements. Tours are not offered on weekends, major holidays, during the week of July 4th or during production changes and year-end maintenance. Closed toe shoes are required for factory floor tour. (Plant tour is for ages 12+, however there are no age restrictions on the museum tour) Note: Tours are wheelchair accessible. Souvenir Shop.*

What little traveler hasn't seen (or better yet - heard) a Harley-Davidson motorcycle pass by? Founded in 1903, Harley-Davidson has become a passion of the American dream. See over 20 vintage and famous Harleys (Malcolm Forbes' custom bike) on the museum tour that is available for all ages (even a Kids Rally area for the little tykes). You will see photographs and videos of the 24 step manufacturing process that produces a completed motorcycle every 6 minutes! They are so confident in their quality and reliability that the first time an engine is started (it contains over 400 parts!) is when the bike is completely finished. An associate takes a few spins around the 1 mile long test track to be sure that it meets all the standards and expectations.

More than 3,000 employees work around the clock assembling Touring

and Softail® models, as well as limited production, factory-custom motorcycles. They perform a variety of manufacturing operations - from machining, polishing and chrome plating, to forming, welding and painting.

At the Tour Center, you'll explore exhibits that detail the plant's history, and guide you through the manufacturing and assembly processes. You'll also have the chance to sit on current production motorcycles and visit the gift shop for tour-related souvenirs. The Kids' Corner, a specially designed area for visitors under the age of 12, makes the York facility an ideal family destination.

AGRICULTURAL & INDUSTRIAL MUSEUMS

York - 480 East Market Street / 217 West Princess Street (US30 to George Street exit, Rte. 462 into downtown) 17403. www.yorkheritage.org. Phone: (717) 852-7007. Hours: Wednesday-Saturday 10:00am-4:00pm. Closes at Noon on Thursdays. Admission: $15 adult, $13 senior, $7 student (6-18) for One ticket to Ag & Industrial, Fire & Historical Museums. Less winters. We recommend the Industrial Museum (Princess Street) most. Educators: Ask for the scavenger hunt before you venture into this maze of artifacts. Pre/Post Visit Resources on Colonial and Civil War times are found on this link: http://yorkheritage.org/ uploads/YCPLessonDescripJAN2013.pdf

Learn about York County's many contributions to agricultural and industrial progress on a visit to the Agricultural and Industrial Museum. Agricultural artifacts produced or used in the county over three centuries include locally made wagons, tractors, steam engines and farm tools. Visit the exhibit Marvelous Milk: From the Farm to Your Table, where students learn about the dairy industry in York County and get the opportunity to milk a (reproduction) cow, Annabelle. A lot of products produced here have clothed, sheltered, transported, fed, and entertained the nation. Learn how the modern day farm evolved from the time of Native Americans.

Then, go a few streets away to explore the numerous products made in York. Begin in an old gristmill, pull a factory whistle or use an old rotary phone to dial up a friend next door (watch the mechanics of the operation station tapping out the numbers). The Pfaltzgraff pottery exhibit is well done with several stages of pottery being made (sometimes a potter comes in for live demonstrations). Don't forget about CAT trucks (get in the cab) and York Peppermint Patties!

For updates & travel games visit: **www.KidsLoveTravel.com**

YORK COUNTY HERITAGE MUSEUMS

York - *250 East Market Street (US 30 to George Street exit, follow signs to downtown) 17403. Phone: (717) 848-1587. www.yorkheritage.org. Hours: Tuesday-Saturday 10:00am-4:00pm. Winter hours closed. Admission: $15 adult, $13 senior, $7 student (6-18) for One ticket to Ag & Industrial, Fire & Historical Museums.*

When you venture downtown, be sure to visit the campus of historical buildings on West Market Street. These buildings include a replica of the courthouse where the Second Continental Congress met, as well as an authentic tavern dating back to 1741. A reproduction of original York village square with Bonham House (beautiful home), General Gates House, and Bobb Log House.

- GOLDEN PLOUGH TAVERN (c. 1741), the city's oldest structure, gives a taste of life during the years when the Tavern housed travelers and served local residents.

- GENERAL HORATIO GATES HOUSE (c. 1751): this English-style house was the General's home while he attended the Continental Congress, and is said to have been the site of LaFayette's famous toast to Washington that sent a signal to conspirators that the French would not support a plot to replace Washington with Gates.

- BOBB LOG HOUSE (c. 1812) is an example of the simple structures popular along the Pennsylvania frontier at the turn of the 19th century.

- HORACE BONHAM HOUSE, with original furnishings of the artist, reveals the social and cultural changes that took place between the Civil War and the turn of the century.

THE BELMONT THEATRE

York - *27 South Belmont Street 17403. Phone: (717) 854-3894. https://thebelmont.org/.*

Family hits like Sound of Music and Annie....Many productions include youth performers. Children's Shows - all tickets are $20.00.

YORK COUNTY FIRE MUSEUM

York - *757 West Market Street 17404. www.yorkheritage.org. Phone: (717) 843-0464. Hours: Saturday 10:00am-4:00pm. Closed winter. Admission: $15 adult, $13 senior, $7 student (6-18) for One ticket to Ag & Industrial, Fire & Historical Museums.*

All seventy-two fire companies of York County are represented here, with some of them dating back to before the American Revolution. The beautiful turn-of-the-century fire house contains a series of displays of how firefighters progressed from the early Leather Bucket Brigades to Hand Drawn Carts and Pumps, to Horse Drawn Apparatus, and finally to Motorized Equipment. All of the equipment is original and full-size. Pull a Fire Alarm Box or visit an old fashioned Fire Chief's Sleeping Quarters, complete with brass slide pole.

CHRISTMAS MAGIC - A FESTIVAL OF LIGHTS

York - Rocky Ridge County Park.   https://yorkcountypa.gov/691/Rocky-Ridge-Park. Christmas Magic is a 0.5 mile long walking trail (accessible to anyone) that meanders through 400,000 Christmas lights, holiday scenes and five enclosed heated pavilions. Walk thru glistening lights in a village with Santa, a mini-train display, Penguin village, food & entertainment. Admission per person. (Thanksgiving weekend thru December)

SHOE HOUSE

York (Hellam) - *197 Shoe House Road (Just south of Rt. 30, 4 miles east of York, north off Hwy 462) 17315. Phone: (717) 840-8339. www.facebook.com/HainesShoeHouse Hours: Wednesday-Sunday 11:00am-5:00pm. Weekends only Spring/Fall. Closed winters. Admission: $3.00-$4.50 (age 4+).*

Haines Shoe House along the Lincoln Highway is a home stuffed into a white, 25-foot stucco boot. The odd shaped building seen from the Lincoln Highway was built by a shoe store chain owner as a promotional gimmick. Colonel Haines was a flamboyant millionaire aptly named the "Shoe Wizard." The house measures 48 ft. in length, 17 ft. in width at the widest part and 25 ft. in height. The interior consists of three bedrooms, two baths, a kitchen and living room. Take a personal tour of the Shoe House and view the interesting rooms on the five different levels. See the curved eating booth in the kitchen located in the heel of the shoe house. Count the number of stained-glass windows with pictures of shoes. Relax in the soul of the shoe with a snack and some homemade ice cream, or picnic on the grounds. Look for the shoe dog house and the shoe mailbox.

Zionsville

STAHL'S POTTERY FESTIVAL

Zionsville - Stahl's Pottery, 6826 Corning Road   www.stahlspottery.org. Tour historic, early 20th century wood-fired kiln and pottery site. Potting techniques demonstrated. Over 15 contemporary potters display and sell their wares. Light lunch available. Admission: $4.00 (third Saturday of October)

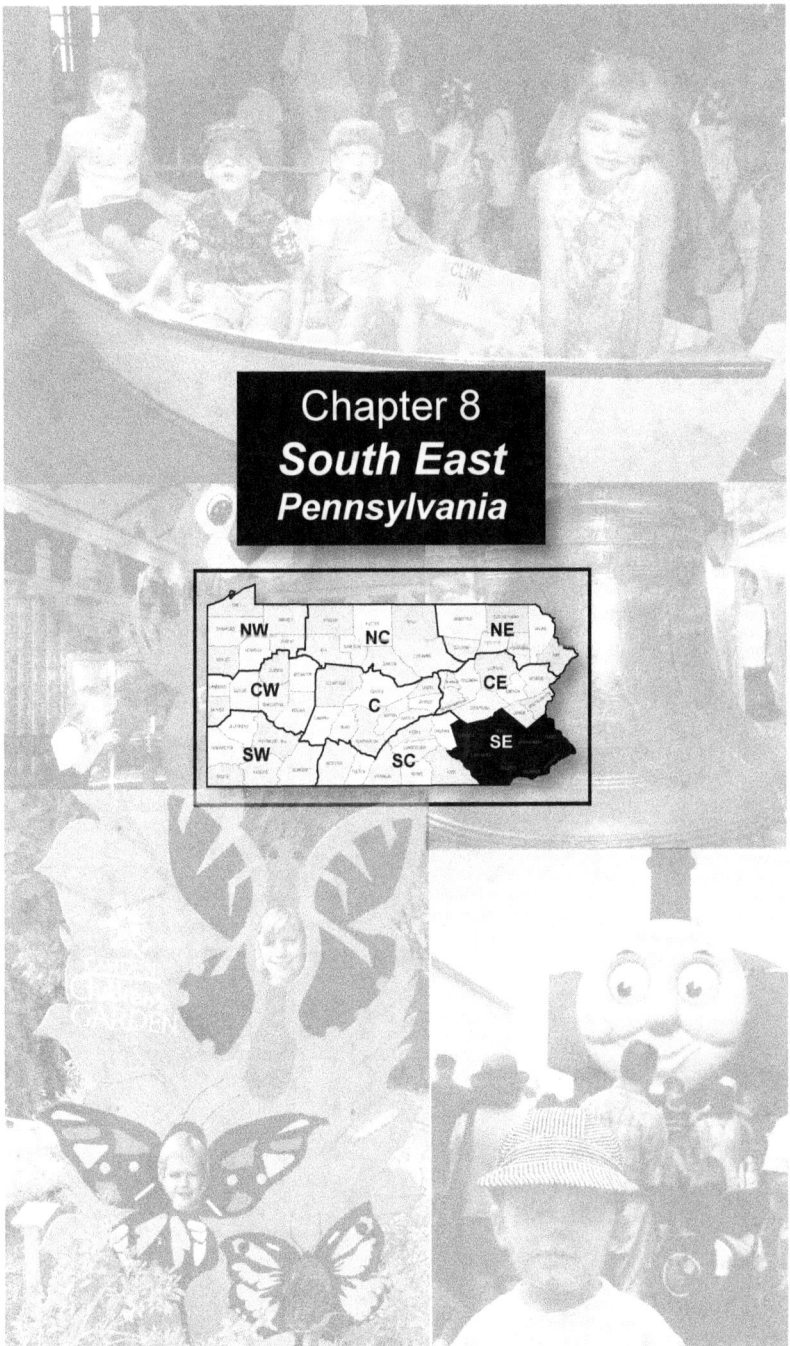

Chapter 8
South East
Pennsylvania

Audubon
- Mill Grove, The Audubon Wildlife Sanctuary

Bensalem
- Neshaminy State Park

Bernville
- Koziar's Christmas Village

Bird-In-Hand
- Americana Museum
- Plain & Fancy Farm

Birdsboro
- Daniel Boone Homestead

Boyertown
- Boyertown Museum Of Historic Vehicles

Chadds Ford
- Brandywine Battlefield Park
- Brandywine River Museum

Collegeville
- Evansburg State Park

Columbia
- National Watch & Clock Museum
- Wright's Ferry Mansion
- Turkey Hill Experience

Cornwall
- Cornwall Iron Furnace

Downingtown
- Marsh Creek State Park

Doylestown
- Mercer Museum
- Moravian Pottery And Tile Works & Fonthill
- Polish American Festival

Doylestown (Chalfont)
- Byers' Choice Ltd

Doylestown (Pipersville)
- Ralph Stover State Park

Elverson
- French Creek State Park
- Hopewell Furnace National

Historic Site

Fort Washington
- Fort Washington State Park

Grantville
- Memorial Lake State Park

Intercourse
- Kitchen Kettle Village

Kempton
- Hawk Mountain
- W.K. & S. Steam Railroad

Kennett Square
- Longwood Gardens

King Of Prussia
- Scottish And Irish Music Festival And Fair, Greater Philadelphia

Kutztown
- Crystal Cave
- Rodale Institute Farm
- Kutztown Folk Festival

Lahaska
- Peddler's Village

Lancaster
- Dutch Apple Dinner Theatre
- Hands-On House Children's Museum
- Landis Valley Museum
- Amish Farm And House
- Biblical Tabernacle Reproduction / Mennonite Information Center
- Dutch Wonderland Family Amusement Park
- Fulton Steamboat Inn
- Lancaster Science Factory
- Lancaster Barnstormers Baseball
- North Museum Of Natural History And Science
- Wheatland
- American Music Theatre

Lancaster (Willow Street)
- Hans Herr House

Lancaster / Strasburg
- Sight & Sound Theatres

Langhorne
- Sesame Place

Langhorne (Newtown)
- Tyler State Park

Lititz
- Sturgis Pretzel Bakery
- Wilbur Chocolate Co.
- Wolf Sanctuary Of PA

Manheim
- Celtic Fling & Highland Games

Manheim
- Pennsylvania Renaissance Faire

Media
- Linvilla Orchards

Media (Newtown Square)
- Ridley Creek State Park

Morgantown
- Hay Creek Apple Festival

Morrisville
- Pennsbury Manor

New Hope
- New Hope & Ivyland Railroad
- New Hope Boat Rides

Norristown
- Elmwood Park Zoo

Nottingham
- Herr's Snack Factory Tour

Penns Creek
- T & D 'S Cats Of The World Wild Animal Refuge

Philadelphia
- Philadelphia Sports
- Philly Cheesesteak
- Philly Transportation & Tours

Philadelphia (cont.)
- Philadelphia Orchestra
- Academy Of Natural Sciences
- Franklin Institute Museum
- Philadelphia Zoo
- Univ. Of Pennsylvania Museum Of Archaeology & Anthropology
- World Café Live
- Betsy Ross House
- Carpenter's Hall
- Christ Church
- City Tavern
- Declaration (Graff) House
- Federal Reserve Bank
- Fireman's Hall
- Franklin Court
- Franklin Fountain
- Franklin Square
- Independence Hall
- Independence Seaport Museum
- Independence Visitor Center (For The Nat'l Historical Park)
- Jones Restaurant
- Liberty Bell
- National Constitution Center
- National Liberty Museum
- Shane's Candies
- Thaddeus Kosciuszko Memorial
- Todd House
- U.S. Mint
- Doubletree Hotel Philadelphia
- Philadelphia City Hall Obsv.Deck
- Reading Terminal Market
- Eastern State Penitentiary
- Philadelphia Museum Of Art
- Fairmount Park
- Please Touch Museum
- Insectarium
- Mummers Museum
- Philadelphia Phillies Park Tours
- Wachovia Center Tours
- Fort Mifflin
- Heinz National Wildlife Refuge
- Philadelphia International Children's Festival
- Battle Of Germantown Re-Enactment

Philadelphia (Chestnut Hill)
- Morris Arboretum

Quakertown
- Nockamixon State Park

Quarryville
- Fulton (Robert) Birthplace

Reading
- Mid Atlantic Air Museum
- Reading Phillies Baseball
- Nolde Forest Environmental Education Center
- Reading Public Museum

Ronks
- Amazing Maize Maze

Schaefferstown
- Alexander Schaeffer Farm Museum

Spring Mount
- Spring Mountain Adventures

Strasburg
- Ed's Buggy Rides
- Amish Village
- Choo Choo Barn, Traintown Usa
- Railroad Museum Of Pennsylvania
- Strasburg Railroad

Strasburg (Paradise)
- National Toy Train Museum

Upper Black Eddy
- Delaware Canal State Park
- Ringing Rocks Park

Valley Forge
- Valley Forge National Historical Park

Washington's Crossing
- Washington Crossing Historic Park

West Chester
- American Helicopter Museum
- QVC Studio Tour

Wyomissing
- Berk's County Heritage Center

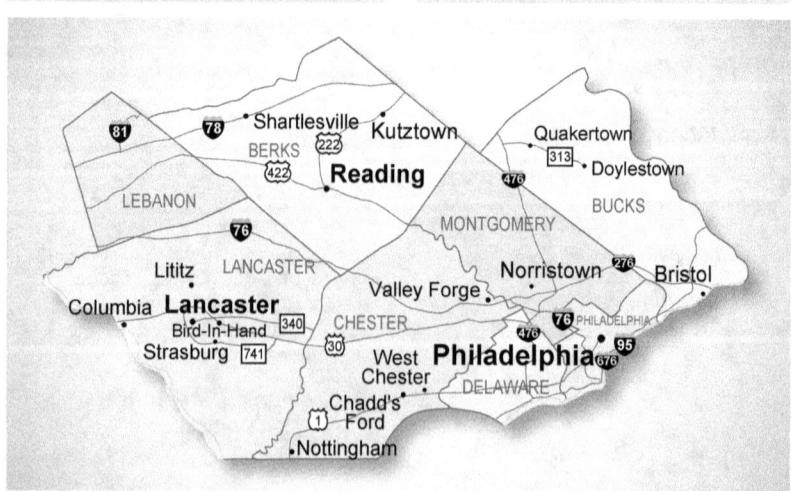

A Quick Tour of our Hand-Picked Favorites Around...

South East Pennsylvania

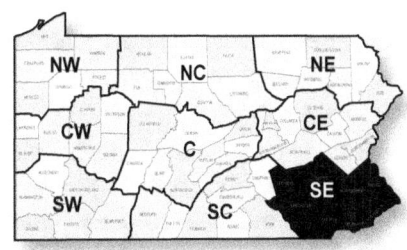

Lancaster County is home to America's oldest Amish settlement, where tens of thousands still live an old "Plain" lifestyle. Horse & buggy remain a primary form of transportation and windmills dot the countryside. **Pennsylvania Dutch Country** offers tours of authentic Amish Homes or, stay on a nearby farm where kids can help milk cows or gather eggs, make preserves, help with planting or harvest activities, and learn about what goes into living an agricultural life.

With the Amish come decisions about food – where to eat and what food stores to visit. Pretzel Factories and buffet dining options abound. There is at least one dozen of each to choose from. The oldest factory, **Sturgis Pretzel**, is in Lititz and still offers a pretzel "ticket" and a quick lesson on twisting your own pretzel by hand. Probably one of the best food factory tours in the USA is found south of Lancaster, off Rte 1 in Nottingham – **Herr's Snack Factory Tour**. Following a curious mascot video tour, your guide takes you through the whole process of making potato chips – with free, warm chip samples at the end-of-the-line!

Families visiting the Lancaster area can enjoy all of the fun and entertainment the county has to offer. Take the kids to Dutch Wonderland for a day of rides (a very manageable park for 2 to 10 year olds), games and live show theaters. Our favorite theater is **Sight & Sound** – it's like the stories you heard as kids come to life.

The **Strasburg Rail Road** and neighboring **Train Museums** also have your ticket to fun. Travel past Amish farms aboard authentically restored passenger cars pulled by a steam locomotive. "Meet" giant locomotives or be dazzled by miniature train displays.

Early America was full of new businesses. One such business was pottery and tile works – best displayed in quirky ways in Doylestown at the **Mercer Museum**. While the tile works are down the street (next to the mansion), kids really gravitate to the old stone castle full of objects made obsolete by the Industrial Revolution. Grab a scavenger hunt worksheet and try to find your way through the most eccentric, yet curiously fun, museum you'll ever find. And, Sesame Place is not too far away.

After grubbing on some delicious Philly Cheesesteaks from a street vendor, head east to the Historic District in Philadelphia, where you'll find **The Liberty Bell**, **Independence Hall** and **Franklin Court**. First check in at the **Independence Visitor Center** to get your free timed tickets (or order them online for a small fee before you arrive) before heading off to see the sights.

Once you've gotten your fill of history, other options like the **Insectarium** (north of town) and Art, Children's (younger set) or Science museums (older kids) like Franklin Institute prevail. The Insectarium allows you to look under a microscope at bugs, crawl like bugs and even eat bugs!

Sites and attractions are listed in order by City, Zip Code, and Name. Symbols indicated represent: 🍽 Restaurants   🛏 Lodging

MILL GROVE, THE AUDUBON WILDLIFE SANCTUARY

Audubon - *1201 Pawlings Road 19403. http://pa.audubon.org. Phone: (610) 666-5593. Hours: Wednesday-Sunday 10:00am-4:00pm. Admission: $14.00 adult, $12.00 senior (65+), $10.00 youth (6-17).*

Early 1800s home of noted artist, author and nature lover, John James Audubon. The house displays Audubon's paintings of birds and a complete set of his greatest work, "The Birds of America". Kids seem to admire the stuffed bird collection and birds' eggs. The new Center delves further: bird banding, walk into "sound forests", bird nests construction, how wings work, and a short movie about Audubon. Grounds with nature trails and bird sanctuary are open dawn to dusk. Fledgling Trail: Children enjoy mimicking the life stages of a young bird from egg to first flight. A sensory garden, water features, accessible play apparatus and benches to relax are on the trail.

HOLIDAY OPEN HOUSE

Audubon - Mill Grove. Celebration of John James Audubon's love of nature. They've brought the outside in and decked the halls of the Audubon art museum with natural decorations and whimsical teasel critters. A critter scavenger hunt for the children and holiday treats await you. Museum gift shop open for holiday shopping. FREE. (first Sunday in December)

NESHAMINY STATE PARK

Bensalem - *3401 State Road (follow PA 132 signs towards Delaware River @ State Road and Dunks Ferry Road) 19020. Phone: (215) 639-4538. www.dcnr.state. pa.us/stateparks/findapark/neshaminy/index.htm Admission: FREE. Pool and camping require fees. Note: The Playmasters Theatre Workshop: The playhouse, on State Road, offers entertainment throughout the year. Visit www.playmasters.org.*

Can you feel the ocean's tides in Pennsylvania? You can at Neshaminy State Park. Waves won't knock you down, but if you watch the river, you'll see it rise or fall an inch a minute. Even though the river flows another 116 miles from here to the ocean, you're at sea level. When the tide comes in at a New Jersey beach, the water rises here also. Because tides affect this part of the river, it's called an estuary.

Neshaminy State Park provides boating access to the Delaware River. The picnic areas and seasonal swimming pool are the most popular park attractions.

River Walk Trail: The trailheads for both River Walk trails begin and end on Logan Walk. The River Walk Trail follows the shoreline and gives views of the river with its boating traffic, and also explores the tidal marsh. The River Trail Inner Loop explores the interior of the park and is a great way to discover animals and plants. The River Walk Brochure compares the past to the present, and describes some of the river inhabitants like sturgeon, shad and eel. Puzzles help children explore the estuary, river and tidal marsh. This self-guiding brochure is available at the park office. Fishing, Boating (unlimited hp motors permitted), and Cross-Country Skiing.

KOZIAR'S CHRISTMAS VILLAGE

Bernville - Off SR 183. www.koziarschristmasvillage.com. Glistening lights. Visit with Santa. Hot chocolate. Freshly baked cookies. Toy/gift shops. Weekend entertainment. Top 10 PA Travel Attractions. Walk-thru. Admission. (Evenings - November through New Year's Day)

PLAIN & FANCY FARM

Bird-In-Hand - 3121 Old Philadelphia Pike (7 miles east on SR340) 17505. Phone: (717) 768-4400 or (800) 441-3505. www.plainandfancyfarm.com. Hours: Monday-Saturday 8:30am-5:00pm, Sunday 10:30am-6:00pm (April-October). Extended summer hours. Monday-Sunday 10:00am-5:00pm (November-March). Admission: $8.95-$12.95 per person/ per activity (Depending on Activity). Combo pricing packages and coupons online. Note: Smokehouse Restaurant - all you can eat home style meals served family style (pass around large tables). Go with an appetite to get your money's worth. There are gift shops, one with ice cream and another serving soft pretzels.

Here's what you can do (choose one or a combo):

*   <u>"THE AMISH EXPERIENCE"</u> - Only one of three "experimental" F/X theatres in North America - they use actual props, 5 projectors, 3D imagery, dramatic stage lighting and "surround sound" to tell a story. The story is of an Amish family and their teenage son who is in a "runabout time" - trying to decide which world he wants to embrace. (85% of Amish teens stay within the church even after experiencing the outside world). It tells a great Amish story (past and present) and is very dramatic - probably best for ages 8 and older. www.amishexperience.com.

The Amish Experience Theater ♥ Bird-in-Hand ♥ Pennsylvania

*   <u>AMISH COUNTRY HOMESTEAD</u> - see how Amish live today through a 9-room house. Learn about Amish living, furniture, chores and clothing, and adapting to life without electricity. Includes new Amish schoolroom.

*   <u>AARON & JESSICA'S BUGGY RIDES</u> - 3.5 mile buggy ride tour of Amish farmlands. Sleigh rides too (winter)! www.amishbuggyrides.com (717) 768-8828. Usually runs $10.00-$14.00 per person. Children half price.

DANIEL BOONE HOMESTEAD

Birdsboro - 400 Daniel Boone Road (off US422 - 1 mile north) 19508. Phone: (610) 582-4900. www.thedanielboonehomestead.org. Hours: Wednesday-Saturday 10:00am-4:00pm, Sunday Noon-4:00pm. Admission: Grounds/Visitors Ctr FREE. Guided tour of Boone House (tours last 45 minutes) is $5.00-$10.00 per person. The House is closed January and February. Self guided tour is $3.00/ person. Tours: Note: The Daniel Boone Homestead offers a variety of walking/ hiking possibilities throughout the site. The gravel path winds around the historic *area and is about ¾ of a mile in distance. A short trail takes you around the Lake and there are hiking/bridle trails. Daniel Boone Lake, created by damming the Owatin Creek, runs through the Homestead property. Fishing is permitted with a valid fishing license during regular visiting hours.*

Courtesy of Pennsylvania Historical & Museum Commission

Historic and legendary, Daniel Boone embodies the cherished American characteristics of rugged individual and adventurer. Born here in 1734, the birthplace interprets the colonial Pennsylvania rural life of Daniel Boone. Daniel spent his first 16 years here before his family migrated to North Carolina. Today, the site tells the story of Daniel's youth and the saga of the region's 18th century settlers by contrasting their lives and cultures. You'll be able to sort through fact and fiction as you tour the historic site which includes the Boone House, 18th century structures, a lake, picnic areas, and recreational facilities. A restored 10 room Boone homestead (originally a log cabin), a similar cabin, sawmill, smokehouse, spring kitchen, blacksmith, and barn are on site. Be sure to watch the video presentation (re-enacted) to get a sense of the Boone family's life here. The Homestead offers many walking/hiking trails - even a ¼ mile sensory trail for the visually impaired.

BOYERTOWN MUSEUM OF HISTORIC VEHICLES

Boyertown - *85 South Walnut Street (SR73 and 562 - South to Warwick) 19512. Phone: (610) 367-2090. www.boyertownmuseum.org. Hours: Daily 9:30am-4:00pm. Admission: $9.00-$10.00 (age 15+).*

See Pennsylvania's transportation heritage - carriages, wagons, trucks, bicycles, and cars. Also on display are 18th and 19th century vehicles built by Pennsylvania Dutch craftsmen and the tools that were used to assemble them. Discover rare and handsome vehicles you won't find anywhere else. See custom bodied cars by Fleetwood, steam and electric vehicle technology, high wheel bicycles, children's vehicles and tools of the craftsman.

Chadds Ford

BRANDYWINE BATTLEFIELD PARK

Chadds Ford - *1491 Baltimore Pike (US1, 1 mile east of SR100) 19317. Phone: (610) 459-3342. http://brandywinebattlefield.org/. Hours: Tuesday - Saturday 9:00am-4:30pm, Sunday Noon-4:30pm (March-November). Closed most federal holidays. Admission: Grounds FREE. General admission $8.00 adult, $7.00 senior (65+), $5.00 youth (3-11). Parking free. Tours: Maps for self-guided tour at Visitor's Center. House Tours Friday and Saturdays only. Tours at 11:30am and 2:30pm. Note: Museum shop. Plenty of picnic areas.*

The peaceful nature of the Brandywine Valley was shattered in the summer of 1777, when British and Hessian forces fought American Continentals and local militia under George Washington and the young Marquis de Lafayette in the largest land battle of the Revolutionary War.

This giant park and museum are focused on actual Revolutionary War events. Watch the audiovisual introduction to the park first, then drive along a tour that includes 28 historic points taking you back to 1777. Remember, this defeat of American forces (led by George Washington) left the Philadelphia area open to attack and conquest by the British.

BATTLE OF BRANDYWINE

Chadds Ford - Brandywine Battlefield Park. Annual re-enactment of the Battle of Brandywine, the largest single day battle of the American War for Independence. Admission. (weekend nearest September 11)

BRANDYWINE MUSEUM OF ART

Chadds Ford - *I Hoffman's Mill Road. US 1 & PA Rte. 100 (from Wilmington, DE head northwest on Rte. 52 to Rte. 1. Left on Rte. 1. Follow signs) 19317. Phone: (610) 388-2700. www.brandywinemuseum.org. Hours: Daily 9:30am-5:00pm. Closed Thanksgiving & Christmas. Winters: Open Wednesday-Monday 10am-4pm. Admission: $18.00 adult, $15.00 senior (65+), $6.00 student/child (age 6-18). FREE for military. Tours: Kuerner Farm Tours (April through November). The historic Kuerner Farm has been a major source of inspiration to Andrew Wyeth. Since his earliest painting of the farm in 1932 at the age of 15, Wyeth has found subjects in its people, animals, buildings and landscapes for more than 1,000 works of art. Educational tours are offered at timed intervals. Due to uneven walking surfaces, the Kuerner Farm is not accessible. Read-Aloud Tours w/Storytimes are offered occasionally. Note: Restaurant open daily 10:00am-3:00pm. FREEBIES: go on a gallery hunt and see if you can find items on the Discovery Game Sheets.*

American art in a 19th century gristmill. Known for collections by three generations of Wyeths. The house where N.C. Wyeth raised his extraordinarily creative children and the studio in which he painted many of his memorable works of art have been restored to reflect their character in 1945, the year of the artist's death.

CHRISTMAS OPEN HOUSE

Chadds Ford - Brandywine River Museum. Tours of decorated, historical buildings. Refreshments and musical entertainment. Admission. Model railroad, Victorian dollhouse and whimsical "critter" ornaments. (Thanksgiving wkend-early Jan)

EVANSBURG STATE PARK

Collegeville - *851 May Hall Road (off US Route 422) 19426. Phone: (610) 409-1150.   https://www.dcnr.pa.gov/StateParks/FindAPark/EvansburgStatePark/Pages/default.aspx. Admission: to PA State Pks is FREE however swimming, marina, camping/lodging fees apply.*

This park is a haven for hikers, equestrians and folks who want to picnic and relax. You can take a walk along Skippack Creek or visit the Friedt Visitor Center that provides insight into German Mennonite living in the 18th and 19th centuries. This farmhouse was built in the early 1700s. This historic building interprets the lifestyles of the German Mennonite families who owned the home for 190 years. Outside, the root cellar, well, and herb and sensory gardens add to the eighteenth century atmosphere. An exhibit room in the house is devoted to the natural history of the area, and the house also provides an area for visitors to watch songbirds and other animals. Fishing, Hiking, Cross-Country Skiing.

Columbia

NATIONAL WATCH & CLOCK MUSEUM

Columbia - *514 Popular Street (off US30 west - follow signs) 17512. Phone: (717) 684-8261. www.nawcc.org/index.php/museum. Hours: Tuesday-Saturday 10:00am-4:00pm (year round). Closed Sunday-Tuesday winters. Admission: $5.00-$9.00 (age 5+). $23 family. Note: Museum Shop. Library. Educators: www.nawcc.org/index.php/museumeducation/teaching-resources*

You've got the time, they've got the place! The National Association of Watch and Clock Collectors have a school (of horology), offices, and this fabulously renovated museum. One staff member described it as the "Disneyland of Clocks and Time". Start at the beginning, Stonehenge, then travel through time as you browse past displays of time-keeping history.

DID YOU KNOW?
This museum houses over 12,000 watches and clocks.

You'll see thousands of watches (many still working), unique water and candle clocks, sundials and even an alarm clock that pinches you when it rings! Bells, chimes, music boxes, and organs sound on the hour as each clock chimes.

TURKEY HILL EXPERIENCE

Columbia. *301 Linden Street (Third & Linden Streets). 17512 www.turkeyhillexperience.com. Hours: generally 10am-4pm (hours vary by season)Admission: Experience is $12.50-$13.50 (age 4+), includes unlimited free samples). Tasting Lab is $9.00 more per person.*

This destination features interactive exhibits highlighting Turkey Hill's role in the agricultural heritage of Lancaster County, including a chance to experience what it's like to be a Turkey Hill Dairy Ice Cream maker for a day by creating your own ice cream flavor. Learn how ice cream is made, sit in a giant milk truck and milk a mechanical cow. Situated in the former Ashley & Bailey silk mill, the venue also includes a café and creamery alongside free samples of ice cream and iced tea.

WRIGHT'S FERRY MANSION

Columbia - *38 South 2nd Street (US30 - Columbia/Marietta Exit SR 441 South) 17512. Phone: (717) 684-4325. https://lancastercountymuseums.org/wrights-ferry-mansion/ Hours: Generally Tuesday & Wednesday, Friday & Saturday 10:00am-3:00pm (May - October). PLEASE VERIFY OPEN HOURS BEFORE VISITING. Admission: $5.00 adult, $2.50 child (6-18).*

Discover the fascinating and visionary life of Susanna Wright, a bright, creative Quaker woman whose diverse talents benefited many. She ran a ferry here, was an unofficial doctor and lawyer, launched the silk industry in this region, and shared ideas with people like Ben Franklin with whom she corresponded regularly. The 1738 house reflects Quaker lifestyles prior to 1750 and its collections are one of the most representative in the country. Because this is an "open" museum (no velvet ropes separating you from the displays) you certainly get the feeling that the occupants have just left for a little while… and may be returning shortly! We recommend close supervision for younger children, or better yet only bring them if your children are age 8 or older.

CORNWALL IRON FURNACE

Cornwall - *94 Rexmont Road (4 miles North of US76 off SR 72 on SR419) 17016. Phone: (717) 272-9711. www.cornwallironfurnace.org. Hours: Friday-Saturday 9:00am-4:00pm, Sunday Noon-4:00pm. Closed most holidays, except Summer holidays. Admission: Visitors Center is FREE. Guided tours are $4.00-$8.00 per person (age 3+). Note: on tour, there is no heat or air conditioning in the furnace building. Educators: an easy-to-follow pre-visit worksheet is found online: www. cornwallironfurnace.org/Vocabulary-Students.pdf.*

A 1742 - 1833 iron making complex. The preserved facility once produced farm tools, kitchenware, stoves, cannons and ammunition. Self-guided tours examine an orientation exhibit that provides a clear understanding of the once active iron plantation. The exhibit tells the story of two families and their iron plantation workers. You can see the original furnace stack, blast machinery, blowing tubs, and a Great Wheel (76 feet around). Remember this site was water-powered. An ironmaster's mansion and the Charcoal House Visitor's Center are on the premises. Start by watching the video showing the making of charcoal and preparing molds for casting in the 19th century. The Visitors Center gallery also provides information on charcoal making, pig iron, and different types of employees, such as indentured servants and slaves. Text is written at the comprehension level of middle school-aged children. There is no admission fee for the gallery or video, which is accessible to all. The property is a 5-acre historic site that offers a picnic area and beautiful grounds for a nice walk on a warm day.

MARSH CREEK STATE PARK

Downingtown - *675 Park Road (two miles west of the village of Eagle on PA 100) 19335. Phone: (610) 458-5119. https://www.dcnr.pa.gov/StateParks/FindAPark/ MarshCreekStatePark/Pages/default.aspx. Admission: to PA State Parks is FREE however swimming, marina and camping/lodging fees apply, with reservation or entrance.*

Marsh Creek Lake is especially popular with sailboaters and windsurfers who take advantage of the prevailing wind to enjoy their sport. Nature lovers will enjoy a pleasant walk on hiking trails or the Larkins covered Bridge located in the northeast section of the park. Pool, Boat Rentals, Sledding, and Fishing.

Doylestown

MERCER MUSEUM

Doylestown - *84 South Pine Street (off SR202, rear SR313 and SR611) 18901. Phone: (215) 345-0210. www.mercermuseum.org. Hours: Tuesday-Sunday 10:00am-5:00pm. Admission: $15.00 adult, $13.00 senior (62+), $8.00 youth (5-17). Combo pricing if touring Fonthill also. Please note: The Mercer Museum is not heated or cooled; plan to dress appropriately for the seasons. Educators: their website has a treasure of downloadable activity sheets, scavenger hunts (highly recommended to print off before you tour), vocabulary and bibliographies. Studying pre-Industrial Revolution history? These materials make it fun: http://mercermuseum.org/education/school-youth-groups/resources/*

The receptionist promised us the best part of the self-guided tour was the walk into the Center Court. It is amazing!  Artifacts are hanging everywhere! While searching through junk in a barn, Henry Chapman Mercer found a jumble of objects made obsolete by the Industrial Revolution. His collection, housed in a "cement castle", represents more than 60 crafts and trades - pre 1850. Called "The Tools of the Nation Maker", play a game to try to find one tool from at least 50 trades (every year, they produce a different themed scavenger hunt worksheet - ask for one). Some are easy to see, but over 40,000 pieces of "junk" are in every nook and cranny. In the museum's Imagination Gallery, located nearby, young children can explore other hands-on activities related to the museum's collection, including puppet play, tile rubbings, puzzles, and storybooks. This is the most eccentric, yet curiously fun, museum you'll ever find! And, the cement and leaded glass windows truly give that medieval.

MERCER MUSEUM FOLKFEST

Doylestown - Mercer Museum. www.buckscountyhistorical.org/folkfest/index.html. Traditional artisans make the skills and trades of early America come to life during this nationally acclaimed festival. Entertainment, militia encampment, and full picnic fare. Admission. (Mothers Day weekend - May)

MORAVIAN POTTERY AND TILE WORKS & FONTHILL

Doylestown - *East Court Street (Court St. and Swamp Rd., off of Rte. 313, which runs north/south of Doylestown) 18901. Phone: (215) 345-6722. www. mercermuseum.org/visit/fonthill-castle/ Hours: Tuesday-Sunday 10:00am-5:00pm. Closed select holidays. Admission: $15 adult, $13 senior (65+), $8 youth (6-17). Discount combo with Mercer Museum. Tours: Guided - every 1/2 hour. Last tour at 4:00pm. Tower Tours for Families (explore basement to tower) the first Saturday morning of every month. Note: Tile Shop.*

This facility, beginning in 1912, produced tiles and mosaics for floors, walls and ceilings. Mercer's artistic floor tiles adorn the rotunda and halls of the Pennsylvania State Capitol, depicting 400 scenes in the Commonwealth's history. Today, the facility makes reproductions of Mercer's original line of tiles. Mercer was a visionary architect who was one of the first designers to work with reinforced concrete as a building material.

Tours are offered every half-hour and consist of a 17-minute video and a self-guided walk through the facility. Watch the clay being prepared, then stamped with designs, then fired, glazed and fired again. Kids will appreciate FONTHILL (Mercer's mansion/castle that is next door) or the Mercer Museum a little more if they understand what made him rich and famous.

JULY 4TH CELEBRATION

Doylestown - City Parks. Parades, music, food, fireworks & contests. Town ball game, Pony rides, contests. Admission.

PUMPKIN FESTIVAL

Doylestown - Moravian Pottery And Tile Works & Fonthill. Pumpkin painting and carving, pie-eating contests. Pumpkin patch (wagon rides out there). Refreshments. Admission. (last weekend in October)

CHRISTMAS OPEN HOUSE

Doylestown - Moravian Pottery And Tile Works & Fonthill. Tours of decorated, historical buildings. Refreshments and musical entertainment. Dolls, toys, crafts. Admission. (weekends in December)

POLISH AMERICAN FESTIVAL

Doylestown - National Shrine of Our Lady of Czestochowa. www.czestochowa.us. Polish folk song dance ensembles, polka bands, entertainment shows, Polish and American foods, and amusements. Admission. (1st two weekends of Sept)

BYERS' CHOICE LTD

Doylestown (Chalfont) - *4355 County Line Road (Just north of Rt.309 & Rt. 202) 18914. Phone: (215) 822-0150. www.byerschoice.com. Hours: Monday-Saturday 10:00am-5:00pm (Closed major holidays). Admission: FREE.*

The Byers Choice factory is the home of America's beloved, handcrafted Carolers® figurine collectibles. What started as a family Christmas gift 40 years ago has grown to a team of 180 artisans. By a walk-through observation deck, you can watch them mold delicate faces and then apply makeup (paint) to add dimension and features. See all the costumes and background landscapes available to make each singing doll unique. What you don't see in production that day, you can watch by pre-taped video. Want more? Stroll down a recreated London street scene and enter the Christmas Museum. You can peer into shop windows and residences filled with Christmas displays, view a short film about the history of the company in a theater reminiscent of Victorian England, and try on a top hat, scarf, muff or bonnet to have your picture taken.

RALPH STOVER STATE PARK

Doylestown (Pipersville) - *6011 State Park Road (State Park Road and Stump Road) 18947. Phone: (610) 982-5560. https://www.dcnr.pa.gov/StateParks/ FindAPark/RalphStoverStatePark/Pages/default.aspx Admission: to PA State Parks is FREE however swimming, marina and camping/lodging fees apply.*

45 acres along the Tohickon Creek. Warm-water fish species found in Tohickon Creek include smallmouth bass, sunfish, carp and catfish. They stock trout, a cold-water fish. There is one mile of easy walking trails that pass through many habitats and near the millrace. The 'High Rocks' section of the park features an outstanding view of a horseshoe bend in Tohickon Creek and the surrounding forest.

FRENCH CREEK STATE PARK

Elverson - *843 Park Road (off Route 345) 19520. Phone: (610) 582-9680. https://www.dcnr.pa.gov/StateParks/FindAPark/FrenchCreekStatePark/Pages/default. aspx Admission: To PA State Parks is FREE however swimming, marina and camping/lodging fees apply.*

French Creek offers two lakes - Hopewell and Scotts Run, extensive forests and almost 40 miles of hiking trails. Adjacent to the park lies Hopewell Furnace. Pool, Boat Rentals, Horseback Riding, Mountain Biking, Campsites, Modern Cabins, Yurts, Fishing, and Cross-Country Skiing.

HOPEWELL FURNACE NATL HISTORIC SITE

Elverson - *2 Mark Bird Lane (PA Rt. 724 East, turn right onto PA Rt. 345 South) 19520. Phone: (610) 582-8773. www.nps.gov/hofu/index.htm. Hours: Wednesday-Sunday 9:00am-5:00pm. Daily summers. Closed holidays. Parking lots, restrooms and hiking trails are open every day except on federal holidays when the park is closed. Admission: FREE. Tours: Self-guided tours enhanced by recorded voices of workers and their families. Note: Younger children prefer summers when living history actors are throughout the village. Older kids like the stories on the tour. Educators: Puzzles/worksheets: www.nps.gov/hofu/learn/education/index.htm*

Hopewell spans two centuries; and presently stands as an example of America's development during the industrial revolution. The Visitor's Center features an audio visual program and exhibits of the original iron castings and tools used in Colonial cold blast charcoal furnaces. See a restored cast house, water wheel cooling shed, tenant houses and ironmaster's mansion (The Big House). Learn about "pig iron" (formed in troughs), and stoves and weapons produced here - recreated by actual blacksmiths shaping the hot slabs of iron alongside molders. This is mostly a living history village (summers and special events) and the "villagers" are well educated on iron casting. Call ahead to be sure you get to see live demonstrations during your visit.

During September and October the park's historic apple orchard is opened for picking by the public. The park's orchard includes many historic varieties not normally available in today's markets. Length of season and availability of varieties depends upon the success of the growing season. The apples are sold by the pound. In December the buildings are decorated for Christmas.

FORT WASHINGTON STATE PARK

Fort Washington - *500 Bethlehem Pike (2 miles from PA Turnpike exit 26) 19034. Phone: (215) 646-2942. https://www.dcnr.pa.gov/StateParks/FindAPark/ FortWashingtonStatePark/Pages/default.aspx   Admission: to PA State Parks is FREE however swimming, marina and camping/lodging fees apply, with reservation or entrance.*

This beautiful park interests historians of the American Revolution. The park takes its name from the fort built by George Washington's troops in the fall of 1777, before heading to Valley Forge. The park is popular with hikers and bikers. Birders enjoy the seasonal migration of raptors from the Observation Deck. Hawks, Washington Encampment, Fishing, Trails, Winter Sports. Disc Golf: The wooded, 9-hole course begins in Lot 2 in the Militia Hill Day Use Area at a kiosk with a map of the course.

MEMORIAL LAKE STATE PARK

Grantville - *RD 1, Box 7045 (I- 81 at exit 29 /Fort Indiantown Gap, take PA Route 934 North) 17028. Phone: (717) 865-6470. https://www.dcnr.pa.gov/StateParks/ FindAPark/MemorialLakeStatePark/Pages/default.aspx Admission: FREE however swimming, marina and camping/lodging fees apply.*

This quaint park has a lake for canoeing, wind surfing and fishing, and hiking trails and lots of beautiful scenery. A short woodland trail winds along the northern shoreline. The open nature of the park allows the visitor to take casual walks through most of the park. Scenic views of the lake provide a tranquil setting, especially during the spring and autumn days. Boat Rentals, Fishing, Cross-Country Skiing.

KITCHEN KETTLE VILLAGE

Intercourse - *Route 340 17534. www.kitchenkettle.com. Hours: Monday-Saturday 9:00am-5:00pm. Closed Sundays.*

Welcome to a village in the heart of Pennsylvania Dutch Country where there's always plenty of shopping, good foods, and a place for everyone to be a kid again. Visit the World Famous Canning Kitchen (samples) or stroll down Pepper Lane and eat as you go: hand-rolled fudge, homemade ice cream, hot pretzels, and freshly baked goodies. Walk that off browsing the shops.

EASTER EGG HUNT

Intercourse - Kitchen Kettle Village. Easter crafts, entertainment, breakfast with Easter Bunny & Yummie. Admission (Saturday before Easter Sunday)

RHUBARB FESTIVAL

Intercourse - Kitchen Kettle Village. Annual festival that teaches us that rhubarb (a red-stalked vegetable) is no longer just for pies. You won't believe the colorful menus of rhubarb-inspired foods, baked goods and beverages, and the Rhubarb Jams made special at festival time. Kids can play games (even build mini-racecars – The Rhubarb Race Car Derby). Food and games. FREE. (third Friday/Saturday in May)

7 SWEETS & SOURS TAILGATE

Intercourse - Kitchen Kettle Village. Celebrate the fall and tailgating season with a celebration of food, music and sports fun. The Village comes alive with a sports themed scarecrow competition, tailgating food demos, pumpkin bowling, musical entertainment and more. Dress in your favorite "team" gear. (third Friday & Saturday in September)

HOLLY DAYS

Intercourse - Kitchen Kettle Village. Join in decking the hall, streets and shops with holiday décor. Caroling, brass bands, cookie baking, roaming musicians and oodles of specialty shopping, Experience Old Fashioned Christmas Friday Nights with Mrs. Claus & Yummie. "Hershey Chocolate S'more Area." Families can enjoy a holiday feast at The Kling House Restaurant (includes family style dining, storytelling with Mrs. Claus & Yummie and a special gift for children).

HAWK MOUNTAIN

Kempton - *1700 Hawk Mountain Road (I-78, exit 9B north to Route 895 east) 19529. Phone: (610) 756-6961. www.hawkmountain.org. Hours: Daily 9:00am-5:00pm. Admission: Trail Fees (to get to lookouts): $10.00 adult, $7.00 senior (65+), $5.00 child (6-12). Educators: www.hawkmountain.org/learn/teachers/teacher-guide/page.aspx?id=279*

Located along the Appalachian Trail, scenic Hawk Mountain Sanctuary offers an outstanding nature experience with its mountaintop vistas, hiking trails, and thrilling autumnal raptor migration. With a total of 2,600 acres, anyone can enjoy these trails rated from easy to challenging. You can spend an entire day at the sanctuary or take an early morning hike and then onto your next stop. Between mid-August and mid-December an average 18,000 hawks, eagles, and falcons fly past this site. Bookstore. Wildlife viewing windows. Exhibits. Trails. FREE Live-raptor programs on weekends (April-November).

W.K. & S. STEAM RAILROAD

Kempton - *42 Community Center Dr (SR143 or SR737 into Kempton. - follow signs) 19529. Phone: (610) 756-6469. www.kemptontrain.com. Hours: Sundays (May thru October). Departures from 1:00pm-4:00pm leave every hour on the hour. Admission: $6.00-$12.00 (age 3+). Note: The station facilities include a gift shop with many railroad-related items, refreshment stand, waiting room, restrooms, and a large picnic area. Large grassy areas provide for the kids to run. No restrooms on train. On Sundays, the Schuykill & Lehigh Model Railroad Club's HO model train display is also open to the public.*

Known as the "Hawk Mountain Line", the WK&S has been open since 1963. Passengers enjoy a three-mile ride to Wanamaker through Pennsylvania's picturesque countryside, passing several historic sites and structures. Nice short ride (40 minutes) where you can get off at picnic groves throughout the countryside and get back on later. What could be better than a 45 minute train ride through beautiful scenic woods on a real locomotive?

EASTER BUNNY TRAIN RIDES

Kempton - W. K. & S. Steam Railroad. Candy treats with the Easter Bunny riding along. Admission. (Easter Weekend)

HARVEST MOON TRAIN

Kempton - W. K. & S. Steam Railroad. Autumn moonlight train ride with musicians and light refreshments. Admission. (third weekend in October)

SANTA CLAUS SPECIAL

Kempton - W. K. & S. Steam Railroad. Join Frosty the Snowman, Santa & his Elves at the WK&S! Free gifts for the children as Santa walks through the train. Admission. (first weekend in December)

Kennett Square

LONGWOOD GARDENS

Kennett Square - *1001 Longwood Road, (take SR 52 northwest to US 1. Left on US 1. Follow signs) 19348. Phone: (610) 388-1000. www.longwoodgardens. org. Hours: Daily 10:00am-5:00pm, closed Tuesdays (open later during peak Spring / Summer & Holiday seasons) Admission: $25.00 adult, $22.00 senior (62+), $13.00 student (5-18). Note: Stop by the Terrace Restaurant for Kids Value Meals. Breakfasts with the Easter Bunny and Santa, and Family Fireworks BBQs are featured seasonally by reservation. Go online to find out more about how you make your visit to the Gardens more enjoyable and worth the admission.*

See exotic plants from around the world, examine insect-catching plants up close, enjoy dancing fountains that shoot water 130 feet in the air, and be dazzled by 40 colorful indoor and outdoor displays every day of the year. Special children's programs like Peter Rabbit, Christmas and Mazes.

Is Longwood Gardens a place for family fun? Yes, if you look for it. Explore three tree houses, have your picture taken next to animal-shaped topiaries and be amused by colorful indoor and outdoor floral displays. The Indoor Children's Garden is an whimsical space of ramps, mazes, grottoes, and lots of running water (30 water features in all). A shooting jet that rings a bell, a spitting fish, a pond with rising steam, a cave with dripping walls, and a gigantic drooling dragon are just a few of the water wonders visitors will enjoy. Two mazes - one square accented by story tiles and shooting jets of water - and one Bamboo offering a jungle of tree-size bamboos for children to explore. Kids will enjoy frolicking in the Bee A-mazed garden designed especially for them. The Garden features three major areas: the Honeycomb Maze, Flower Fountain, and Buzz Trail. All the children's areas are accessible for kids of any age. We noticed lots of moms pushing strollers on the pathways. Within reason, kids can romp and squeal to their hearts content.

CHRISTMAS OPEN HOUSE

Kennett Square - Longwood Gardens. Tours of decorated buildings. Refreshments and musical entertainment. Admission. (Thanksgiving thru early January)

Kutztown

CRYSTAL CAVE

Kutztown - 963 Crystal Cave Road (Off US 22. Follow signs) 19530. Phone: (610) 683-6765. www.crystalcavepa.com. Hours: Daily 9:00am-5:00pm (March-November) Holidays & Weekends to 6:00pm. Admission: $14-$19.00 (age 4+). Tours: 45 minutes includes video about cave formation. Note: Food. Gift shop. Rock shop. Mini-golf. Gem Panning (extra fee). Museum and nature trails. Caution: there are many steps to climb to get to the cave entrance and stairs to navigate inside the cave. Heavy or unhealthy persons may find this a challenge.

The most visited cave site in Pennsylvania, Crystal Cave is known for its profuse and varied formations. The 45 minute tour begins with an eight minute video presentation in the theatre. Trained guides take you past milky white formations enhanced by indirect lighting. Look for the Giant's Tooth, Prairie dogs, Indian Head, Totem Pole, Natural Bridge and the Ear of Corn formations. Although the cave isn't spectacular, the added adventure of the guide momentarily turning off the lights is an interesting feature. We liked how the guides point out formations and tell some stories of why they named them. This site includes shops, fast food, trails, 125 acres and a museum.

RODALE INSTITUTE FARM

Kutztown - 611 Siegfriedale Road (off US222, just northeast of town) 19530. Phone: (610) 683-1400. www.rodaleinstitute.org. Hours: Monday-Saturday 9:00am-5:00pm, Sunday 10:00am-3:00pm (early May - mid-October). Admission: Self guided tours are FREE. Average $3.00 per person (age 5+) Tours: Monday - Friday morning (By appointment, group fee charged). Note: Gift shop - light fare and samples - suggest you try homemade organic apple sauce or butter.

Regenerative Organic Farming and Gardening - Do you know what that means? The Rodale Institute is located on a 333-acre organic certified farm devoted to research, education and certified organic production. Learn the connection between healthy soil, healthy food, and healthy people, all through demonstrations and children's gardens. A tour highlight for children is watching how earthworms help aerate and fertilize the soil. Initial shrieks turn to keen interest as the children handle the subterranean workers, feed them kitchen scraps and watch them burrow. They can then take a trip through a child-size "Earthworm Tunnel™" for a first-hand experience.

KUTZTOWN FOLK FESTIVAL

Kutztown - Fairgrounds. www.kutztownfestival.com. An annual celebration of the Pennsylvania Dutch lifestyle with demonstrating craftsmen, entertainment, food, nature center, antique farm museum, etc. Delightful baby farm animals, puppets, make-and- take crafts, hay mazes, story time, and singalongs. Admission. (first full week in July)

PEDDLER'S VILLAGE

Lahaska - *Routes 202 & 263. www.peddlersvillage.com. Phone: (215) 794-4000.*

Lightspace Play, an LED-lighted floor programmed to create games and activities, is the newest addition to Giggleberry Fair, a family-friendly attraction at Peddler's Village that includes an old-fashioned Grand Carousel, Giggleberry Mountain, Discovery Land, the Game Room and the Painted Pony Café.

STRAWBERRY FESTIVAL

Lahaska - Peddler's Village. Sample strawberry treats like fresh strawberry shortcakes and strawberry ice cream or sundaes. From great beverages and tempting sweets to colorful side dishes and barbecued meats grilled with berry sauces. Entertainment, demonstrations, contests and prizes. Kids' activities. FREE. (first weekend in May)

CELEBRATION OF FREEDOM

Lahaska - Peddler's Village. Live entertainment, children's activities, and picnic-style favorites await you at this patriotic event. Fireworks display at 9:15pm. Free admission. Music accompanying fireworks. (July 3rd)

SCARECROW COMPETITION & DISPLAY

Lahaska - Peddler's Village. Unusual and delightful bird-chasing creations compete for over $1400 in prizes. Vote for your favorite traditional, contemporary, whirl-a-gig and amateur. Displayed throughout the village. Pumpkin painting, square dancing. Make one workshop. (Mid-September to Mid-October)

APPLE FESTIVAL

Lahaska - Peddler's Village. Live music, marionettes, pie-eating contests. Apples served up in fritters, pastries, butter, dipped in chocolate and caramel, or plain. Take home a bushel fresh from the orchard. Juried Artisans sell their wares and demonstrate their skills. Live entertainment. FREE. (first weekend in Nov)

Lancaster

DUTCH APPLE DINNER THEATRE

Lancaster - *510 Centerville Road (off US 30west) 17601. Phone: (717) 898-1900. www.dutchapple.com.*

Children's matinee and Sunday twilight. Dine while watching children's musicals like Pinocchio, Adventures of Huck Finn, Willy Wonka or Cinderella. Regular show Tickets start at $22.00. Children's Theatre Schedule Ticket Price: For Kids of all ages $20.00 includes children's lunch and show.

TINY TOWN

Lancaster - *533 Janet Avenue (off US 30west) 17601. Phone: (717) 947-7350 or tinytownpa.com. Hours: Monday-Saturday 9am - 4pm. Admission: $15 general (age 13 months +). Free for children 12 months and under.*

It's a miniature version of a town square, where youngsters can fix the engine on a 1950s Chevy, be a server at a cafe or scan canned goods at a grocery store cashier's station. Kids can climb up a ladder in the firehouse and slide down the pole, or pull the nozzle from the toy gas pump outside the mechanic's shop. These things that in real life would be far above their heads are right at eye level for young kids. Each house is several feet tall, and can accommodate about five or six kids at a time. There's a whirring plastic blender on the counter of the cafe, floor-to-ceiling books in the library and toy dryers in the hair salon. There are costumes that go with each (playhouse), from plastic capes in the hair salon to a firefighter jacket in the fire station. While the kids are in the playhouses, their parents can sit in the cafe and lounge area across the room and socialize over coffee and a snack.

HANDS-ON HOUSE CHILDREN'S MUSEUM

Lancaster - *721 Landis Valley Road (US 30 to Oregon Pike N exit) 17601. Phone: (717) 569-KIDS. www.handsonhouse.org. Hours: Tuesday-Friday 9:00am-5:00pm, Saturday 9:00am-6:00pm, Sunday 11:00am-5:00pm. Open Mondays and extended hours, seasonally. Closed major winter holidays. Admission: $10.50 adult, $12.00 child (ages 2-10), $9.00 Military. Everything is simply explained.*

All of the exhibits at Hands-on House are custom-designed and unique. There exhibits include a variety of activities appropriate for children ages 2-10 years. Each exhibit has a theme with a variety of activities to do that relate to the theme. Favorite "spaces" include: a Lancaster Farming Area, Grocery Store and Art Smart Fun. In Marty's Machine Shop, you'll wear safety goggles to work on an assembly line or sort and deliver mail at a kid-friendly factory. The Space Voyage Checkpoint takes kids on a spaceship ride to learn about health and wellness as earthlings get a checkup before their journey into space. At Feelings, talk to a giant stuffed bear.

LANDIS VALLEY MUSEUM

Lancaster - *2451 Kissel Hill Road (3 miles north on Oregon Pike - SR272) 17601. Phone: (717) 569-0401. www.landisvalleymuseum.org. Hours: Tuesday-Saturday 9:00am-4:00pm, Sunday Noon-4:00pm. Closed some major holidays and winter Tuesdays. Admission: $12.00 adult, $10.00 senior (65+), $8.00 child (3-11). Note: Weathervane gift shop.*

The largest Pennsylvania German museum in the U.S. (100 acres) includes 20 buildings including the craft shop, schoolhouse, country store, leather crafts, farmstead, blacksmith, transportation building, hotel, pottery shop plus others. Exhibits interpret rural life prior to 1900 through artisans and demonstrations of traditional skills. Children can try their hands at woodworking and mingle with lambs. If they are conducting lessons in the schoolhouse, mind your ways as you might get sent in the corner with a dunce cap. Special performances, craft demonstrations and living history programs change monthly. The tavern, log home, family home and general store are the most informative presentations. Don't forget about the traditional walkways of dirt, pebble or brick. Lots of walking here. Besides the festivals listed below, they often have less formal events which are the ideal time to visit - events or festivals - as there are always more costumed guides leading the kids in hands-on activities.

HARVEST DAYS

Lancaster - Landis Valley Museum. Tractor pulls, antique steam engines, parades, food (made with steam), threshing, baling, cider and apple butter making, hayrides, children's activities, petting zoo & fall crafts. Admission. (second weekend in October)

AMISH FARM AND HOUSE

Lancaster - *2395 Route 30 East 17602. www.amishfarmandhouse.com. Phone: (717) 394-6185. Hours: Daily 8:30am-6:00pm (Summer). 9:00am-5:00pm (Spring & Fall). Admission: $12.95 adult, $11.95 senior (60+), $8.95 child (5-11). For an additional fee you can take a Countryside Bus Tour. Tours: 35 minutes Note: Amish Chicken BBQ (April - Oct). Weekend craft demos. Buggy rides (extra fee).*

Guided tours of an Amish home (10 rooms) - learn the history, religious customs and a simple way of life. Self-guided tour of a working farm with local crops, barns, and farm animals. Most interesting is a unique Lancaster County device - a water wheel powered pump operates a larger pump via wire. In the Spring House, a large water wheel powers a pump which forces cold spring water into a kitchen refrigerator. A limestone quarry on the property supplied stone to build this barn and house. New to the property is a tour of the Amish One Room Schoolhouse.

FALL FARM DAYS

Lancaster - Amish Farm And House. Fall celebration of the apple harvest. See cider being pressed, apple "schnitzing", taste historic apple varieties. Games for children. Corn maze, buggy rides and wood carving. Admission. (second wkend in Oct)

MENNONITE LIFE VISITORS CENTER

Lancaster - *2215 Millstream Road - Off US30 17602. Phone: (717) 299-0954. www. mennonitelife.org. Hours: Tuesday-Saturday 9:00am-5:00pm (April-October). 9:30am-4pm (November-March). Admission: FREE for info center. $10.00 adult, $7.00 child (age 6-16). Guided group tours. 45 minutes on the hour. Gift shop.*

Film and displays explaining the faith and culture of Amish and Mennonites

called The "Lancaster Amish" movie, which requires tickets, offers a first-hand look into the Amish, their faith, and life. Shown every hour. Included is a reproduction of a Hebrew Tabernacle with lecture tours given on the history, construction, function, and significance on the hour (every 2 hours in the Winter). Most kids leave with an understanding of the Arc of the Covenant and can answer as to why the 66 lumps in the candleholder were prophecy of the future. Even if you know little about Biblical history, this presentation is fascinating. You will also find walk-through exhibits and fair trade crafts.

DUTCH WONDERLAND FAMILY AMUSEMENT PARK

Lancaster - *2249 Route 30 East 17602. www.dutchwonderland.com. Phone: (717) 291-1888. Hours: Daily 10:00am-7:00pm (Memorial Day-Labor Day), Weekends only 10:00am-6:00pm (Spring & Fall). Admission: $49.99 (ages 3+). Online discounts. Preview Plan is FREE if you go the night before and pay for the next day. Note: Also Wonderland Mini-Golf.*

It's a Kingdom for Kids. Come and meet "Duke The Dragon" and the "Princess of Dutch Wonderland". Merlin's Mayhem is the newest roller coaster ride at Dutch Wonderland. Sitting in seats suspended below the track, you'll rise 60 feet in the air, zoom through two helix turns, and spin along many twists and drops — all while receiving clues and encouragement from Merlin via the on-board audio system. It's cute…with many clean, safe rides for kids (probably best age range is 4-12, with their adults). Cute little interactive shows and a wonderful "High Dive" show. It's hard to believe those guys really dive from 30 to 80 feet…until you see it! Rides include: Roller Coaster, Giant Slide, Splash Flume, Flying Trapeze, Riverboat,Train rides, Skyride, and Duke's Lagoon waterplay.

WINTER WONDERLAND

Lancaster - Dutch Wonderland. Selected rides and attractions open. Santa. Decorate cookies. Storytelling. FREE (rides & crafts, pay as you go). (late Nov-Dec)

FULTON STEAMBOAT INN

Lancaster - 1 Hartman Bridge Road (US30 & SR896) 17602. Phone: (717) 299-9999 or (800) 922-2229. www.fultonsteamboatinn.com. From the first "Welcome Aboard" to the last splash in the Indoor Atrium pool – your kids will think it's cool to overnight in a steamboat. They have an indoor pool, jacuzzi, playground and an observation deck that looks onto the duck/koi pond and walking trail. Check out all of the ship's wheels and Victorian flare – esp. the lobby. The family-favorite Promenade Deck Queen w/Bunk rooms are located on the first level of the hotel and have one queen bed & a set of bunk beds. All rooms on board include HDTV's, refrigerator, microwave. Average daily rate runs about $100. After you spend the night sleeping on a steamboat, enjoy a meal in a room full of steamboat antiques. As you hear seagulls sounds, select from Steamboat or Mid-Ship Specialties for breakfast, lunch or dinner.._____

LANCASTER SCIENCE FACTORY

Lancaster - *454 New Holland Avenue (and Plum St.) (near Industrial Area of downtown) 17602. Phone: (717) 509-6363. www.lancastersciencefactory.com. Hours: Tuesday-Saturday 10:00am-5:00pm, Sunday Noon-5:00pm (September-June). Opens Mondays also (June-August). Admission: $12.00 general.*

Through exhibits, work stations and mini-labs, children can experiment and create as they learn the principles of science in engineering and technology. Exhibits include a large Water Lab, Flight Test Zone featuring airplane launchers and a Wind Tube, Topographic Box, Sustainable Energy Dance Floor, Giant Turntable, Pneumatic Tubes, and much more. Can you make a long-lasting bubble? What about a building that withstands an earthquake? Next, run some electric or design and put a roller coaster in motion. And, our favorite - the maze that is a Kinetic Energy Machine.

LANCASTER BARNSTORMERS BASEBALL

Lancaster - *Clipper Magazine Stadium, 650 North Prince Street (downtown) 17603. Phone: (717) 509-HITS. www.lancasterbarnstormers.com. Single tickets run $13-$17.00.*

The Barnstormers are part of the Atlantic League of Professional Baseball and play from early May until October. The state-of-the-art stadium offers affordable and fun family entertainment. Fans enjoy the largest Kids' Play Area in minor league baseball, concession stands offering a "taste of Lancaster," unique promotions and giveaways and "up close" seats.

NORTH MUSEUM OF NATURAL HISTORY AND SCIENCE

Lancaster - *400 College Avenue (Franklin Marshall College) 17603. Phone: (717) 291-3941. www.northmuseum.org. Hours: Wednesday-Sunday 10am-3pm. Admission: $18.00 (ages 3+). Small fee for planetarium.*

The North Museum has generated excitement and curiosity about natural history, science and technology for more than 50 years. Close to downtown, the Museum features exhibits from outer space to local Native American peoples, from rocks and minerals to dinosaurs, from the Living Animal Room to the Discovery Room. Twist a 20-foot spiral wave machine, see how a tidal wave spreads across the Earth, play with a tornado, examine hundreds of birds, or explore the galaxy in the planetarium. The Tech area features Lego Lab. Linger to enjoy incredible images from the Hubble telescope and NASA

WHEATLAND

Lancaster - *1120 Marietta Avenue (PA 23 off US30west) 17603. Phone: (717) 392-8721. www.wheatland.org. Hours: Tuesday-Saturdays 10:00am-4:00pm. Open Mondays, too (spring and summer). Closed all major holidays. Admission: $15.00 adult, $13.00 senior (65+), $8.00 student (11-17), FREE child (10 and younger). Tours: Costume guides for general or pre-arranged hands-on tours. Last tour begins at 3:00pm. Note: Gift shop. Snack bar. Educators: click on Learn icon for biographies of Buchanan and others.*

The Federal Style mansion was home to the nation's 15th President (and the only President from Pennsylvania), James Buchanan. Tours begin in the carriage house where you view a film about Mr. Buchanan and see the actual carriage his family used to travel around town. Also, see the library that served as a headquarters for his Presidential campaign. Kids are invited to dress in top hats or hoop skirts and may be asked questions like, "How often did people take baths in the mid-1800s?" Guess? (Answer - An average of 2 times per year!) His response to inquiries about "Wheatland" was…"I am now residing at this place, which is an agreeable country residence…I hope you may not fail to come this way…I should be delighted with a visit…"

CHRISTMAS OPEN HOUSE

Lancaster - Wheatland. Tours of decorated, historical buildings. Refreshments and musical entertainment. Admission. (first and last week in December)

AMERICAN MUSIC THEATRE

Lancaster - *2425 Lincoln Highway East (US 30) 17605. Phone: (717) 397-7700 or (800) 648-4102. www.amtshows.com.*

American Sights. American sounds. American Songs. American spirit. Musicals plus 30+ celebrity concerts year round. Morning, matinee and evening shows. Spring thru the Holidays. From concerts and Broadway Tours, to original musical revues that are fun for the whole family, there's something on stage for everyone at AMT. $25.00-$49.00 avg. Friday Family Night Rates (discounted early shows).

HANS HERR HOUSE

Lancaster (Willow Street) - *1849 Hans Herr Drive (between Pennsylvania route 741 / U.S. route 222 (Beaver Valley Pike) and Penn Grant Road) 17584. Phone: (717) 464-4438. www.hansherr.org. Hours: Friday-Saturday 10:00am-4:00pm (April-October). December special events. Admission: $15 adult, $7 child (7-12).*

The 1719 Hans Herr House, built in that year by Hans' son Christian, is the oldest surviving dwelling place of European settlers in what is now Lancaster County, Pennsylvania. It is the oldest still-standing Mennonite meeting house in the Western Hemisphere. The 1719 House, or "Hans Herr House" as it is known locally, was a home to several generations of Hans Herr's family until the 1860s, after which it was used as a barn and storage shed. It was restored to colonial-era appearance in the early 1970s. It is now part of a Museum complex which includes three Pennsylvania German farmhouses, several barns and other outbuildings, and an extensive collection of farm equipment spanning three centuries. Check their website for special events when re-enactors bring this place to life. Three regularly scheduled special events throughout the year include Heritage Day, a farm festival with many demonstrations and workshops; Snitz Fest, celebrating the apple in Lancaster County; and Christmas Candlelight Tours.

SIGHT & SOUND THEATRES

Lancaster / Strasburg - *Route 896 (off Rte. 30), 300 Hartman Bridge Rd (Millennium Theatre & Living Waters Theatre) 17579. Phone: (717) 687-7800. www.sight-sound.com.* Seasonal shows each Christmas and Easter, too.

Sight & Sound continues the same mission to share the Word of God by turning stories you've always loved into shows you'll never forget. This special effects theatre is known for live Easter and Christmas performances. Shows the rest of the year focus on familiar bible characters like Ruth or Daniel. Through inspirational productions, they seek to encourage others to be dedicated and wise stewards of our God-given talents and resources.

Epic stories unfold in front, beside and even above you! With innovative dream "cloud" sequences, lavish staging, colorful characters and vibrant music, this energy packed production is for all ages and is certain to stir your emotions with life-changing messages. Don't be afraid of the price, it's worth it. Tickets range from $39.00-$84.00.

SESAME PLACE

Langhorne - *100 Sesame Road (I-95 to US 1 north to Oxford Valley exit. Next to Oxford Valley Mall) 19047. Phone: (215) 752-7070. www.sesameplace.com. Hours: Daily 10:00am-8:00pm (mid May - Labor Day Weekend), Weekends (early May, September & October) - current schedule online. Admission: ~$49.00 general admission (online). Parking $10.00. Note: Late afternoon and family discounts. Bathing suits required for water attractions. We'd recommend staying all day to get your money's worth. Eateries, cafes.*

While your kids continue to peek over their shoulders for a glimpse of a Sesame Street character like Big Bird, they'll be pulling your hand in every direction so they won't miss anything. Big Bird, Elmo and the other stars of Sesame Street come out and play at Sesame Place. Usher you and your little ones aboard Oscar's Wacky Taxi™. Catch a show like "Rock Around the Block", then jump on Ernie's Bed Bounce or scale "Cookie Mountain". Rides include: A roller coaster called "Vapor Trail", or, a 40-foot high balloon tower ride carries you up in a balloon baskets - providing a bird's eye view of the park, and, also a character themed tea cup ride. Everybody's favorite character hosts Elmo's World ride area. There's also 14 refreshing water attractions. As you float, zoom or chute through Big Bird, Ernie's and Slimey's Rides, you'll be splashed or trickled by a giant rubber ducky. Toddlers can be water trickled in Teany Tiny Tidal Waves. Bet your kids can't wait to walk down a full-sized replica of Sesame Street and take pictures to show their friends.

TYLER STATE PARK

Langhorne (Newtown) - *101 Swamp Road (Follow I-95 north to the Newtown-Yardley exit 49) 18940. https://www.dcnr.pa.gov/StateParks/FindAPark/TylerStatePark/Pages/default.aspx. Phone: (215) 968-2021. Admission: FREE however swimming, marina and camping/lodging fees apply.*

The meandering waters of Neshaminy Creek flow through the park along with 10 miles of paved bicycling trails, a playhouse--Spring Garden Mill (www.langhorneplayers.org), and several children's play areas. Maze Picnic Area: is popular with families with young children because of the Children's miniature play barn and maze, sand box, and large play field. Gravel hiking trails to the east of Neshaminy Creek link picnic areas. Anglers may fish along the banks of the Creek or from a canoe. A 27-hole Disc Golf course begins by the Upper Plantation Picnic Area. Neshaminy Creek offers calm, easy boating (electric motors only) upstream from the canoe rental. Horseback Riding, Trails, Winter Sports like Ice Skating, Ice fishing, Sledding & Tobogganing.

Lititz

STURGIS PRETZEL BAKERY

Lititz - 219 East Main Street (Route 772 - off Route 501) 17543. Phone: (717) 626-4354. www.juliussturgis.com. Hours: Monday-Saturday, 9:00am-5:00pm, Sunday Noon-4pm. Closed winter holidays. Admission: General $4.00-$5.00 (A pretzel is given as your admission ticket) Tours: Every half hour. Monday-Saturday 9:30am-4:30pm, Sunday Noon-3:30pm. Note: Gift shop with all sorts of fresh baked pretzels to purchase.

Boy, did the memories flow at this place! Over 20 years ago, my family took the same tour, in the same building and I still have my "Official Pretzel Twister" (see right) certificate. (By the way, they still do that - our daughter now has one too!). This is the first pretzel bakery in America (1861) and they still make their original soft pretzel by hand in the original 200 year old ovens. Julius Sturgis started the pretzel industry with a recipe he learned from a hobo. Learn the history of the "pretiola" derived from monk's gifts to nearby children if they said their prayers. As you learn to fold your own pretzel, you'll learn how each step is related to prayer or marriage or the trinity. Definite "must see" while in Amish country.

WILBUR CHOCOLATE CO.

Lititz - 45 North Broad Street - (Route 501) 17543. www.wilburbuds.com. Phone: (717) 626-3249. Hours: Monday-Saturday 9:00am-5:00pm. Admission: FREE. Note: Gift shop. The original factory is nearby - converted into a boutique Hilton hotel.

Visitors to the modern candy kitchen can watch handmade chocolates created right before their eyes, including homemade marshmallow, almond bark, peanut butter meltaways, heavenly hash, mint drizzle, and almond butter crunch. They also make unique flavors of fudge in the Candy Shop.

While browsing, check out the memorbilia - antique metal molds, tin boxes, and advertisements. Everyone walks out with a bag full of store bought variety chocolates and yes, they still offer FREE Wilbur Bud Samples to guests. P.S. - For a walk back in time, try their hot cocoa mix that you prepare over a stove - it's worth shoveling snow just to enjoy entering a warm house full of an aroma of the rich liquid chocolate.

WOLF SANCTUARY OF PA

Lititz - 465 Speedwell Forge Road (Follow Rt.501 North, at Rt.322 in Brickerville, turn left. Take the first left onto Long Lane, and follow to end, left onto Speedwell Forge Rd) 17543. Phone: (717) 626-4617. wolfsanctuarypa.org. Tour rates - $15 adults, $14 senior, $13 child (4-11). Tours: Weekend tours at 10am (summers) and noon (rest of year) only. Arrive one half hour early to register. Weekday tours (Tuesday & Thursday).

Located in the heart of Pennsylvania Dutch country on 22 acres of natural woodland, Wolf Sanctuary of Pennsylvania is the unlikely home of the

Speedwell Wolves. Kids enjoy meeting the wolves most of all. They enjoy hearing the wolves' stories and learning about their behaviors, personalities, and interactions with other wolves as well as volunteers. If they would like, they may bring dog treats to share with the wolves. Even though they love doggy treats, wolves make very bad pets. Find out why. Twice a year they have special events that include face painting, wolf identification, and other kid friendly activities. See website for updates. They also have numerous cats on the property that kids enjoy. Check out their "howling" full moon tours too!

CELTIC FLING & HIGHLAND GAMES

Manheim - Mount Hope Estate & Winery (83 Mansion House Road, Route 72 & PA Turnpike Exit 20). www.parenfaire.com. Held on the festival grounds of the PA Renaissance Faire turns Amish Country into the Celtic Capital of the US! This Irish and Scottish heritage celebration covers the Faire's 35 acres in kilts, cabers and Celts with each day featuring musical sets, competitions and demonstrations. $10-$25 admission (age 5+). (third or last weekend in June)

PENNSYLVANIA RENAISSANCE FAIRE

Manheim - Mount Hope Estate. www.parenfaire.com. The Faire, with a cast of 100's of colorfully costumed merriemakers, is a rollicking recreation of a 16th Century country festival celebrating a visit by Her Majesty, Queen Elizabeth I. Shows include knights jousting, cuttings from Shakespeare's immortal plays, Commedia Del Arte, puppet shows, juggling, rope walking, and much more. Strolling minstrels and memorable street characters delight visitors hither and yon about the Shire. Admission. (weekends, mid-August thru mid-October)

Media
LINVILLA ORCHARDS

Media - *137 W. Knowlton Road (Rte 352 north 3.5 miles. Left onto Knowlton Rd.) 19063. Phone: (610) 876-7116. www.linvilla.com. Hours: Regular hours are 9:00am-6:00pm daily with longer fall hours and shorter winter hours. Open every day of the year except Dec 25 and Jan 1. Indoor mini golf (extra fee), barnyard animals and playland, too.*

Linvilla Orchards is one of the last working farms in the Delaware Valley. With more than 300 acres, Linvilla hosts a variety of family-friendly events throughout the year. Families can pick their own seasonal fruit, hop on a hayride and buy fresh-baked pies. Try a Hayride to Bunnyland or Pumpkinland. Go out to look at the blossoms in spring and the autumn leaves each fall. After getting a nice lunch at the food stands, head out into the fields to pick some blue- or blackberries — they'll make a nice souvenir for your ride back home!

- AUTUMN HAYRIDE AND TOUR – After a hayride, a tour guide will lead your group through a series of displays that teach about Johnny Appleseed, the Native Americans that lived on this site, different varieties of apples and squash, and the process of making cider. Fee

- SPRING / SUMMER HAYRIDE AND TOUR – After a hayride, a tour guide will lead your group through a discussion of planting and growing our food, how the Lenni Lenape planted in the spring, and show you some of the equipment we use today. Fee

RIDLEY CREEK STATE PARK

Media (Newtown Square) - *Sycamore Mills Road or 351 Gradyville Road (entrances on PA3, PA 252 or PA352) 19073. Phone: (610) 892-3900. https://www.dcnr.pa.gov/StateParks/FindAPark/RidleyCreekStatePark/Pages/default.aspx Admission: FREE into park. Fee charged for Plantation tours.*

Shaded equestrian, hiking and bicycling trails lace the woodlands and old meadow.

Within the park is the *Colonial Pennsylvania Plantation* (www. colonialplantation.org) that depicts a Delaware County Quaker farm prior to the American Revolution. On weekends from April to November, visitors can observe the farm family cooking over the open hearth, preserving foods, processing textiles, tending field crops and performing other chores necessary for survival in the 18th century world (small fee). There are hundreds of picnic tables in 14 picnic areas. Each area is equipped with restrooms and charcoal grills. Fishing and Winter Sports.

INDIAN POW WOW

Media (Newtown Square) - Ridley Creek State Park. Native American singing and dancing. Arts and crafts. Native food storytelling and much more! Ridley Creek State Park. (610) 566-1725. Native Americans of the Delaware Valley present a Pow Wow at Colonial Pennsylvania Plantation. Admission. (second wknd in Sep)

HAY CREEK APPLE FESTIVAL

Morgantown - Historic Joanne Furnace. www.haycreek.org/festivals.htm. Homemade apple specialties. Scarecrows, pumpkin paintings, hay and pony rides. The Hay Creek Festival is known for its delicious homemade foods - Mabel's kettle soups, Schnitz Un Knepp (Apples & Ham), Ice Cream Floats, Apple Butter, Mint Tea, and Hamburgers & Hot Dogs. Entertainment. Historical activities for young children include rubber stamp and rubbing stations. Civil War Encampment. FREE. (mid-Sept long wknd)

PENNSBURY MANOR

Morrisville - *400 Pennsbury Memorial Road (Rte. 1 north, Morrisville to Rte 13 south. Exit onto Tyburn Road East. on the Delaware River) 19067. Phone: (215) 946-0400. www.pennsburymanor.org. Hours: Wednesday-Saturday 10:00am-5:00pm, Sunday Noon-5:00pm (March - December). Admission: $9.00 adult, $7.00 senior (65+), $5.00 child (3-11) Tours: 90 minutes long - a little difficult for pre-schoolers. Note: Best for kids to visit (April - October) Sundays for living history days. Picnic areas. Grounds only pass = $3.00/person.*

A quaint, Quaker, simple homestead of William Penn, the founder of Pennsylvania. In 1682, William Penn sailed to Pennsylvania with one hundred other passengers on The Welcome. See a replica of the boat Penn used to "commute" to Philly. Horses, cattle, sheep and even a few peacocks roam the grounds as 17th century costumed interpreters demonstrate crafts and activities of the day. They may be baking bread (up to 30 loaves at one time!) or check out the farm where sheep and geese roam. Inside the Visitor's Center try writing with the original "pen" - a quill pen.

For updates & travel games visit: **www.KidsLoveTravel.com**

CHRISTMAS OPEN HOUSE

Morrisville - Pennsbury Manor. Tours of decorated, historical buildings. Refreshments and musical entertainment. Admission. (second weekend in December)

NEW HOPE AND IVYLAND RAILROAD

New Hope - *32 West Bridge Street (I-95 exit 51 west. Taylorsville Rd 5 miles. Rte. 32 north 5 miles. Depot at West Bridge and Stockton Street) 18938. Phone: (215) 862-2332. www.newhoperailroad.com. Hours: Daily (April-Holidays). Admission: Generally $26.00-$28.99 per ticket. Toddlers $4.99. Special trains more (Easter, Christmas). Tours: 45 min tours.Departure times vary, visit website for schedule.*

Climb aboard the New Hope & Ivyland passenger train and travel into a scene from the past. Relax and leave your cares behind as you journey into history, learning what rail travel was like for your grand parents and great-grand parents. This ride is famous for the trestle called "Pauline" upon which actress Pearl White was bound to in the 1914 silent film "The Perils of Pauline".

ELMWOOD PARK ZOO

Norristown - *1661 Harding Blvd (I76 to Rte. 202 to Johnson Hwy.) 19401. Phone: (610) 277-BUCK. www.elmwoodparkzoo.org. Hours: Daily 10:00am-5:00pm. Closed major winter holidays. Admission: $12.95-$19.95 (ages 3+). Note: Feedings & Rides add $3-$4.00. Snack shop. Gift shop. Picnic area. Easter Egg Hunts each spring. Butterflies in the summer.*

This is not a big city zoo but it is a calm, friendly atmosphere where you have the opportunity to leisurely observe animals. Highlights of the zoo include: Petting Barn (goats & sheep), Duck Lake, Prairie Dog exhibits, Aviary Wetland (waterfowl, beaver, otters), and The Bayou (murky home to lovely alligators, turtles, and snakes - everything that hisses or snaps!). There's also your basic natural Grasslands (bison, elk, and new "bears" area). Animal shows on Summer weekends are entertaining as they play with and share stories about unique animals in the park.

HERR'S SNACK FACTORY TOUR

Nottingham - *20 Herr Drive (US 1 and SR272 to Herr Drive) 19362. Phone: (800) 63-SNACK. www.herrs.com. Admission: $8.00 adult, $4.00 student (age 4-17). Tours: Monday - Wednesday 10:00am -4:00pm. All tours take approximately one hour. When scheduling, please indicate the time of day (on the hour) you wish to take tour. Note: Gift shop. Chippers Café. Very reasonable snack bar prices.*

There's no fake machinery or actors - it's the REAL factory, the REAL workers, and the REAL process. "Watch a groovy-chip movie" starring "Chipper" your tour guide and mascot. The whimsical tour takes you through the simple process of snack food production. Lots of hot oil and hot air drying, moisturizing and "spritzing" going on - a salon for snacks! Try samples warm off the "beltway" - those were a favorite point of the tour. Yes, you can have more than one! Also see other snacks made like cheesepuffs (corn meal dollops filled with air), tortilla chips, popcorn (huge poppers!) and pretzels (how do they make the outsides brown?).

Your kids will be amused at the sideway mixers churning out 10 pound mounds of pretzel dough. The dough takes a long trip on a conveyor and then a "dough-bot" (robot) removes them to be shaped & baked. Like to try new things? Try Grilled Cheese Curls, sweet Chocolate Covered Pretzels or baby back Ribs Potato chips (yes, meat flavored!) An excellent, organized tour - voted our best pick of snack food tours.

T & D 'S CATS OF THE WORLD WILD ANIMAL REFUGE

Penns Creek - *Mountain Road (off rte. 104) 17862. www.tdscats.com. Phone: (570) 837-3377.   Hours: T & D's is a not for profit refuge and is opened May to September for visitors but only 40 select days per year. Admission: $10.00 per person (ages 3+). Arrive early. Tours start on time.*

One family owns and operates an exotic wildlife refuge for unwanted, abused and confiscated animals. The tour through the woods takes approximately an hour and half to complete. Students will learn about the native habitat, diet, distribution, and adaptations of each species; as well as conservation activities, how the animals came to T&D's, and why these animals should not be kept as pets. Students will be able to get within four feet of the animals-- close enough to count the whiskers on the lions and tigers! They will also have the opportunity to feed deer, goats, and ducks.

Philadelphia

PHILADELPHIA SPORTS

- **PHILADELPHIA EAGLES FOOTBALL** -www.philadelphiaeagles.com. Lincoln Field. NFL Professional football team (August-December). Meet and greet players at the annual Eagles Carnival in August.

- **PHILADELPHIA FLYERS HOCKEY** - https://www.nhl.com/flyers/. Wells Fargo Center. National Hockey League (October-March).

- **PHILADELPHIA UNION SOCCER** - https://www.philadelphiaunion. com/ Subaru Park, a soccer-specific stadium located in Chester, Pennsylvania on the banks of the Delaware River.

- **PHILADELPHIA PHILLIES BASEBALL** - https://www.mlb.com/phillies. Citizens Ballpark. Take a romp in the Phanatic Phun Zone, the largest Softplay area for kids in the MLB. Take a stroll through Ashburn Alley, an outdoor entertainment area - All-Star Walk, Games of Baseball, Memory Lane, Rooftop Bleacher Seats, Wall of Fame, Alley Store, etc! Opens 2 1/2 hours prior to game time so fans can watch batting practice. Hungry? Order at Shake Shack, famous cheesesteaks, or roast pork.

PHILLY CHEESESTEAK

People usually come to Philadelphia for two things: the history and the cheesesteak. So what is an authentic cheesesteak and how do you order it? Here's the lowdown on this region's favorite sandwich:

A cheesesteak is a long, crusty roll filled with thinly sliced sautéed ribeye beef and melted cheese. Originally, the cheese of choice was Cheez Whiz, but American and provolone are common substitutions. Other toppings include fried onions, sautéed mushrooms, ketchup and hot or sweet peppers. The onions, cheese and beef are the most common. You'll find Cheesesteaks sold on every corner of historic and south Philly...mostly at small, family-owned pizza shops or delis. Some of the best we've had were from food carts stationed around the Liberty Bell. When ordering, there are two critical questions to answer: First, what kind of cheese do you want? (Whiz? Provolone? American?) Second, do you want onions? Be forewarned: Lines are often long at lunchtime and if you don't have your order and money ready to go, you might be asked to step back to the end of the line until you decide. This isn't your mall cheesesteak - these babies are dripping with juices.

Here's some of our favorites to try:

- More famous for its creative menu of hoagies, **CAMPO'S DELI** cooks up a respectable traditional cheesesteak. It's a small place but fun. Great for lunch. 214 Market Street. (215) 923-1000.

- **JIM'S STEAKS** has multiple locations, but the classic smell of fried onions wafting down South Street makes that location the most memorable. 400 South Street. (267) 519-9253 or www.jimssteaks.com.

PHILLY TRANSPORTATION & TOURS

Philadelphia - *(Downtown). Admission: Call for rates. Pay as you board.*

Parking can be difficult and pricey around downtown Philly. During their spring/summer and fall season they offer the Phlash, a Visitors' loop bus. The rates are very reasonable. Many parking garages give significant discounts to guests who park in their garage (all day) and then transport to museums and sites via Phlash. Street parking is available for around $4.00 per two hours at meters. For a full day downtown, budget $20.00 for parking and enjoy as many free attractions as you can!

- **SEPTA** (Southeastern Pennsylvania Public Transportation Authority) Part of Philadelphia's subway system. Fares start at $2.50 on board, at station pay stations, and Regional Rail Ticket Offices or online: www5. septa.org.

- **PHILADELPHIA TROLLEY WORKS** ('76 Carriage Company): www. phillytour.com. This longtime Philadelphia company offers several exciting options for touring town, including Victorian Trolley Tours, Horse Drawn Carriage Tours, walking Tours and Double Decker Bus Tours. Entertaining staff will treat you to a fun and informative trip around the city. $17-$36 each ticket. www.bigbustours.com

- **PHILLY PHLASH** - (215) 4-PHLASH or www.phillyphlash.com. Look for Philadelphia Trolley Works Purple Phlash Trolleys for a quick, cheap and easy way to get around Center City Philadelphia. Phlash is the quick and easy connection between Penn's Landing and the Philadelphia Museum of Art, with stops at 21 key destinations covering most downtown hotels. $5 for an individual all-day pass. Runs May thru end of October.

- **RIVERLINK FERRY** - https://www.delawareriverwaterfront.com/places/ riverlink-ferry Passenger ferry across the Delaware River between Penn's Landing and the Camden waterfront sites. Seasonal

PHILADELPHIA ORCHESTRA

Philadelphia - *260 South Broad Street, 16th Floor (most performances at Kimmel Center) 19102. Phone: (215) 893-1900. www.philorch.org.*

Sound All Around Series (ages 3-5), learn about the different families of instruments. Family Concert Series (ages 6-12) - music featuring puppets, magicians, storytellers, and young soloists. (Saturday mornings). Each summer The Philadelphia Orchestra performs free outdoor concerts in neighborhoods around the Philadelphia region.

ACADEMY OF NATURAL SCIENCES

Philadelphia - *1900 Benjamin Franklin Parkway (off I-676 and corner of 19th Street) 19103. Phone: (215) 299-1000. www.acnatsci.org. Hours: Wednesday-Friday 10:00am-4:30pm, Saturday, Sunday & Holidays 10:00am-5:00pm. Closed Thanksgiving, Christmas, and New Year's Day. Admission: $25.00 adult, $22.00 senior (65+), $21.00 child (2-12). Online discount. Part of CityPass discount card. FREEBIES: Ask for Scavenger Hunts sheets (age appropriate) when you enter. The kids stay focused this way. Note: Films show daily. Academy Café and gift shop.*

The oldest dinosaur and natural science exhibit in the world is here. Most families' favorite area is the Dinosaur Hall. This is hands-on paleontology including a fossil dig (equipped with goggles and tools), fossil prep lab, and Time Machine (get your picture image appearing with dinosaurs!). You'll also meet T-Rex, plus 11 friends, and even get to climb into a dinosaur skull.

The North American Hall has some stuffed large animals that are almost 200 years old. Ocean Bound! Discover the importance and vulnerability of watersheds, identify solutions to pollution problems and see how you can make a difference. There are live animal shows and "Outside In"... hands-on, touching mice, snakes, frogs, and huge bugs. Touch a real meteorite, view a stream from underneath, crawl through a fallen log, look for fossil footprints, pan for shark teeth, watch a working beehive, build a sandcastle or read a book on Lucy's Back Porch. There's also a crystals and gems exhibit that features a 57 pound amethyst and "Living Downstream" - a showcase of life in a watershed or Egyptian Mummies.

FRANKLIN INSTITUTE SCIENCE MUSEUM

Philadelphia - *222 North 20th Street (intersection of 20th Street and the Benjamin Franklin Parkway, downtown) 19103. Phone: (215) 448-1200. www.fi.edu. Hours: Daily 9:30am-5:00pm. Closed major winters holidays only. Admission: $25.00 adult, $21.00 child (3-11). Sci-Pass includes museum, science demos, and planetarium. IMAX and special exhibits extra. Note: Ben's Bistro - Lunch, Café, Museum Stores.*

What began as a national memorial to Ben Franklin is now a hands-on exhibit and demonstration complex. Some exhibits have been there forever. Spark your curiosity about the wonders of Electricity in this classic exhibit inspired by our namesake, Benjamin Franklin. Walk through "Your Brain" - What is the brain? What does it do? How does it work? Or, walk explore a Giant Heart - hear a heart beating as "blood" races through the arteries. Also, see a full-size train or airplane cockpit! Learn how Sports and Physics mix or how Art & Physics collide. Highlights include The SportsZone, which uses virtual-reality technology to illustrate the physics of sports; The Train Factory's climb-aboard steam engine; Space Command's simulated earth-orbit research station; a fully equipped weather station; and exhibits on electricity. Our favorite area is Space Command where you visit a research station right here on Earth! Locate your house using a satellite device. Embark on a mission to discover a lost, unmanned space probe. Check out equipment used by real astronauts to explore space. Films lassume grand proportions on the IMAX Theater's 79-foot domed screen; galaxies are formed and deep space explored in North America's second-oldest planetarium sporting the continent's most advanced technology. Don't miss the 3D Theater.

PHILADELPHIA ZOO

Philadelphia - *3400 West Girard Avenue (I-76, exit 36) 19104. Phone: (215) 243-1100. www.philadelphiazoo.org. Hours: Daily 9:30am-5:00pm (March-November). Thursday-Sunday 9:30am-4:00pm (December-February). Closed major winter holidays. Admission: $24 adult, $19 child (2-11). Zoo. $6-$8 Wildworks ropes. Swan boat, train & carousel extra. Parking $17.00. Seasonal Zoo Trolley transport from Independence Visitor Ctr. Is only $2.00. Educators: https://www.philadelphiazoo. org/Learn/schoolvisits/CurriculumConnections.htm Note: Zoo shop. Cafes w/ burgers, pizza, chicken, tacos. Victorian picnic groves. Stroller & wheelchair rentals. Wkends in December Santa visits.*

The first zoo in the country - now has 1800 animals on 42 acres of beautiful landscape. Favorites include the famous white lions, Jezebel and Vinkel, the first white lions ever to be exhibited in North America. Big Cat Falls! - home to endangered big cats from around the world, including snow leopard cubs, puma kittens and a black jaguar cub. Water is Life has the country's only giant otters. Bear Country allows you to interact (viewing, that is) with playful bears that love to show off. Check out the primate habitat. The KidsZooU has your typically petted animals plus cow-milking and other live demos. Creatures of Habitat is a fantastical adventure visiting 12 amazing life-size vignettes made with LEGO® bricks situated throughout the Zoo. WildWorks Ropes course lets guests explore at their own pace and pick their own path. Take to the air 34 feet up to cross bridges, balance on ropes, and climb through obstacles, and take a quick zip right to the bottom....all while safely hitched to a climbing harness!

UNIVERSITY OF PENNSYLVANIA MUSEUM OF ARCHAEOLOGY & ANTHROPOLOGY

Philadelphia - *3260 South Street (I-76 to South Street exit to 33rd and Spruce Streets) 19104. Phone: (215) 898-4001. www.penn.museum. Hours: Tuesday-Sunday 10:00-5:00pm (Closed Mondays, Holidays). Admission: $18.00 adult, $16.00 senior (62+) and $13.00 student (age 6-17). Reduced admission times each month - $10. Tours: Guided on Weekends at 1:30pm during school year. Note: Snack café. Pyramid Gift Shop. Most fun to come during a Family Fun Day.*

Did You Know?
The Penn Museum is the only museum in the world to exhibit such a significant portion of an Egyptian royal palace.

Exhibits of findings from Ancient Egypt, Asia, Central America, North America, Mesopotamia, Greece, and Africa, uncovered by University staff and student expeditions. Find more than 1,200 objects - from a clay footprint left by a worker in Iraq to 4,500-year-old jewelry of a Mesopotamian queen to a child's first writing primer all. See a giant Sphinx and real mummies. Gaze at an Apache tipi or a Navajo walk-in sky theater. On one side of each gallery the exhibition focuses on the use of objects to display status and to transfer laws and traditions to upcoming generations. The other side displays objects of everyday life and invites you to compare the lifestyle of hunter-gatherers with the lifestyle of farmers by looking at the objects each uses. The stories of the archeologists' thoughts and accompanying pictures of "digs" might inspire a budding career.

WORLD CAFÉ LIVE

Philadelphia - 3025 Walnut Street 19104. http://worldcafelive.com. Phone: (215) 222-1400. World Cafe Live is about creating fun and interactive live music experience for kids and parents. Join them on a Saturday morning for the show and snacks. Doors generally open at 11am with show starting at 11:30am, but you should always check each performance listing for times. Show admission: $12 per person. ⬤

ARCH STREET FRIENDS MEETING HOUSE

Philadelphia - *320 Arch Street, 19106 (at the corner of 4th Street in Old City). http://www.HistoricASMH.org/ (215) 413-1804. Hours: Wednesday-Sunday 10am-4pm. Donations encouraged.* Arch Street Meeting House was built in 1804 on a burial ground originally deeded by William Penn in 1701. Step inside this active Quaker meetinghouse to learn more about the stories of the people, the building, and the grounds of Arch Street. Despite criticism and persecution, Quakers throughout history have acted against injustices and led humanitarian efforts that align with their faith. Notable members of the Religious Society of Friends who worshiped at this meetinghouse include abolitionists and woman rights advocates. Many other notable early colonists are buried here, too. Kids, why touring the meeting house, note the large soundboard in the main room. Try your hand at speaking to the crowd under it. Does it make your voice louder?

BETSY ROSS HOUSE

Philadelphia - *239 Arch Street, Historic area (Between 2nd & 3rd Streets)*

19106. Phone: (215) 686-1252. www. betsyrosshouse.org. Hours: Daily 10:00am-5:00pm (March-November). Closed Tuesdays & Holidays (December-February). Admission: $6-$8.00 per person. Tours: Self-guided audio tours are $8-$10.00 (includes admission). Self-guided tour lasts about 25 minutes. Note: Hot dogs, drinks and snacks are offered in the courtyard. FREEBIES: Ask for the "house hunt" sheet for kids.

The nation's most famous seamstress, credited with the creation of the first American flag, stitched her way into history in the small workroom on display at this house. In 1777, the first American flag made by Colonial Mrs. Ross was sewn here. Betsy, who made a living as a furniture upholsterer, rented the 1740 home, and the teeny-tiny rooms and tight little staircases give a good portrayal of a working class woman's life in colonial America. You can tour her modest home. Each room has a description, in Betsy's words (in old English), of what led up to her sewing the flag. She and the fellas that made the Liberty Bell were just ordinary folks who had a skill needed to help the cause of Independence. What was considered a routine job lead to national recognition! After you tour the house, make sure to meet Betsy Ross and plan to spend some time relaxing in the shady courtyard where you'll enjoy family friendly programming, hear storytelling and see colonial crafters at work.

CARPENTER'S HALL

Philadelphia - *320 Chestnut Street, Historic area (exit for Indep. Hall. Follow signs for 6th st to Chestnut, left on 2nd) 19106. https://www.carpentershall.org/. Phone: (215) 925-0167. Hours: Tuesday-Sunday 10:00am-4:00pm (Closed January & February Tues).Admission: FREE. FREEBIES: scavenger hunt under LEARN.*

Displays of early carpenter's chairs and tools used by the First Continental Congress in 1774. A 10 minute video chronicles the history of the carpenter's company (they still own and operate the hall). Because the site is dedicated to the craft of carpenters and builders, supplementing with a scavenger hunt is the best way to engage the kids. That, and the model of Carpenter's Hall which looks like a colonial "doll house".

CHRIST CHURCH

Philadelphia - *20 North American Street 2nd Street (between Arch & Market Streets) 19106. Phone: (215) 922-1695. www.christchurchphila.org. Hours: Tuesday-Sunday 10:00am-4:00pm (March-December). Admission: Suggested Donation $2-$5.00 to help maintain church. Note: Services held on Sunday mornings and Wed at Noon.*

Christ Church is bordered by a tree-lined brick path, small park and a cobblestone alley, which provide the perfect setting for this historic treasure. Fifteen signers of the Declaration of Independence worshiped here including George Washington and Benjamin Franklin. A brass plaque marks each pew of famous Colonists including Betsy Ross. Families and groups can visit the church and burial ground to gain a deeper understanding of our early history and the importance of religious freedom. Tours given throughout the day. The church was built in 1727 and originally had dirt or wood floors. Ask a guide what those marble rectangles are in the floor. Careful - though they won't mind, you may be stepping on the memory of a notable patron of the church!

FEDERAL RESERVE BANK MONEY IN MOTION

Philadelphia - *100 N. 6th Street, ground floor of Federal Reserve (next to National Constitution Center) 19106. https://www.philadelphiafed.org/education/money-in-motion. Hours: Monday-Friday 9:30am-4:30pm. Reduced hours each winter. Admission: FREE. FREEBIES: Besides the souvenir pack of $, ask the hostess for a Scavenger Hunt worksheet.*

This permanent exhibit explains the way our financial system works. The exhibit's 16 different stations offer artifacts ranging from wampum, the original colonial money, to a $100,000 bill, which was produced for one year (1934). Kids will gasp at the giant tube stuffed with $100 million in shredded cash and giggle at the "Match wits with Ben" game. At the end of the exhibit, visitors get a packet of shredded money worth $100.

FIREMAN'S HALL

Philadelphia - *147 North 2nd Street (Historic district near Elfreth's Alley) 19106. Phone: (215) 923-1438. www.firemanshallmuseum.org. Hours: Tuesday-Saturday 10:00am-4:00pm. Admission: FREE.*

Take a look at this restored 1902 firehouse that holds some of the nation's earliest blaze-fighting equipment and important historical artifacts. See memorabilia, films, too. Did your kids know Benjamin Franklin founded the first Philadelphia Fire Department in 1736? See old-fashioned leather buckets, fire wagons and an "around the world" display of firefighter helmets. Play pretend in the re-created living quarters or steer a fireboat. Taped firemen's stories recall high level exciting moments on the job. The Spider Hose Reel (1804) has a chariot look with brass bells and shiny mirrors. Also be on the lookout for the fire pole and injured firemen's hats (charred & broken).

BENJAMIN FRANKLIN MUSEUM & COURT

Philadelphia - *3rd, 4th, Chestnut & Market Streets (I-95 exit 22, Phila/Indep.Hall/ Callowhill to 6th & Race Sts) 19106. Phone: (215) 597-8974. www.nps.gov/inde. Hours: Usually daily 9:00am-5:00pm but can vary. Post Office not open Sundays. Admission: FREE for court bldgs. $2.00-$5.00 for Museum.*

Today the site contains a steel "ghost structure" outlining the spot where Franklin's house stood and features an underground museum with a film and displays about his personal life. "Bump into" Mr. Franklin as you roam his court and he'll invite you to gather around to hear stories of his life. What a wonderful way to study this amazing historic man! Once owned by Ben

Franklin who lived in Philadelphia from 1722-1790, the complex includes:

- PRINTING OFFICE - Working reproduction of 1785 printing press and bindery.

- BEN FRANKLIN MUSEUM - Check out Franklin's numerous inventions, then walk and talk in the Phone Room where dozens of phones can call famous friends of Franklin. Hear "voices" of historic men such as Thomas Jefferson and Mark Twain talk about Franklin. In the courtyard, peek in the pits below to see excavations of rooms of Franklin's home.

- POST OFFICE - In 1775, Ben Franklin was appointed as the first Postmaster General. The name "Free Franklin" was used as the hand cancellation signature because Mr. Franklin was referring to America's struggle for freedom. See actual hand-canceled letters, then, purchase a post card & send it from this working post office!

FRANKLIN FOUNTAIN

Philadelphia - 116 Market Street (exit Indep. Hall and follow signs to Market St. Head east (left) on Market) 19106. Phone: (215) 627-1800. www.franklinfountain. com. Hours: Noon to Midnight every day. The Franklin Fountain, in Old City, is an authentic early 20th century soda shop with tin walls and ceiling, original marble counters and mosaic floors. Servers dressed as old-fashioned soda jerks serve homemade hard ice cream, banana splits, thick shakes, egg creams, sundaes and flavored soda water creams. Favorites: The Franklin Mint (mint chip ice cream, crème de menthe topping) or The Lightning Rod (dark chocolate brownie, espresso, choco espresso beans, coconut and pretzel rod). Adventuresome foodie - ever thought of ordering green tea or Pistachio flavors? Most sundaes run ~$16.00 and are generally 3 scoops of ice cream (very sharable portions). With the menu's use of words like covered, glazed, bathed, cascading, blanketed, doused, and ruffled...how can you go wrong? __ 🍽

FRANKLIN SQUARE

Philadelphia - *6th and Race Streets (close to the National Constitution Center) 19106. http://historicphiladelphia.org/day/franklin-square/. Hours: Daylight hours. Admission: Carousel $3.00 per person (age 3+). Mini-Golf $7.00-$9.00.*

Franklin Square is one of Philadelphia's five original squares - and the only one dedicated just to fun.

A day outside around Franklin Square could include a ride on an old-fashioned carousel, a game of mini-golf, a romp on a modern playground and a family picnic. Day and night at the fountain, free choreographed shows feature dancing water, lights and music from Philadelphia artists. On the bridge is the Electric Philadelphia Mural. SquareBurger sells burgers, hot dogs, fries, drinks and frozen treats. The 18-hole Philadelphia-themed course allows guests to putt through favorite icons including Elfreth's Alley, Benjamin Franklin Bridge, LOVE statue, and on the 18th hole, putt through the crack in the Liberty Bell and land in front of Independence Hall. Winters they offer street Curling.

INDEPENDENCE HALL

Philadelphia - *520 Chestnut Street, Historic area (5th & 6th Streets on Chestnut - across from Liberty Bell) 19106. Phone: (215) 965-7676. www.nps.gov/inde Hours: Daily 9:00am-5:00pm. Admission: FREE. Tours: Guided tours only throughout the day. Long lines move pretty fast. You must reserve a free timed ticket from the Visitor Center OR online ($1.50 handling fee per ticket) to enter. Educators: Any angle of our country's founding is at this website: www.independencehall.org.*

Note: Congress Hall (where the first US Congress met and inaugurations of Presidents occurred) and Old City Hall (Supreme Court original house) are across the street. Hours vary but it is a must see for kids studying the setup of the United States Government.

You will get a patriotic chill as you enter the hall where the Declaration of Independence was adopted and the U.S. Constitution was written. They risked everything — "their lives, their fortune and their sacred honor." During the blistering summer of 1776, 56 courageous men gathered at the Pennsylvania State House and defied the King of England. George Washington's "rising sun" chair dominates the Assembly Room which is arranged as it was during the Constitutional Convention. The Assembly Room looks just as it did in 1776 (you'll feel like you're in a movie) and you can see the original inkwell the Declaration signers dipped quills in to sign the famous freedom document.

INDEPENDENCE SEAPORT MUSEUM

Philadelphia - *211 South Columbus Blvd, Penns Landing (I-95 exit 20) 19106.*

Phone: (215) 925-5439. www.phillyseaport. org. Hours: Daily 10:00am-5:00pm. Closed major winter holidays. Admission: $14.00. $12.00-$15.00 additional fee for touring Olympia and submarine Becuna. Educators: an excellent Teacher's Activity Packet is downloadable to print by clicking on: EDUCATION, then TEACHER RESOURCES. Note: The Museum Store. Ask about the Philadelphia Citypass - it's a great value if you're seeing more than just historic area. Seafarin Saturdays at the Seaport is a programs where kids craft while pretending to be a pirate or ship captain.

With historic vessels to board, a ship's hull to rivet, and cargo to unload with miniature cranes, Philadelphia's maritime museum conveys what the Delaware and Schuylkill Rivers have meant to the city over the years. "Climb in, Pull this, Please"…are common signs here. For example, ride a waterbed boat, blow a fog horn, play the Crane Game or climb aboard bunks on a ship. In clever dioramas, hear and see immigrant and crew stories. Take a few moments to watch and talk to boat builders as they build skiffs, then head outdoors to the walk-on battleship Olympia and submarine Becuna. This is what the kids come for! The Olympia is the nation's oldest floating steel warship (1892)

and most famous for being Admiral Dewey's flagship during his Spanish-American war victory in Manila Bay. The Becuna is a classic World War II submarine that fought battles in the South Pacific. Self-guided tours lets kids "feel" like sailors, captains, or pirates. The kids will move quickly following the self-guided arrows so try to keep up!

History lessons are woven between these additional exhibits:

*   <u>RIVER ALIVE!</u> - focuses on the wonders and challenges of the Delaware River watershed, our place within that system, and the increasingly sophisticated science we use to understand the watershed's complexity. The exhibition features multiple interactive and hands-on experiences, including a Science Lab and Fisharium.

INDEPENDENCE VISITOR CENTER (FOR THE NATIONAL HISTORICAL PARK)

Philadelphia - *525 Market Street, Historic area (northeast corner of 6th & Market Sts - across from the Liberty Bell) 19106. https://www.nps.gov/inde/planyourvisit/ independencevisitorcenter.htm. Phone: (215) 597-8974. Hours: Daily 9:00am-5:00pm. Extended summer hours. Admission: FREE. Parking garages in downtown Philadelphia are very steep ($5.00 per half hour up to $25.00). Cheaper alternatives: Philly Phlash buses, 2-3 hour parking meters (esp. on Walnut & Chestnut sts). Tours: sign up for free programs or walking tours (daily summers, weekends only rest of year). Cell Phone Audio Tours are available using special code numbers attained at various stops or thru maps at the Center. Note: This is where to park (below center) and purchase tickets or schedule times for tours. Plan to spend 5-8 hours in the Independence Historical Park. Secure areas (I. Hall & Liberty Bell) Do Not have restrooms so use them here. Hersheys Kitchens Cafe. Educators: click on FOR TEACHERS link and download Lesson Plans & worksheets. FREEBIES: you can pick up the Junior Ranger Activity booklet at the Center. Search for stamps found in the park, complete some activities and earn a Ranger Badge. Coloring pages, too. This JR activity book is one of the best ever!*

Start here before you explore the well-known sites. See award winning historical and tourism films shown throughout the day. Ben Franklin, George Washington, John Adams and others come back to life to tell the Independence story. Older children will want to sign up for the walking tour here (little ones up to grades 1 or 2 will want to wander at their own pace and usually aren't interested enough to stay with the group). To keep attention spans high, we noticed they create a theme (seasonally) of historical significance. Actors called "Town Criers" present impromptu conversations and "street stage" presentations along with that theme. They admired our "carriage" (known to you and me as a wagon) and our "horse" that was pulling it (Daddy!) Most events are daily in the summer and weekends the rest of the year.

JULY 4TH CELEBRATION

Philadelphia - Independence Visitor Center. www.americasbirthday.com. Welcome America Festival. Top name musical groups and dramatic readings by famous actors. FREE. Parades, music, food, fireworks & contests.

What does a cracked bell sound like?

Try clanging the sample cracked bells that show how a bell sounds before and after repairs.

LIBERTY BELL

Philadelphia - *6th Street, between Market and Chestnut Streets (across from Independence Hall, entrance on Market Street) 19106. Phone: (215) 597-8974. www.nps.gov/inde. Hours: Daily 9:00am-5:00pm. Extended summer & weekend hours. Admission: FREE Tours: Given by park rangers, relates the bell's history. Long lines (for security checks) - but they move fast. Note: Glass encased bell is viewable 24 hours a day. Interpretive kiosk displays explain details of the Bell.*

Made a few blocks away by two crafters who only made pots and pans (usually), its famous "crack" has many folklore stories associated with it. It would be nice to believe that each crack was the result of zealous ringing; however, it just wasn't cast properly to withstand its large size and temperature variances. Initially, it was just a bell ordered to be placed in the tower of the meeting hall (now called Independence Hall). Later, abolitionists used it as a symbol of freedom for slaves and proclaimed it the Liberty Bell (not until 1840 though!) - and the name stuck! X-rays give an insider's view, literally, of the Bell's crack and inner-workings. "*In Quiet Alcoves*", a short History Channel film, available  in English and eight other languages, traces how abolitionists, suffragists and other groups adopted the Bell as its symbol of freedom. It'll give you goosebumps to stand inches from it. Be sure to take advantage of the photo opportunity time provided by park rangers.

MUSEUM OF AMERICAN REVOLUTION

Philadelphia - *101 S 3rd St, Philadelphia, PA 19106. https://www.amrevmuseum. org/ Hours: Daily 10am-5pm. The Museum is closed Election Days, Thanksgiving Day, Christmas Day, and New Year's Day. Admission: $21.00 adult, $13.00 student (age 6-17). Small senior, teacher, military discount. FREEBIES: https:// www.amrevmuseum.org/learn-and-explore/for-kids-and-families/at-home-crafts-activities. SCAVENGER HUNT:https://www.amrevmuseum.org/at-the-museum/ kids-and-families-at-the-museum. EDUCATORS: https://www.amrevmuseum. org/learn-and-explore/for-students-and-educators/resources-opportunities-for-educators/mini-lesson-plans.*

Follow George Washington's remarkable journey and sit in the presence of his original Revolutionary War headquarters tent. It is eerie, yet awe inspiring when you're in this signature room, imagining the intel and decisions shared within that tent!

Stand beneath the branches and lanterns of a life-size reproduction of the Boston Liberty Tree. Read the list of grievances leveled the against the King from authentic printings of the Declaration of Independence. Stand among life-size replicas of members of the Oneida Indian Nation and listen to the intense debate that led to their decision to break with the Iroquois Confederacy and join the American cause. Experience the fear and frenzy of the front lines as you are confronted by an all-out British infantry charge at the Battle of Brandywine. Climb aboard a replica privateer ship to experience the war at sea. Learn about the wartime reality that faced many freed and enslaved African Americans and explore the contradictions between the fight for American liberty and the persistence of American slavery. The best part for kids: the many interactives among stellar exhibits (like the walk on Privateer Ship) and especially, The Revolution Place.

The Museum's family discovery center, Revolution Place, brings to life the Museum's lively, diverse Old City neighborhood during the late 1770s and invites visitors to learn through hands-on exploration of a soldiers' encampment, a tavern, a parlor, a house of worship, and even a privy! A variety of replica objects, dress-up clothes, and digital interactives await visitors young and old.

PRESIDENT'S HOUSE

Philadelphia - 6th Street, and Market (next to the Liberty Bell) 19106. Phone: (215) 597-8974. www.phila.gov/presidentshouse. Hours: Daily 24/7. FREE

This Independence National Historical Park site is open around the clock so that visitors can see the exposed underground remains of the home where Presidents Washington and Adams lived during their terms. Through interpretive panels, videos, etc. the site recognizes nine enslaved people who served the first president as he led the young country in its pursuit of freedom and equality. It reveals the contradiction of slavery in the new nation.

For updates & travel games visit: **www.KidsLoveTravel.com**

NATIONAL CONSTITUTION CENTER

Philadelphia - *525 Arch Street, Historic area (Independence National Park, between Arch & Race, 5th & 6th Streets) 19106. www.constitutioncenter.org. Phone: (215) 923-0004. Hours: Wednesday - Sunday 10:00am-5:00pm (except Thanksgiving Day, Christmas Day, and New Years Day) Extended summer hours. Admission: $11.00 - $14.50 (age 6+). Active Military w/ID are FREE. Parking*

garage under the museum runs $8.00-$18.00. Educators: click online on RESOURCES page, then Bill of Rights game or civics lesson plans for all grades. FREEBIES - click on EDUCATION, then Students, then Studying the Constitution for resources, games and puzzles just for you.

The first-ever national museum honoring and explaining the U.S. Constitution and the Constitution's relevance to our daily lives so that all of us -- "We the People" -- will better understand and exercise our rights and our responsibilities. It's only four pages long, but the U.S. Constitution is among the most influential and important documents in the history of the world. Wandering a "street scene" in 1787 Philadelphia, you can eavesdrop on fellow citizens and discover the forces that inspired the creation of the document. You then enter a theater-in-the-round, where you view The Founding Story, a dramatic multi-media production which orients you to the major themes of and the basic historical context of the Constitution. The newest space, Reconstruction Amendments—the 13th, 14th and 15th—which ended slavery and pledged equality for all in the U.S. in the years after the Civil War. The first of its kind in the country, the exhibit features personal stories, documents and artifacts that highlight the debates and key figures in the amendments' formation and ratification. "Signers Hall," is where visitors are invited to play the role of Signer amidst life-size statues of the Founding Fathers. Place notes or sign a modern Constitution book and then hang out taking pictures with famous folks present at the 1st signing. High-tech, interactive exhibitions let everyone-even those under 18-vote on legislative bills, weigh in on court cases and take the Presidential Oath of Office. Kids get to dress up in robes and push buttons and play games.

NATIONAL LIBERTY MUSEUM

Philadelphia - *321 Chestnut Street (Washington Ave. exit , left on Columbus. Follow signs to Market & Second St) 19106. www.libertymuseum.org. Phone: (215) 925-2800. Hours: Daily 10:00am-5:00pm (Memorial Day - Labor Day). Limited hours remainder of the year. Admission: $12.00 adult, $10.00 senior, $8.00 student, $6.00 child (6-17). Educators: Lesson plans and activities/follow up questions are under EDUCATION, then PRE-VISIT MATERIALS.*

This museum is home to more than 100 works of glass art by Dale Chihuly. The exhibits celebrate heroes who fight for freedom around the world. From the stories of thousands of heroes of all walks of life... to awesome glass art... to lively discussions on youth-oriented topics, try to stop in and see some of the spaces that really engage questions because the art if so fun! Parents love the interactive themes including anti-bullying and non-violence, pride in oneself, civic responsibility, character education and more. The Jelly Bean People and Flame of Liberty are must sees!

SHANE'S CANDIES

Philadelphia - *110 Market Street (between 2nd & Front Sts.) (exit Indep. Hall/ Callowhill, bottom of ramp turn left onto 2nd St, then left onto Market) 19106. Phone: (215) 922-1048. shanecandies.com.*

America's oldest candy store still makes candy the old-fashioned way. Handmade, hand-dipped chocolates in traditional and novelty shapes have been tempting palates since 1876. It claims to be the oldest candy store in the country and the place hasn't changed much. Shane's Candies famous creamy buttercreams are slowly cooked the old-fashioned way in a copper kettle while being stirred with a wooden paddle. These irresistible delicacies are super creamy. The ladies behind the counter try and stuff you with vanilla cream samples. They love kids!

THADDEUS KOSCIUSZKO NATL MEMORIAL

Philadelphia - *301 Pine Street (I-95 Independence Hall exit/ Columbus Blvd. Follow signs to Society Hill) 19106. Phone: (215) 597-9618. www.nps.gov/thko. Hours: Saturday-Sunday Noon-4:00pm (April-October). Admission: FREE.*

Visit the house where wounded Polish freedom fighter Thaddeus Kosciuszko lived and hear how this brilliant military engineer designed successful fortifications during the American Revolution. See the room where he received notable visitors such as Chief Little Turtle and Thomas Jefferson, who said he was "as pure a son of liberty, as I have ever known..." Exhibits & audiovisual displays (English & Polish language) describe the help Thaddeus gave to the American Revolution. Learn why he was loved and then kicked out of his native Poland, why he carried a crutch and how his skills helped Americans strategically beat the British. He was a genius engineer!

TODD HOUSE

Philadelphia - *4th & Walnut Streets, Historic area (just west of Carpenters Hall) 19106. Phone: (215) 597-8974.   https://www.nps.gov/inde/learn/historyculture/ places-dolleytoddhouse.htm. PLEASE CHECK WEBSITE BEFORE VISITING. REPAIRS TO PROPERTY ONGOING.*

This was the home of Dolley Todd before her marriage to James Madison. Dolley, by most accounts, was a fabulous and spirited hostess. Here fish, meat, fruit, and baked bread all purchased fresh daily from vendors at the High Street headhouse (now Market Street) would be prepared for the Todds, their two children, Dolley's younger brother and sister, and two law clerks who worked under Barrister Todd. Add to that a pet bird and a dog named Pointer and one has at the least a quite lively household. Representing a middle-class Quaker home, she became quite a First Lady when she moved from this house and married James Madison, fourth President of the United States.

U.S. MINT

Philadelphia - *5th & Arch Streets (Take I-95 to Exit 22 for "Central Phila/I-676". Follow signs for Phila/ Independence Hall/Callowhill Streets) 19106. Phone: (215) 408-0112. https://www.usmint.gov/about/mint- tours-facilities. Admission: FREE Tours: Weekdays 9:00am-4:30pm, except Federal holidays. Open Saturdays in summer. If the Dept of Homeland Security level is elevated to CODE ORANGE, the US Mint will be CLOSED to the public unless otherwise noted. All tours are free and self-guided; no reservations. Note: The United States Mint does not provide parking.*

While in the historic district of Philadelphia, be sure to take your family to the world's largest coinage operation (seen through a glass enclosed gallery). They make a million dollars worth of coins per day! (29 million coins!). See them start with blanks that are cleaned and then stamped, sorted, and bagged. To see coins in large bins or spilling out of machines is mesmerizing! Even little kids eyes sparkle. A "Stamp Your Own Medal" machine (press a big red button to operate) is located in the Gift shop. Great souvenir idea!

DOUBLETREE HOTEL PHILADELPHIA

Philadelphia - 237 S. Broad Street (neighborhood: Convention Ctr /Market East-Broad St. exit south about 5 blocks) 19107. www.doubletree.com. Phone: (215) 893-1600. Guests who want to stay in the middle of the action check in to the Doubletree Hotel Philadelphia, located on the Avenue of the Arts. Families can spend some time at the rooftop pool, sundeck and courts, and kids get a free cookie at check-in. Especially nice if you want to stay in between the Science Museums and the Historic Area. The views of the city are pretty cool, too. Parking is $45.00 per day or more. You can walk to everything (or take the Phlash) but that means 10 blocks each way. _____

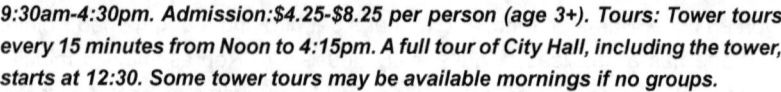

PHILADELPHIA CITY HALL OBSERVATION DECK

Philadelphia - *Broad & Market Streets (Broad St. exit south about 4 blocks) 19107. Phone: (215) 686-2840. www.phila.gov/virtualch . Hours: Weekdays 9:30am-4:30pm. Admission:$4.25-$8.25 per person (age 3+). Tours: Tower tours every 15 minutes from Noon to 4:15pm. A full tour of City Hall, including the tower, starts at 12:30. Some tower tours may be available mornings if no groups.*

Every city has one building that stands as one of the tallest in town and usually it has a lot of history behind it. Most noted is the courtroom (available to view on the tour only) where a motion picture film was made and the 548 foot tall tower that has a statue of William Penn on top. At the base of the statue is the observation deck. Its observation deck provides a panoramic view of the city. This building is so breathtakingly beautiful and stands in the center of downtown…believe us, you can't miss it!

READING TERMINAL MARKET

Philadelphia - 12th and Arch Streets (neighborhood: Convention Ctr/Chinatown/ Market East-Broad St. exit south, follow signs) 19107. www.readingterminalmarket. org. Phone: (215) 922-2317. Hours: Monday through Saturday: 8:00am-6:00pm. Sunday: 9:00 am-5:00 pm. Wednesday - Saturday only hours for Pennsylvania Dutch vendors & they close at 4 or 5pm. Begin your adventure at the Reading Terminal Market, the nation's oldest continuously operating farmer market. Family-run vendors sell virtually every type of farm-fresh cuisine, to go or ready to eat there. A corner of the market is devoted to Amish merchants from Lancaster, who bring their products and distinctive dishes to the Market four days a week. Watch as Amish bakers twist and bake soft pretzels right in front of you - then try one while it is still warm from the oven. You can get a traditional Amish-style meal - or get an authentic Philadelphia cheesesteak. This is a foodie paradise! _____

EASTERN STATE PENITENTIARY

Philadelphia - *2124 Fairmount Avenue (I-95 exit 22, follow I-676 west. Get off at Art Museum/Benjamin Franklin Parkway Exit. Turn right and go five blocks past the Museum of Art) 19130. Phone: 215-236-3300. www.easternstate.org. Hours: Daily 10:00am-5:00pm. Closed winter holidays. Admission: $23.00 adult, $21.00 senior and $19.00 student, child (7-12). Online discounts. Children under the age of 7 cannot be admitted to the site.*

Let's go to jail. This Penitentiary introduced Americans to a new- and a supposedly more humane-form of housing criminals: solitary confinement. Kids are fascinated by the massive cellblocks, dark cells, and stories of punishment and escapes. Tours include: The central rotunda, restored cells, the solitary confinement yards, the baseball diamond, death row and Al Capone's Cell. A "Voices of Eastern State" audio tour is available during all hours. Although the subject matter is family friendly, it's recommended for kids 12 and up. Special Guided Tours with themes on Escape! Or Prison Life are highlighted versions of the audio tour. These tours are hands-on, interactive experiences, designed for visitors to engage in the spaces more.

PHILADELPHIA MUSEUM OF ART

Philadelphia - *2600 Ben Franklin Parkway (follow I-676 west. Get off at "Art Museum/Benjamin Franklin Parkway" Exit. Turn right) 19130. Phone: (215) 763-8100. www.philamuseum.org. Hours: Thursday-Monday, 10:00am-5:00pm. Friday*

The famous steps from the movies...

evening until 8:45pm Admission: $25.00 adult, $23.00 senior (62+), $14.00 child & students (age 13+). First Sunday of each month: Pay what you wish all day. Museum restaurant.

The 3rd largest museum in the country. 2000 years of fine and applied arts (crafts, interiors, architecture) with 200 galleries. Many rooms have themes that transport you back to when the works were created. Sundays are family days at the museum. The pay-what-you-wish admission is budget friendly, and gallery games, musical performances and art projects entertain the whole family. Families can also take advantage of Self-Guided Family Tours & Children's Audio Tours to explore collections on their own.

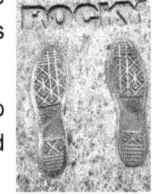

Outside, your kids will love running up the numerous steps to the top like Rocky (from the movie). Pretend you hear the crowd cheer as you step onto the imprints of Rocky's shoes!

FAIRMOUNT PARK

Philadelphia - *Benjamin Franklin Parkway (info at Visitor's Center at Memorial Hall) 19131. www.fairmountpark.org or www.smithplayhouse.org. Phone: (215) 685-0000.*

Along both sides of Schuylkill River, one of the world's largest city park's features include:

- **SMITH PLAYGROUND & PLAYHOUSE** - (215) 765-4325. Emphasis on playhouse (3 story) for preschoolers with trains, foam blocks and comfortable reading rooms. Pick up a Cozy Car and drive along the play roads with stop signs and traffic lights. This century old playground has a Giant Wooden Slide that four generations have slid down.

- **ENVIRONMENTAL EDUCATION CENTERS**: Come check out Fairmount Park's two environmental education centers and its 112-acre working livestock farm. The Pennypack and Wissahickon Environmental Centers are open year-round. Experience their interpretive exhibits, wildlife viewing areas, picnic areas and miles of trails. Fox Chase Farm is an enjoyable place to visit and explore. Open House the first Saturday of each month. Come experience Maple Sugar Day (Feb-March), Sheep Shearing or Apple Fest too. https://www.facebook.com/ExplorePEC/ and https://www.facebook.com/WissahickonEC/

- **FAIRMOUNT WATER WORKS INTERPRETIVE CENTER**: 640 Water Works Drive https://fairmountwaterworks.org/ Who cares that you don't know the difference between a watershed and a woodshed? At the Interpretive Center you and your family can learn about watersheds and have a ton of fun doing it. Fly a helicopter simulation from the Delaware Bay to the headwaters of the Schuylkill River. Or visit Pollutionopolis, America's most contaminated and disgusting town, to see how a city can really mess up its water supply. The Water Works is a pumping station from 1815 to 1909 where visitors can create rain, view historic photos and play with high-tech exhibits. Wednesday-Saturday Noon-4:00pm.

- **WISSAHICKON CREEK GORGE** - hiking trails.

- **DISCOVERY CENTER** @ Strawberry Reservoir - The Discovery Center is situated on an historic 19th century reservoir, and serves as a critical habitat for more than 150 migratory and native bird species. Exhibits, a trail and bird spotting activities. *https://pa.audubon.org/chapters-centers/discovery-center*

PLEASE TOUCH MUSEUM

Philadelphia - *4231 Avenue of the Republic, Fairmount Park (Memorial Hall, GPS - Use 4231 North Concourse Drive for directions) 19131. Phone: (215) 581-3181. www.pleasetouchmuseum.org. Hours: Monday and Wednesday-Saturday 9:00am-4:30pm, Sunday 11:00am-4:30pm. Closed New Years, Thanksgiving and Christmas. Themed Shows presented several times each day. Admission: General $19.00 (over age 1). Parking fee $16.00. Note: Please Taste Café. The Kids Store - take ideas from the museum home as souvenirs or projects. Nature's Pond and Fairy Tale Garden toddler areas for kids 3 and under.*

PLEASE TOUCH MUSEUM has moved and improved! The museum space is divided into six learning-through-play environments – based in the real world and fantasy themes. Here are some highlights: Real Victorian era carousel & model of the Statue of Liberty's torch made of toys. Kid-scaled city-scape; Road-side kid "mechanics" can work on real Toyota Scion or "ride/drive" a real SEPTA bus; and an indoor Treehouse. Exploration of space where kids can pedal a propeller bike, play hopscotch on clouds or spin inside a giant hamster wheel.  Nature-inspired instruments that play music; Collection of 12,000 toys and games from 1945 to the present. Or, River Adventures. Race sailboats in water currents, play with bubbles, and rainbows. This hands-on museum for kids 8 and under also kept our favorite: <u>WONDERLAND</u> - The tale is explained in miniature (little doors to peek through) and then full size. Try on cover ups and pretend you're the Queen of Hearts ready for a tea party with Mad Hatter & rabbit (great photo op).

Although the setups are classic in here, the fresh aspects of creativity through role playing are really different. It's pricier than most kid's museums we've been to in our travels, but its uniqueness is often worth it.

PHILADELPHIA INSECTARIUM & BUTTERFLY PAVILION

Philadelphia - *8046 Frankford Avenue (1-95 Cottman Avenue exit 30 thru to right on Frankford for several blocks) 19136. Phone: (215) 338-3000. https://www.phillybutterflypavilion.com/ Hours: Tuesday-Sunday 10am-5pm. Admission: $20.00 adult, $15.00 senior, military, teachers, students, first responders. FREE Street parking on streets nearby.*

While in Philly, maybe add a creepy trip over to the INSECTARIUM, north of downtown. The all-bug museum exhibits thousands of live and mounted insects from Africa, Tanzania and other exotic locations, as well as interactive displays and movie room. Did you know we eat bugs every day? They're ground up in plants as they are harvested. See a glow in the dark scorpion or bugs with noses. There's giant bugs and little bees (do you know what honey really is?). Pet live bugs like Martin the cockroach or Harry the millipede (yes, actually pet them!). Interact as you climb thru a spider web, eat fried worms, or push buttons. The highlight has to be the Cockroach Kitchen & Bathroom! How do they keep them inside the room? They live here and are welcome! Great photo ops and their gift shop has inexpensive craft kits and bug food and toys. You will learn so much here and the guides really add the "magic".

Outside, there's a learning garden where you go on bug hunts and the Butterfly Pavilion (year round space). The tropical ecosphere is filled with 2000 native and tropical butterflies. Wear bright colors so the butterflies land on you!

MUMMERS MUSEUM

Philadelphia - *1100 South 2nd Street & Washington Avenue (I-95 exit 20 west. Turn left on to Columbus Blvd. Take first left onto Washington Avenue. 2 lights up on left) 19147. Phone: (215) 336-3050. www.mummersmuseum.com. Hours: Tuesday-Friday 10am-5pm, Saturday 10am-3pm (October - April). Adm: $5.00.*

What is a mummer? Opened in 1976, the museum is dedicated to the Philly celebration of the new year. Audio and interactive displays, musical instruments, costumes, and artifacts from the traditional New Year's Day parade. Some of the spectacular costumes date back to the turn of the 20th Century. See videos of past parades or watch how those colorful sparkly costumes are made.

PHILADELPHIA PHILLIES BASEBALL BALLPARK TOURS

Philadelphia - *Citizens Bank Park (south Philadelphia) (off exit 17 onto Broad St. & follow signs) 19148. http://philadelphia.phillies.mlb.com/phi/ballpark/index.jsp. Tour Pricing: Tickets are $20.00 for adults, and $15.00 for children (3-14 years)* *and senior citizens. Tour Times: Tours are offered year round, during the season, on non-game days. Off Season Tuesday & Thursday at 1:30pm.*

Come get an inside look at the Phillies home. Tour guests will be treated to a brief audio/visual presentation of Citizens Bank Park, followed by an up-close look at the ballpark. Tour stops include the Phillies dugout, Diamond Club (which features the glass-enclosed batting cages), broadcast booth and media room, and the unique Hall of Fame Club. Tours last approximately 75 minutes and start and end at the Phillies Team Store.

WELLS FARGO CENTER TOURS

Philadelphia - *3601 South Broad Street (South Broad Street & Patterson Avenue) 19148. Phone: (215) 389-9543. www.wellsfargocenterphilly.com/tours.aspx. Tours: Tours are approximately 60-90 minutes long, include a commemorative photo and frame for each guest, and will start at the Broad St. Doors. Weekdays (provided no events are scheduled). By reservation. $14.00 per person.*

Guided tours of the home of the Philadelphia 76ers & Flyers. In your personal guided tour through the Wells Fargo Center, you will be given an exclusive chance to visit and explore the private luxury seating levels, the press box, Arena Vision studio control room, Comcast SportsNet, and the official NBA and NHL locker rooms. See playing floors and learn great inside scoops on the history of favorite players and teams.

FORT MIFFLIN

Philadelphia - *Fort Mifflin Road (I-95 to Island Avenue Exit 15 west - follow signs) 19153. Phone: (215) 685-4167. www.fortmifflin.us. Hours: Wednesday-Sunday 10:00am-4:00pm. (March-mid-December) Admission: $10.00 adult, $8.00 senior (65+) & $6.00 child (6-12) and veterans. Extra $2.00 for Living History Events. Note: Sundays suggested as there are military drills & craftspeople demonstrating skills. Ask for educational Treasure Hunts.*

"What Really Happened at Fort Mifflin?" Starting in 1772, it was built by the British to protect the colonies. Ironically, in 1777, it was used by Americans trying to protect the Philadelphia and Delaware River from the British (7 long, grueling weeks of siege). It also protected the city of Philadelphia during the War of 1812 and was active as a Confederate and Union prison camp during the Civil War. Until 1954, it was still used to store ammunition for the United States military. A great place to study several wars in one spot.

HEINZ NATIONAL WILDLIFE REFUGE

Philadelphia - *Lindbergh Blvd. & 86th Street (I-95 exit 10west. left onto Bartram Ave, left onto 84th St, left onto Lindbergh Blvd) 19153. Phone: (215) 365-3118. http://heinz.fws.gov/. Hours: Wednesday-Saturday 9:00am-4:00pm. FREE.*

The refuge was established by an act of Congress in 1972 to protect the last 200 acres of freshwater tidal marsh in Pennsylvania. Hiking trails to explore butterflies, muskrats, frogs, flying geese, and loads of wildflowers is open dawn to dusk. Observation tower. Education Center.

PHILADELPHIA INTERNATIONAL CHILDREN'S FESTIVAL

Philadelphia - University of Penn. Annenberg Center for Performing Arts. www.annenbergcenter. org/events/childfest.php Performances throughout each day...you pick & choose from international acts like a circus from Finland, a dance company from the Ivory Coast, comedy from Denmark, fairy tales from England, or folk singers from the USA. The Playworks area is where international artisans teach their art and help kids create crafts such as drums, tapestry, egg painting, dream catchers and sundials. Stageworks is where regional performers share their talent. Adm.(first week of May)

REVOLUTIONARY GERMANTOWN FESTIVAL

Philadelphia - Germantown Avenue on Market Square. www.cliveden.org. (215) 848-1777. This historic district is home to Cliveden (family homestead w/ original furnishings & bullet marks still visible) plus a museum with an overview of America's first German settlement. This land was the scene of a Revolutionary Battle of Germantown, the birthplace of writer Louisa May Alcott, and a stop on the Underground Railroad. Normally boring historical sites become more interesting at re-enactments.(first Saturday inOct)

MORRIS ARBORETUM

Philadelphia (Chestnut Hill) - *100 Northwestern Avenue (University of Pennsylvania) 19118. www.business-services.upenn.edu/arboretum/. Phone: (215) 247-5777. Hours: Daily 10:00am-4:00pm (year round). Open until 5pm on Saturday & Sunday (April - October) Admission: $20.00 adult, $18.00 senior (65+) and $10.00 student, military & child (3-17).*

Romantic 92 acre Victorian garden with many of Philly's rarest and largest trees, a sculpture garden, a rose garden and the Fernery. A stairway brings visitors front and center into one of the Arboretum's most spectacular groves of trees called meta Metasequoia. The model trains in the Garden Railway Display change each season. Kids are sure to find hidden paths and coves.

NOCKAMIXON STATE PARK

Quakertown - *1542 Mountain View Drive (PA Route 563, Northeast Extension of the PA Turnpike, Exit 32) 18951. Phone: (215) 529-7300 or -7308 (marina). https:// www.dcnr.pa.gov/StateParks/FindAPark/NockamixonStatePark/Pages/default. aspx. Admission: to PA State Parks is FREE however swimming, marina and camping/lodging fees apply.*

The name Nockamixon is synonymous with boating. Four public launching areas are provided on the lake and boats may be rented from a park concession. Visitors enjoy watching sailboats from a bench at the marina, and the equestrian, bicycle and hiking trails. Pool, Visitors Center, Horseback Riding, Modern Cabins, Fishing, and Winter Sports.

ROBERT FULTON BIRTHPLACE

Quarryville - *1932 Robert Fulton Hwy (Rte. 30 west to Rte. 372 west to US222 South of Quarryville) 17566. Phone: (717) 548-2679. www.facebook.com/pages/ Robert-Fulton-Birthplace/112190615460149 Hours: Saturday 11am-4pm, Sunday 1-5:00pm (Summer). Admission: $4.00 adult, $2.00 child (11 and under).*

Robert Fulton, the inventor, the artist, and the engineer was born here in 1765. On display are many of his drawings,portraits, and models (located throughout the living room). Being most famous for his steamboat, "Claremont" (the first steamboat), you'll see a strong connection between his artistic ability and his engineering ideas. Because his drawings were so well done, supporters could easily visualize his inventive ideas.

Reading

MID ATLANTIC AIR MUSEUM

Reading - *11 Museum Drive - SR183 (Reading Regional Airport) 19605. Phone: (610) 372-7333. www.maam.org. Hours: Saturday, Monday-Thursday 9:30am-4:00pm. Closed major holidays. Admission: $10.00 adult, $8.00 senior (65+),$3.00 child (6-12). Note: Aviation gift shop. Airplane rides weekends in summer for additional fee. Museum annually hosts a WWII Weekend 1st weekend in June.*

Restored, ready to fly, classic civilian and military aircraft. This museum highlights the Mid Atlantic's contribution to flight as well as the general history of aviation, including military aviation. Take a tour and walk through the exhibits, hangar and go out on to the ramp. Of special interest are the commercial airliners, and the first night fighter ever built, and aviation movies and toys.

READING PHILLIES BASEBALL

Reading - *1900 S. Centre Avenue (FirstEnergy Stadium) 19605. Phone: (610) 370-BALL or 375-8469. www.readingphillies.com. Admission: $8.00-$11.00*

Minor League AA Class affiliate of the Philadelphia Phillies. While parking is always free and the concessions remain affordable, every game is a unique experience. Giveaways, fireworks, The Mascot Band, and the five-member R-Phils Mascot Team keep things hopping throughout the season.

NOLDE FOREST ENVIRONMENTAL EDUCATION CENTER

Reading - *2910 New Holland Road 19608. Phone: (610) 775-1411. https://www.dcnr.pa.gov/StateParks/FindAPark/NoldeForestEnvironmentalEducationCenter/Pages/default.aspx.* Education&Interpretation Ctr.

Nolde Forest encompasses more than 665 acres of deciduous woodlands and coniferous plantations. A network of trails (one accessible) makes the center's streams, ponds and diverse habitats accessible to both students and casual visitors. Teaching stations offer places for students to work and benches for those who wish to sit. Park open daylight hours year-round.

READING PUBLIC MUSEUM

Reading - *500 Museum Road (follow 222 South/422 East to West Reading/Penn Avenue exit) 19611. Phone: (610) 371-5850.   www.readingpublicmuseum.org. Hours: Daily 11:00am-5:00pm Closed most holidays. Admission: $10.00 adult, $6.00 seniors/students (4-17). These costs apply to the Museum only. Star & Laser Shows @The Planetarium are separate and listed on The Planetarium page.*

The Museum houses galleries and collections as well as events showcasing the discovery of art, science and civilizations. While the art of many nations and people is represented in the permanent collection, the fine art collection includes more than seven hundred oil paintings by American and foreign artists such as: N.C. Wyeth, George Bellows, Raphaelle Peale, and Edgar Degas - names students are familiar with in art history class. In addition, the Museum possesses over one hundred sculptures. Learn about life in the Middle Ages, the code of chivalry, and how one became a knight in the Arms and Armor Gallery of Knights in shining armor. Mounted Specimens are prepared to resemble the organism as it would normally appear in the wild.

Visit the planetarium for a star or laser show. With specials on black holes, astronauts, and icy worlds plan on an informative trip. Public Star Shows on Sundays, Public Laser Shows on Saturdays (separate fee).

AMAZING MAIZE MAZE

Ronks - Cherry Crest Farm. www.cherrycrestfarm.com. Different design each year. (i.e. Noah's Ark). Petting zoo, refreshments, pumpkin patch, corn maze, pony or wagon rides. Also 4 smaller mazes and hay jump on property. Pedal carts. Sack slides. Admission. (weekends each fall, especially in October)

CHERRY FAIR

Schaefferstown - Alexander Schaeffer Farm Museum. Phone: (717) 949-2244. www.hsimuseum.org. Lots of cherry goodies to eat, cherry pie eating and pitting contests, cake walks, a family corner, a pig roast, demos and crafters, horse wagon rides, and saw mill demonstrations. Stage shows along with a violin maker, and wheelwright shop, the spinners, and many others. Adm. (last Sat in June)

HARVEST FAIR

Schaefferstown - Alexander Schaeffer Farm Museum. Phone: (717) 949-2244. www.hsimuseum.org. Tractor pulls, antique steam engines, parades, food (made with steam), threshing, baling, cider and apple butter making, hayrides, children's activities, petting zoo & fall crafts. Admission. (second weekend in September)

SPRING MOUNTAIN ADVENTURES

Spring Mount - *757 Spring Mount Road (minutes from the Lansdale exit of the Pennsylvania Turnpike) 19478. www.springmountainadventures.com. Phone: (610) 287-7900. Note: Sunday night is Family Night.*

Spring Mountain has always been Pennsylvania's perfect place to learn to ski and snowboard, but now it's also the perfect place to experience the thrill of a canopy tour and rock climbing. Skiers and Boarders participate in terrain park, half-pipe and eight trails. Plus, they have two tubing runs and a skating rink.

Strasburg

ED'S BUGGY RIDES

Strasburg *(Ronks)- 253 Hartman Bridge Rd, SR 896 (across from Sight & Sound Theatre) 17572. Phone: (717) 687-0360. www.edsbuggyrides.com. Admission: $10.00 adult, $5.00 child (35 min ride).*

3 mile tour through Amish farmlands in an Amish buggy. Experience the beautiful Pennsylvania Dutch Country landscape, while watching the everyday routine of the Amish through hilly back roads in an authentic Amish buggy. Experience riding in an authentic Amish buggy. They have open and closed Amish family carriages and open Amish spring wagons. Daily, year-round.

AMISH VILLAGE

Strasburg (Ronks) - *199 Hartman Bridge Rd, Route 896 (1 mile south of US30 & 2 miles north of Strasburg) 17572. Phone: (717) 687-8511. https://www.amishvillage. com/. Hours: Daily 9:00am-5:00pm (Spring/Fall). Til 6pm (summers). Open at 10:00am on Sunday. Admission: $12.00 adult, $7.00 child (5-12). Tours: 20-25 minutes. Note: Amish Village store.*

Tour an authentic 1840 Amish farmhouse, explore the farmland and animals, walk to school to the one-room school house built and furnished by the Amish. Visit the Smokehouse and taste the flavor of the 1800's. The highlight is an educational tour of an 1840 Old Order Amish home, authentically furnished. The site includes a blacksmith, water wheel, spring house and windmill.

CHOO CHOO BARN, TRAINTOWN USA

Strasburg - *Route 741 East, 226 Gap Road, 17579. www.choochoobarn.com. Phone: (717) 687-7911. Hours: Monday, Tuesday, Thursday, Friday, Saturday 10:00am-5:00pm (April- December). Closed major winter holidays and Easter. Admission: $10.00 adult, $6.00 child (3-11).*

Gigantic model train display! A 1700 square foot mini display of Pennsylvania Dutch County with area landmarks, 20 operating trains plus over 150 animated and automated vehicles and figurines. The kids shriek with delight - esp. when it changes from daylight to nighttime. Look for the skiers zooming down the slopes and the dump truck that really moves. The working fire display shows a house burning and then the fire truck comes to put it out. Most displays can be seen from "kids-eye" level. You have to pass the well-stocked gift shop in and out of the exhibit so plan extra time for shopping.

RAILROAD MUSEUM OF PENNSYLVANIA

Strasburg - *300 Gap Road - SR741 East 17579. Phone: (717) 687-8628. www.rrmuseumpa.org. Hours: Wednesday-Saturday 10:00am-5:00pm, Sunday Noon-4:00pm. Admission: $10.00 adult, $9.00 senior (65+), $8.00 child (3-11). Note: Whistle Stop Shop.*

Outdoor yard restoration available in good weather. Hands-On-Center. Orientation video. 2nd floor observation deck. Strasburg Railroad is across street. Christmas Open House (2nd Sunday in December)

Sit in an engineer's seat, explore a caboose, experience a turn-of-the-century passenger station. Trainworks hands-on area — Stewart Junction, Steinman Station, and the Diesel Simulator, have been revamped. Docents are on hand to explain special locomotives and show you how they worked, and other cars are opened during special events. Meet "Diesel", GG 1 Electric, Logging, Freight and Passenger (actually get to walk in) trains! More access than most train museums. In the center of the museum is the railroad workshop where you can actually walk under a train! Great place to bring grandmas and grandpas to pass along stories to younger generations.

STRASBURG RAILROAD

Strasburg - *SR741 East - 17579. www.strasburgrailroad.com. Phone: (717) 687-7522. Hours: Daily 10:00am-7:00pm (July & August), 11:00am-3:00pm (May, June, September, October, November to Thanksgiving). Mostly long weekends (weather permitting) Noon-3:00pm (Rest of the year). Admission: Train Rides: $28.00 adult, $14.00child (2-11), $2.00 toddler. Activities: $5.00 per activity (tokens). Tours: 45 minutes, depart on the hour. Schedule online. Note: Several gift shops with train souvenirs, books and loads of Thomas stuff! Restaurants with casual dining, picnic lunches and sweet treats on premises.*

Offering the most authentic train ride experience of the period, the Strasburg Railroad takes visitors back to a simpler time. The restored Victorian open-air and coach cars offer wide views of the landscape (some cars even offer snacks and the dining car offers meals). Visitors travel through farm fields still plowed by horses and mules. Amish buggies wait patiently at railroad crossings. Train travelers can stop at an old-fashioned picnic grove and enjoy a treat while the trains rumble by. Each train has a narrator who tells the railroad's history spiced with a few tall tales.

Other activities on the premises: Hand-propelled cars, which date back to the 1930s, allow little ones to take control as they crank their way around a track; Cagney Train - built around 1920, this miniature steam train was originally used at an amusement park; President's Car Tour - Take a self-guided tour aboard the stationary "mansion on rails." Also, tour the freight equipment display; and the Switch Tower Tour - Built in 1885, this is a classic example of Pennsylvania Railroad signal tower design. Your young engineers are really going to enjoy the train ride and be sure to plan one or two extra activities because they'll be begging for more! Classy railroad. Easter & Christmas themed trains too.

Be sure to check on seasonal events that your "little engineers" will love like "A Day Out With Thomas the Train!" (A life-size Thomas plus storytelling, Sir Topham Hatt, Play Tables, Thomas Coloring and Videos, and Live Musical Entertainment for the wristband price of ~$25 per person/ages 2+.

NATIONAL TOY TRAIN MUSEUM

Strasburg (Paradise) - *300 Paradise Lane (off SR 741 East & US 30) 17579. Phone: (717) 687-8976. www.nttmuseum.org. Hours: Daily 10:00am-5:00pm (June, July, August), Weekends in April, May, September thru December. Admission: $8.50 adult, $8.00 senior (65+), 5.50 child (4-11), $25.00 family.*

Five operating push button layouts in panoramic viewing. Meet toy trains from the 1800s to the present in use as part of the layout. The Train Collectors Association operates it (they are often featured on national TV). A continuously running video show in the Museum's Theater area features cartoons and comedy films about toy trains.

DELAWARE CANAL STATE PARK

Upper Black Eddy - *11 Lodi Hill Road (Rte. 611 and Rte. 32 18972. Phone: (610) 982-5560. https://www.dcnr.pa.gov/StateParks/FindAPark/DelawareCanalStatePark/Pages/default.aspx Admission: to PA State Parks is FREE however swimming, marina and camping/lodging fees apply, with reservation or entrance.*

A walk along the 60-mile towpath of the Delaware Canal is a stroll into American History. The Delaware Canal is the only remaining continuously intact canal of the great towpath canal building era of the early and mid-19th century. Mule drawn canal boat rides and the Lock Tender's House Visitor Center are at New Hope. Also, Horseback Riding, Mountain Biking, Fishing, Trails, Cross-Country Skiing.

RINGING ROCKS PARK

Upper Black Eddy - *(9 miles south of Easton) 18972. Phone: (215) 348-6114 or (215) 757-0571 Bucks Co. Parks n Rec. https://www.buckscounty.gov/Facilities/Facility/Details/Ringing-Rocks-Park-5*

Southbound, the site lies just off Route 32, two miles past its intersection with Route 611 at Kintnersville. From there, Narrows Hill Road runs past the General Store to Ringing Rocks Road. A quarter-mile trail meanders from a picnic area to the field of boulders. Take along your own hammer. Why? This vast field of boulders all ring like bells, with tones ranging from high ping to low bong. This is literally a rock concert. Whatever the score, "heavy metal" would lie at its heart, it is the iron content that makes them ring. No one knows where the boulders came from. No guards are needed to protect the singing stones at the field itself; they must weigh from half-a-ton up. Ringing Rocks Park also boasts a beautiful waterfall and lots of lovely flora and fauna, rich in the lore of magic and mystery. Can you solve the mystery?

VALLEY FORGE NATL HISTORICAL PARK

Valley Forge - *1400 North Outer Line Drive SR23 & N. Gulph Road - (I-76 to exit 24 - SR202 south to SR422 west to SR23 west) 19406. Phone: (610) 783-1077. www. nps.gov/vafo/index.htm. Hours: Daily 9:00am-5:00pm. Closed Thanksgiving, Christmas. Admission: FREE. Tours: By trolley (summers) or self-guided driving with audio tape. Ranger led tours 2 times per day in the summer. Note: Expanse of outdoor park areas available. Hiking and bike trails. Stop at the Visitor's Center first. Valley Forge Canteen open 10:00am-2:00 pm Saturday and Sunday. Educators: wow, an outstanding and thorough Valley Forge Curriculum Guide is here online: http://www.nps.gov/vafo/forteachers/upload/CurriculumGuide.pdf.*

Explore the site of the Winter of 1777-78 encampment that was a difficult time for battling elements and disease. Some of the sites that you won't want to miss are:

- VISITOR'S CENTER - An eighteen-minute film, "Valley Forge: A Winter Encampment," is shown every 30 minutes on the hour and half-hour, starting at 9:30am, ending at 4:30pm. Be sure to take that in first and look over the dioramas.

- BRIGADE HUTS - Reconstructed huts built to Gen. Washington's specifications. Also, this is the main site for Valley Forge's Living History program. Get out a stretch and run areas.

- WASHINGTON'S HEADQUARTERS - Isaac Potts' House - looks exactly as it did when General George Washington and his wife, Martha were in residence. (Initially he shared the rough conditions with the soldiers in the field tents). Interpreters are excellent here (weekends and summers).

- GRAND PARADE - learn about the other hero (Von Steuben) who turned tattered, confused young men into soldiers.

Summer weekends are the best time to visit because the Muhlenberg Brigade is recreated in living history encampments - bringing the drudges of winter camp to life. Remember, these "huts" replaced tents but still only offered a little more warmth.

Brave a visit Winter weekends to see scout troops living under similar conditions as the soldiers did. Battles may not have occurred here, but after months of training in the worst conditions - those soldiers were a fighting force.

WASHINGTON CROSSING HISTORIC PARK

Washington's Crossing - *1112 River Road SR32 and SR532 (off I-95, exit 31, head northwest on Rte. 532) 18977. Phone: (215) 493-4076. https://www. washingtoncrossingpark.org/. Hours: Daily 10am-5pm. Closed some holidays.*

Admission: $7.00 (age 5+) for tour of Village or Farmstead or Tower. Park charges $1.00 per vehicle at entrance. Cash & check only. Tours: Guided tours of the Village and the Thompson-Neely section occur everyday but select holidays/special events. Tours begin on the half hour. During winter months, tours may conclude earlier in the day due to low light levels in the historic structures. Village takes one hour to tour. Allow 30 minutes to tour the Thompson-Neely House. The Thompson-Neely grist mill is open seasonally for tours. Allow additional time to tour the grist mill. Note: Events occur each month on the weekends, especially Sundays. Every Christmas (at 1:00pm) the park re-enacts Washington's crossing and special events also occur on his birthday. Also on grounds is the Bowman's Hill and Wildflower Preserve. FREEBIES: click on FOR KIDS icon to browse thru several games and FAQ. Be sure to print a copy of the Washington Crossing Scavenger Hunt to complete while you're on site.

It's December 25, 1776. Washington planned his attack on the British, first crossing the Delaware River by boat. In the Durham Boat House, you can see the boats that were actually used. A larger than life copy (20 ft. X 12 ft.) of the painting "Washington's Crossing" creates the best image of this historic Christmas Day for freedom. A total of 13 historic buildings are on site and your tour ticket includes Bowman's Hill Tower observation point, Thompson-Neely House (where Washington ate and slept), The Ferry Inn (where Washington dined before crossing the icy Delaware) and the Memorial Building where the giant painting stands. Picture the life of an early American colonist at the newly renovated Thompson-Neely House & Farmstead, which served as a temporary regimental army hospital during Washington's winter campaign of 1776-1777. All of this, plus a short historical film is shown of the event. It'll give you goosebumps!

AMERICAN HELICOPTER MUSEUM

West Chester - *1220 American Blvd.* *(Brandywine Airport - Next to QVC Studios) 19380. Phone: (610) 436-9600. www. helicoptermuseum.org. Hours: Thursday-Saturday 10:00am-5:00pm, Sunday Noon-5:00pm. Admission: $15.00 adult, $14.00 senior (65+) and child (3-11) or student. Note: Older kids will want more information about the engineering of the rotocraft. Films and mechanics are available to fill in all of the details. Helicopter Rides (every 4th Saturday for $40 per person) - ask for adventure here! Fly-bys...wow!*

This very kid-friendly museum exhibits the adventure and history of "rotary wing flight" at the country's only helicopter museum. Helicopters from the earliest to the most modern are here, inside and outside (Coast Guard, Navy, Army, M.A.S.H.), plus interactive exhibits. Climb aboard and play with the controls inside the giant helicopters being restored. Visitors come back here frequently because the kids can actually go on many units and work the rotors and play pretend. Plus a very exciting miniature wind tunnel blows air in the

face of anyone in its path.

BERK'S COUNTY HERITAGE CENTER

Wyomissing (Reading) - *940 Centre AveRed Bridge Road (off Route 183) 19601. Phone: (610) 374-8839. www.berkshistory.org. Hours: Wednesday-Saturday 10:00am-3:00pm (May - October). Admission: $4.00-$7.00 (age 4+) per museum. Discount combo prices.*

The Berks County Heritage Center is a historical complex honoring important eras of our local transportation and manufacturing history. The Society's 20,000 artifacts tell many stories behind the development of the county. Three levels of museum exhibits interpret colorful history from the Conestoga Wagon to the 1902 Duryea to toys, crafts, fine arts, all related to our social history. This includes the Trades to Industry Room, Pennsylvania German Gallery, Firefighting & Toy displays and the Hands On History Room. Start learning about more Berks County heritage by taking a tour through landmarks of local history; including the Gruber Wagon Works and the C. Howard Hiester Canal Center.

<u>GRUBER WAGON WORKS</u> - Survives as one of the most complete examples of an integrated rural manufactory of its kind in the nation. Wagon wheels were constructed in the bench shop, and wooden parts of the wagon were made from patterns in the wood shop. Wheels were "tired" and wagons were "ironed" and assembled in the blacksmith shop. The distinctive striping and scrollwork were applied by hand in the paint shop.

<u>C. HOWARD HIESTER CANAL CENTER</u>: Canals saw their rise and fall in the 19th century. They offered means of bulk transportation and travel in the era prior to railroads when the only alternative to walking was the horse and wagon. Red Bridge (longest covered bridge in the state).

CIVIL WAR ENCAMPMENT

Wyomissing - Berk's County Heritage Center. The year is 1863, and Pennsylvania Federal Regiment try to enlist new recruits and demonstrate military life. Free. (second weekend in July)

Chapter 9
South West
Pennsylvania

Brownsville
- Nemacolin Castle

Champion
- Seven Springs Mountain Resort

Clinton
- Hozak Farms Fall Festival

Donegal
- Living Treasures Animal Park

Elizabeth
- Round Hill Exhibit Farm

Farmington
- Fort Necessity Nat'l Battlefield
- Laurel Caverns
- Nemacolin Woodlands Resort
- Friendship Hill Nat'l Historic Site

Finleyville
- Strawberry Festival

Greensburg
- Westmoreland Museum Of American Art
- Overly's Country Christmas

Harrison City
- Bushy Run Battlefield

Hidden Valley
- Hidden Valley Ski

Latrobe
- Pittsburgh Steelers Summer Training Camp

Latrobe (Derry)
- Keystone State Park

Laughlintown
- Compass Inn Museum
- Forbes State Forest

Ligonier
- Fort Ligonier
- Idlewild Park & Soak Zone
- Ramada Inn Historic Ligonier

McMurray
- Simmons Farms Fall Playland

Meyersdale
- Pennsylvania Maple Festival

Mill Run
- Fallingwater

Monongahela
- Reilly's Summer Seat Farm

Mt. Pleasant
- Mt. Pleasant Glass & Ethnic Festival

North Huntington
- Big Mac Museum Restaurant

Ohiopyle
- Ohio Pyle State Park

Pittsburgh
- Pittsburgh Sports
- Primanti Brothers
- Sand Castle
- Pittsburgh Zoo & Aquarium
- The Frick Art & History Center
- Duquesne Incline
- Carnegie Science Center
- Children's Museum Of Pittsburgh
- Heinz Field Tours
- National Aviary
- Photo Antiquities
- Soldiers And Sailors Museum
- Allegheny Observatory
- Gateway Clipper Fleet
- Grand Concourse Restaurant
- Monongahela Incline
- Ft Pitt Museum/Point State Park
- Heinz History Center
- Society For Contemporary Crafts
- Strip District Dining
- Beechwood Farm Nature Preserve
- International Children's Festival
- Pittsburgh Vintage Grand Prix
- Pittsburgh Light Up Nights
- Kids Holiday Crawl

Pittsburgh (Avella)
- Meadowcroft Rockshelter/Village

Pittsburgh (Canonsburg)
- Little Lake Theatre Company

Pittsburgh (Carnegie)
- Pittsburgh's Motor Speedway

Pittsburgh (Gibsonia)
- Pittsburgh Holiday Train Show

Pittsburgh (Monroeville)
- Boyce Park Ski Area

Pittsburgh (Oakland)
- Carnegie Museum Of Art
- Carnegie Museum Of Natural History
- Phipps Conservatory
- Pittsburgh Playhouse Jr.
- Rodef Shalom Biblical Gardens
- Cathedral Of Learning Nationality Classrooms

Pittsburgh (West Mifflin)
- Kennywood Park

Rector
- Linn Run State Park

Rockwood
- Laurel Ridge State Park

Scenery Hill
- Westerwald Pottery

Scottdale
- West Overton Museums

Shanksville (Friedens)
- Flight 93 Memorial Chapel & Impact Site

Somerset
- Kooser State Park
- Laurel Hill State Park
- Somerset Historical Center

Tarentum
- Tour-Ed Mine And Museum

Uniontown
- Searight Toll House Museum

Washington
- Pennsylvania Trolley Museum
- Washington County Museum

Waynesburg
- Greene County Museum
- Battle Of The Bulge Re-Enactment

Wind Ridge
- Ryerson Station State Park

A Quick Tour of our Hand-Picked Favorites Around...

South West Pennsylvania

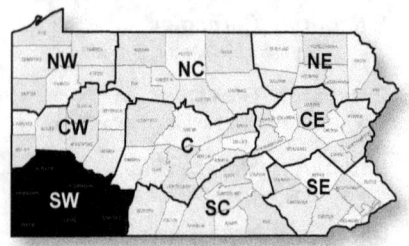

A Weekend in Pittsburgh and Its Countryside. Pittsburgh is so exciting! Pittsburgh is also so interactive! On any trip to the city by the Three Rivers, you'll find an overflowing handful of surprises.

Check out Mister Roger's Neighborhood exhibit, a hometown favorite at the **Children's Museum of Pittsburgh**, coupled with a very different approach to typical museums including "The River" water play space where you build bridges and water fountains to the sky.

Union Station and The Strip District have lots of dining and shopping options but it's also the depot for one of our favorite riverboat tours - **Gateway Clipper Tour**. Venture aboard a large riverboat for a short, one-hour tour of Pittsburgh from the three rivers. Try "PIttsburgh only" famous foods on land.

On the outskirts of downtown are two other fabulous family sites. **The Pittsburgh Zoo** & PPG Aquarium is a double hit of animals in one place. You won't want to miss the polar bears and sea otters. What a treat to see these playful, curious water creatures from all angles. The setup actually allows you to look above, beside and below the water in a cute seaside town motif.

At **Meadowcroft** Rockshelter and Village re-live rugged rural life from 200 years ago as you walk the dirt and stone roads of this reconstructed village. By touring a settler log house, schoolhouse, country store, barn and blacksmith shop - you'll be introduced to inhabitants like the Native Americans, frontier settlers, farmers, lumbermen, coal miners, and conservationists who have worked the land. Get involved by taking a real school lesson. Shear sheep and then spin and weave wool. Then, dig some ancient rock at Rock Shelter.

Be sure to include a ride up the **Inclines** at least one evening during your visit. Wait until you see the view. And, if you get lost meandering

Pittsburgh streets around construction zones, just stop any native and they'll be glad to help you find your way. Some even wrote a map on napkins, others volunteered to drive ahead with us following.

The thriving metropolis of Pittsburgh, just one hour north of the Laurel Highlands, sits well amongst big cities. But every major town has countryside and the Laurel Highlands is such an area. Their natural area consists of 10 state parks and forests. Named for the Mountain Laurel, the hills and streams of these sleepy towns bloom with different colors from March through October. But quiet towns and beautiful blossoms don't wow the kids as much as The **Big Mac Museum**, a storybook forest, and a resort zoo or some French & Indian War forts!

Located in the scenic Laurel Highlands on 2800 acres, the 335-room **Nemacolin Resort** features an enormous variety of amazing activities. But did you know they have a Wildlife Academy? Just east of the main entrance, folks can schedule nursery tours or safari tours for a fee or just a pop in visit meandering near habitats of wolves in the wild, dozens of horses or maybe a panther. Or, scattered throughout the resort property, catch special Wildlife Habitats (black bears, zebras, elk, bison, and moose have habitats scattered around the golf course).

Forts – fun forts just for playing. **Fort Necessity** and **Fort Ligonier** commemorates the mid-1700s battles – George Washington battles – of the French and Indian War. The Visitor Center is the best place to begin your visit. After their movie introduces you to the park's story, sight and sound experiences engage the kids to listen closely as you enter exhibit spaces.

Now, I know we boast about few amusement parks but **Idlewild** and Storybook Forest are too fun to not shout about! Story Book Forest is a timeless walk through Nursery Rhymes but the park also has manageable rides, Mister Rogers Neighborhood and a Soak Zone waterpark.

Sites and attractions are listed in order by City, Zip Code, and Name. Symbols indicated represent: |⦿| Restaurants   ◣   Lodging

SEVEN SPRINGS MOUNTAIN RESORT

Champion - *RR#1 Box 110 (I-76 exit 9 or 10, follow Rte. 31 or 711) 15622. Phone: (814) 352-7777, www.7springs.com.*

Longest Run: 1.2 miles; 30 Slopes & Trails. Pennsylvania's largest ski and year-round resort. Be sure to get all of the latest details by calling or visiting their website. A perfect winter getaway resort, Seven Springs can accommodate more than 5,000 overnight guests in its 10-story high-rise hotel and nearly 1,000 condominium, town homes, cabins and chalets. The "resort cam" shows live pictures that are updated every 5 minutes. Tons of lodging & restaurants, indoor bowling, roller skating, swimming & mini-golf. Outdoor summer alpine slide, craft days, golf, outdoor pool, downhill bike park, zipline, horseback riding and tennis.

AUTUMNFEST

Champion - Seven Springs Mountain Resort. Petting zoo, refreshments, pumpkin patch, corn maze, pony or wagon rides. Scenic chair lift rides, Alpine slide, open-spit cooked foods. (all October weekends)

HOZAK FARMS FALL FESTIVAL

Clinton - Hozak Farms. www.hozakfarms.com. Petting zoo, refreshments, pumpkin patch, corn maze, pony or wagon rides. Admission. (October weekends)

LIVING TREASURES ANIMAL PARK

Donegal (Jones Mills) - *288 SR 711 (south of Rte. 31) 15628. www.ltanimalpark. com. Phone: (724) 593-8300. Hours: Daily 10am-8pm (Summer). Daily 10am-6pm (April, May, September, Oct). Admission: $16.99 adult, $14.99 senior (62+), $13.99 child (3-11).*

Watch kangaroos, tigers and wolves and ride the miniature horses. Kids love the petting area (babies, reindeer, camels) and feeding areas (bears, otters, monkeys, goats, sheep, giraffe & llamas). Cups of animal feed are available in the gift shop or at coin-operated food dispensers throughout the park. The Laurel Highlands location has several new additions each year including Black Leopards, Prairie Dogs and Dingos. But the "biggest" addition is their Grizzly Bear family or baby camels!

ROUND HILL EXHIBIT FARM

Elizabeth - *651 Round Hill Road (SR51 & SR48 to Round Hill Road) 15037. Phone: (412) 384-4701. www.alleghenycounty.us/parks/rhfac.aspx. Hours: Daily 8:00am-DUSK. Admission: FREE*

A small scale working farm dating back to the late 1700s. A brick farmhouse with barns and fields including dairy and beef cattle, pigs, chicken, sheep, horses, and a duck pond. Be ready to watch the cows being milked daily at 8:30am and 4:30pm. You can tour the grounds, play with the animals, plan a picnic, romp and play on the soccer fields, splash in Spray Park, and walk the trails.

Farmington

FORT NECESSITY NATIONAL BATTLEFIELD

Farmington - *1 Washington Parkway - US40 15437. https://www.nps.gov/fone/ index.htm Phone: (724) 329-5805. Hours: 8:00am-Sunset (park), Visitor's Center 9:00am-5:00pm, Closed many holidays. Admission: FREE. Tours of the Mount Washington Tavern are available when staffing permits. The Tavern is a museum of life along the National Road and operated from 1828 to 1855. Note: Picnic areas. Short 1/5th to 1/2 mile trail walks to fort and other museum sites along the National Road. Educators: Free lessonplans:www.nps.gov/fone/ learn/education/classrooms/ curriculummaterials.htm*

Commemorating the 1754 battle - George Washington's first battle of the French and Indian War, this war was a clash of British, French and American Indian cultures. It ended with the removal of French power from North America. The stage was set for the American Revolution.

The Visitor Center is the best place to begin your visit. The twenty-minute movie "Road of Necessity" introduces the park story. Begin at Jumonville Glen - the site where the first skirmish occurred with the French. Washington feared they would return with backup forces, so, he had this fort built quickly, out of "necessity". It's a sight and sound experience as you enter spaces - ex. crossfire, characters talk at the roadside rest while you pull up a seat and listen in. Whose story of how the war started do you believe? Outside - soft play fort and Conestoga wagon with mini slides; pop in heads picture photo ops. Next, walk along the short marked trail to see the reconstructed fort - 53 feet in diameter, the gate is only 3.5 feet wide. Talks, tours, and historic weapons demonstrations are offered during the summer months.

LAUREL CAVERNS

Farmington - *1065 Skyline Drive (Chestnut Ridge in Laurel Highlands, off US 40) 15437. Phone: (800) 515-4150 or (724) 438-3003. https://laurelcaverns.com/. Hours: Daily 9:00am-4:00pm (Mid April-October). Admission: $11.00-$17.00 (age 5+). $6.00 extra per person for mini-golf course - recommended. Tours: 1 hour. Constant temperature, 52 degrees Fahrenheit. Note: Visitors center, picnic areas.*

DID YOU KNOW?

Kavernputt is the largest simulated cave in the world.

Pennsylvania's largest cave 2.3 miles. - well-lit tours of the "Grand Canyon" on the Family Tour. Laurel Caverns is a natural cave which follows the natural slope of the mountain. The family tour goes down approximately 1,700 feet. Kavernputt is so unique (additional activity fee required). A ten thousand square foot simulated cave is an eighteen hole golf course. The course is handicapped accessible with each hole conveying some unique aspect of caves.

NEMACOLIN WOODLANDS RESORT

Farmington - *1001 LaFayette Drive 15437. www.nemacolin.com. Phone: (800) 422-2736.*

Located in the scenic Laurel Highlands, the 335 room resort features a spa; golf course; the shooting academy; the off-road driving academy, mystic mountain ski area; adventure course (ropes, Zipline, paintball, rock climbing wall, mountain bike rentals); miniature golf; every sport court imaginable; equestrian - trail rides, surrey rides, and sleigh rides; 6 swimming pools (2 indoor, one of which is just for children/families); and The Marina at Paige's Beach - canoes, kayaks, pedal boats and small sailboat rentals. Once you're settled in, your hardest decision is what to do first?

Lodging - as you step inside the Chateau foyer, modeled after the famed Ritz Paris, you may wonder if the place is a bit pretentious. That feeling leaves almost immediately as you quickly find families in every corner. Sightings of beach towels and the pit-pat of flip-flops makes you want to start exploring. But first, check into your Lodge room - original to the resort, the lodge is an English Tudor style hotel with room decor reminiscent of a comfortable English country inn. (This is upscale, yet comfortable elegance. Be prepared for overnight room rates starting at $400/night during non-peak times. Look for packages for the whole family so you get the most perks to make this fairy-tale place a special event).

Hungry? The Tavern has the world's largest free-standing cylindrical salt water aquarium with a wrap-around breakfast bar for dining. The menu is casual, American fare with offerings like root beer floats and pizza.

Retail stores - little 'streetside' shops and whimsical sculptures fill many corridors but the kids especially like the 50s soda shop and the arcade. The kids activities and pool area is based from this same space so the kids can just settle into one area and feel comfortable.

- NEMACOLIN'S WILDLIFE ACADEMY - (nursery tours for a fee or safari tours) Just a pop in visit includes wolves in the wild, dozens of horses or maybe a panther. We fed a bear, a big black bear! Special wildlife habitats of black bears, zebras, elk, bison, and moose have habitats scattered around the golf course. You can take the shuttle around, walk the property, or drive and park near the featured stops in the woodlands or around the links.

- MYSTIC MOUNTAIN SKI AREA: Mystic Mountain is Western Pennsylvania's ideal learning environment for first-time skiers, with 25 acres of short lines, friendly trails and experienced instructors. Downhill skiing and snowboarding are available on 10 slopes at Mystic Mountain, with slope difficulty ranging from beginner to expert. Mystic Mountain has a 300-foot vertical drop, three lifts, and is 100 percent illuminated, making night snowsports great fun. Longest Run: .5 miles; 7 Slopes & Trails.

FRIENDSHIP HILL NATIONAL HISTORIC SITE

Farmington - *223 New Geneva Road (US 119 to PA 166) 15474. Phone: (724) 725-9190. www.nps.gov/frhi/index.htm. Hours: Daily 9:00am-5:00pm (May-September). Winter hours are Saturday-Sunday only. Closed Christmas day only. Admission: FREE. Educators: Curriculum materials: www.nps.gov/frhi/learn/ education/classrooms/curriculummaterials.htm*

Visit the home of Albert Gallatin (a famous local financier, scholar and diplomat of the early republic). "A country, like a household, should live within its means and avoid debt", says Albert Gallatin. Albert Gallatin is best remembered for his thirteen year tenure as Secretary of the Treasury during the Jefferson and Madison administrations. In that time he reduced the national debt, purchased the Louisiana Territory and funded the Lewis & Clark exploration. Gallatin's accomplishments and contributions are highlighted in his restored country estate, Friendship Hill. Ranger guided tours (summer) and self-guided Audio tours (rest of year).

STRAWBERRY FESTIVAL

Finleyville - Trax Farms. www.traxfarms.com. Sample strawberry treats like fresh strawberry shortcakes and strawberry ice cream or sundaes. From great beverages and tempting sweets to colorful dishes and barbecued meats grilled with berry sauces. Entertainment, demos, contests and prizes. Kids' activities. Watch them make strawberry jam. Pick your own. (second weekend of June)

WESTMORELAND MUSEUM AMERICAN ART

Greensburg - 221 North Main Street (downtown) 15601. Phone: (724) 837-1500. www.wmuseumaa.org. Hours: Wednesday-Sunday 10:00am-5:00pm. Admission: FREE. Suggested donation $5.00 (age 12+). Cafe.

"Arty-Facts" educational programs for children. Kidspace interactive area - Exhibitions include artwork from the permanent collection on display together with accompanying hands-on activities and a well-stocked reading corner. Regional industry, rural and cityscapes, toys of yesteryear, historical heroes.

OVERLY'S COUNTRY CHRISTMAS

Greensburg - Westmoreland Fairgrounds. www.overlys.com. Glistening lights. Visit with Santa. Hot chocolate. Freshly baked cookies. Toy/gift shops. Mini-railroad display. Talking & dancing trees. Train ride. Weekend entertainment. Admission. (Evenings - mid-November thru early January)

BUSHY RUN BATTLEFIELD

Harrison City - Bushy Run Road (off US22 to Bus66 to SR993) 15636. Phone: (724) 527-5584. www.bushyrunbattlefield.com. Hours: Wednesday-Saturday 9:00am-5:00pm, Sunday Noon-5:30pm (May-October). Admission: $3.00-$5.00.

The battle that opened Western Pennsylvania to settlement - Pontiac's War in 1763. Native American forces lead by Chief Pontiac had occupied nearby forts. The British finally stopped advancements at Bushy Run - this reopened supply routes. See a life-size mannequin of an Indian Warrior dressed for battle with war paint from head to toe. Children can take turns dressing up like a British soldier (check out all the buttons!). Learn what "lock, stock, and barrel" means or discover different ways they used nature to provide basic needs (trees for gun stock, food, and dyes). View the 3D movie and electronic map of the battle - then walk outside to markers of the actual battlefield ground.

ANNIVERSARY OF THE BATTLE OF BUSHY RUN

Harrison City - Bushy Run Battlefield. Live re-enactment of the Battle of Bushy Run, 1763. Period British and Native American campsites, and a variety of other programs. Admission. (first weekend in August)

HIDDEN VALLEY SKI

Hidden Valley - *One Craighead Drive (PA Route 31) 15502. Phone: (814) 443-2600. Snow Report: (800) 443-7544. www.hiddenvalleyresort.com.*

Longest Run: 1 mile; 17 Slopes & Trails. Sleigh rides, Children's Snow Play area, Snowtubing and snowboarding. Year-round sports and recreation at Hidden Valley Resort from golf, outdoor swimming, indoor swimming, and mountain biking in the spring, summer and fall. Lodging in condos.

PITTSBURGH STEELERS SUMMER TRAINING CAMP

Latrobe - *US30 at Fraser Purchase Road (St. Vincent College) 15650. https:// www.golaurelhighlands.com/things-to-do/steelers-training-camp/ Hours: Daily practice - get a schedule at the field. (Mid-July - August) Admission: FREE.*

Since 1967, this has been the site of the NFL - Pittsburgh Steelers pre-season training camp. Young fans can root for their favorite team member in a more intimate setting. Children can also learn that the glory of the NFL only comes from hard, focused work each day on the practice field. If you're lucky, you might have a chance to get some autographs. Be sure to bring a pen (a Sharpie is best), paper, old program, or Steeler's memorabilia for the players to sign! A wonderful children's area offers face painting with Steeler's logos,

photo boards and 3-D player props, plus kicking, passing, and running games. From our experience, it's tough to see the practice and get autographs on the same visit. If you want autographs, stay up on the hill near the dorms by the entrance to the camp. The practices take place on the lower fields and the coaches
usually enter from the dorm driveway farthest from the entrance.

KEYSTONE STATE PARK

Latrobe (Derry) - *RD 2, Box 101 (on SR 1018, the park is three miles from SR 981/ SR 22) 15627. https://www.dcnr.pa.gov/StateParks/FindAPark/KeystoneStatePark/ Pages/default.aspx Phone: (724) 668-2939. Admission: to PA State Parks is FREE however swimming, marina and camping/lodging fees apply, with reservation or entrance.*

Camping, modern cabins, trails of all sorts, a lake, and a swimming beach provide an ideal setting for a summer outing. The park offers a variety of trails open year-round for hiking, cross-country skiing and snowshoeing. A sand beach is open summers 8:00am to sunset. A food concession is in the Beach House Complex. Visitor Center, Year-round Education & Interpretation Center, Boat Rentals, Horseback Riding, Yurts and Camping, Sledding, Fishing.

COMPASS INN MUSEUM

Laughlintown - *1386 US30 East, (3 miles east of Fort Ligonier) 15655. Phone: (724) 238-4983. www.compassinn.org. Hours: Tuesday-Sunday 11:00am-4:00pm (May-October) Admission: $14.00 adult, $12.00 senior (62+), $10.00 child (6-17). Tours: Costumed tour guides take you on a 1 1/2 hour tour. Christmastime tours in Nov/Dec. Note: ask for the scavenger hunt.*

A great chance to see a restored 1799 stagecoach stop that was a typical roadside inn - with cramped sleeping quarters. In the reconstructed cookhouse, you'll learn terms like "uppercrust" (the bottom of the bread was sooty from the stove - so the upper crust was much better). Also view the contents of The Barn & Blacksmith Shop. The tour utilizes many comparisons to modern-day things, so that students can relate the historical to the familiar while emphasizing the work children did and the important contribution this made to a family.

FORBES STATE FOREST

Laughlintown - *1291 Rt. 30E, 15655. Phone: (412) 238-9533. https://www.dcnr. pa.gov/StateForests/FindAForest/Forbes/Pages/default.aspx*

Fishing, Camping, Trails, Winter Sports.

- BLUE HOLE DIVISION - a deep hole with water appearing blue, located on Blue Hole Creek and Cole Run Falls is located a few yards west of the Cole Run Road.
- BRADDOCK DIVISION - Pine Knob is an observation point overlooking Uniontown. Cabin Hollow Rocks is an interesting rock formation. Wharton Furnace was one of the last active iron furnaces in Fayette County. Old Water-Powered Grist Mill and Ponderfield Fire Tower.
- LINN RUN DIVISION - Grove Run Spring is a walled, much used, spring. Adams Falls is a miniature water fall. Rock formations and Bluestone Quarry (stone from this quarry was used to pave the streets of Pittsburgh).
- KOOSER DIVISION - Beck Springs, Old Sawmill Site, & Kooser Fire Tower, Old Logging Railroad Grades & Bridges remain throughout the area.
- NEGRO MOUNTAIN DIVISION - many rock formations and Tarkiln is a kiln used to extract tar from the knots of pitch pine.

FORT LIGONIER

Ligonier - *200 South Market Street (US30 & SR 711) 15658. Phone: (724) 238-9701. www.fortligonier.org. Hours: Daily 10:00am-5:00pm (mid-March thru mid-November). Winters only open Friday-Sunday. Admission: $15.00 adult, $12.00 senior (62+), $8.00 child (4-17) and military. Note: reenactments in summer. Quaint town shops within walking distance - some are toy stores!*

Built by the British during the French and Indian War (1758), it was a vital link to the supply line to the West. You'll be able to view gun batteries, the very visibly and painful sharp wooden pickets of re-trenchment, the quarter master's store, a home, hospital (saws made from bone), and the commissary. Because you're free to roam in and out of buildings within the fort, it's ideal for antsy or playful children. The Museum displaying models and realistic dioramas, as well as a new audiovisual presentation about General Washington, serves as your gateway to the Fort.

FORT LIGONIER DAYS

Ligonier - Fort Ligonier. Commemorates the key battle of the French and Indian War. Hear the roar of the cannons and thunder of musketry at battle demonstrations. Visit the British and French military encampments, and journey back in time to an eighteenth century fort community. Experience the pageantry and color of Scottish Highlanders, American Provincial Troops and French Marines. Admission to fort. (second weekend of October)

IDLEWILD PARK & SOAK ZONE

Ligonier - *Route 30 East, PO Box C (I-80 to I-76, exit 9, Donegal to 711, Left at Route 30) 15658. Phone: (724) 238-3666. www.idlewild.com. Hours: Opens at 10:00am (summers). Admission: $40.00-$50.00 GENERAL for Funday Pass (age 2 and under FREE). Note: Goofy golf, rental boats extra.*

I know we boast about few amusement parks but our recent visit to Idlewild and Storybook Forest was too fun! Story Book Forest is timeless. Founded in 1878, Idlewild offers 16 unusual rides. Don't miss the Story Book Forest or the life-size tribute to Daniel Tiger's Neighborhood®, complete with the TV show's famous residents. They just aren't anywhere else! You can still meet Goldilocks, Snow White, the Old Woman in the Shoe, and even get a lollypop from the Goodship Lollypop captain. Ride a real trolley into the Neighborhood of Make-Believe. This village is like being zapped into a giant TV set!

Some other featured spots include:

- JUMPIN' JUNGLE - crawl, climb, swing, and bounce.

- SOAK ZONE - water slides, pool, Little Squirts Kiddie area.

- HOOTIN HOLLER - mining town with Cowboy shows, Old West games and food, Confusion Hill and Loyalhanna Railroad.

- OLDE IDLEWILD - roller coasters, merry-go-round, and Raccoon Lagoon kiddie rides (largest kiddie area in the US!)

School-aged kids can ride most every ride in the park and waterpark and families can bring in picnic baskets and grill. If you don't want all that fuss, they offer reasonable prices at Hootin' Holler' and the food is varied and good. Well before or after you eat, try a ride on the "Howler" replica tornado ride around a

funnel cloud. There's entertainment from foot stompin', hand clappin' music and dancing to street actors. Every part of the park is clean and easy to manage, even with younger kids. Still a great place for old-fashioned family amusement.

RAMADA INN HISTORIC LIGONIER

Ligonier - 216 West Loyalhanna Street (entrance off US 30) 15658. Phone: (724) 238-9545. https://www.wyndhamhotels.com/ramada/ligonier-pennsylvania/ramada-ligonier-pa/overview. The closest family-friendly lodging to IDLEWILD (they almost always have seasonal Family Fun Packages to Idlewild-good value). Cozy doubles to spacious kings or suites at reasonable prices. Start your day with their free hot breakfast buffet. Enjoy dinner at the casual Bistro, see the sites, or relax by the outdoor heated pool. Great food in kid-friendly atmosphere featuring steaks, seafood and salads. Kids 10 and under eat for cheap off the select children's menu. Walking distance to quaint shops and eateries or Fort Ligonier. Fees start @ $119.00_____

SIMMONS FARMS FALL PLAYLAND

McMurray - Simmons Farms, 170 Simmons Road. www.simmonsfarm.com. Petting zoo, refreshments, pumpkin patch, corn maze, pony or wagon rides. Admission. (daily in October)

For updates & travel games visit: **www.KidsLoveTravel.com**

PENNSYLVANIA MAPLE FESTIVAL

Meyersdale - US 219 Meyers Avenue Historic Buildings. www.pamaplefestival. com. Actual tapping of trees. Syrup making. Demonstrations of coopering and sugaring off in a realistic sugar camp. Pancakes and syrup served. War encampment, too. (last two weekends in March)

FALLINGWATER

Mill Run - _1491 Mill Run Road, State Route 381 (I-76 exit 91, to SR31 East to Rte 381 south. 19 miles south of the Donegal exit) 15464. Phone: (724) 329-8501. www.fallingwater.org. Hours: Daily except Wednesdays & winter holidays 10:00am-4:00pm. (mid March thru December). Closed January and February. Admission: $35.00 per person. For safety reasons, children must be at least 6 years old to tour. Tours: 45 minutes - 1 hour. If you will be bringing very young children to Fallingwater, you may use their on-site Family Room. The Family Room is an unsupervised area where a member of your party must stay with your children while you wait for your party to complete their house tour. Note: Try the guided grounds Family Tour ($25 per person) - a tour around the grounds plus activities that explain how Fallingwater stands up. Grounds only Admission is $15/person. Falling Water restaurant. Want to see more, visit nearby Kentucky Knob, in Ohiopyle._

One of the most famous houses in America - and a memorable experience that is sure to delight all ages. The Edgar Kaufmann family used to vacation on this exact spot in the woods during the summer months and loved to picnic by this waterfall. They loved it so much that they commissioned Frank Lloyd Wright (the famous architect) to build a home that would allow them to live on

this spot, but not take away from its natural beauty.

Wright commented, "I wanted you to live with the waterfall, not just look at it." The home is built from several cantilevers (stacked like Legos) that hang over the waterfall (actually - the stream goes right through the inside of the house!). Boulders were used as flooring and windows and walls on the first floor. Closer cave-like spaces were used as bedrooms. Children think Fallingwater is cool, with the waterfall, the natural landscape and all mysterious nooks and crannies throughout the house. As you tour, try to answer some questions: How many leaks in the stone? How many cantilevers in the building?

REILLY'S SUMMER SEAT FARM HARVEST FESTIVAL

Monongahela - Triple B Farms, 823 Berry Lane. www.triplebfarms.com. Petting zoo, refreshments, pumpkin patch, corn maze, pony or wagon rides. Storybook Pumpkinland - with 200 pumpkin-headed, cartoon, storybook, and nursery-rhyme characters. Rope maze. Admission. (October Weds-Friday nights & weekends)

MT. PLEASANT GLASS & ETHNIC FESTIVAL

Mt. Pleasant - Washington Street & Veterans Park. Over 100 arts, crafts and ethnic food booths. Two stages of national and regional entertainment. Parade, contests, rides and glass blowing demonstrations. https://www.facebook.com/MPGlassFestival/ (last weekend of September)

BIG MAC MUSEUM RESTAURANT

North Huntington - *9051 Route 30 (Rte. 30 just off the PA turnpike at Exit 67) 15642. Hours: Lobby open 5am to midnight. https://uncoveringpa.com/big-mac-museum*

Titled "the most tasteful museum in the world," the combo museum and restaurant features the world's largest Big Mac statue (measuring 14 feet high and 12 feet wide), and hundreds of historic artifacts and high-tech exhibits that celebrate the Big Mac, which was invented 40 years ago in Uniontown by Jim Delligatti. Say Cheese in front of the world's largest Big Mac replica and have a big bite of fun in the state-of-the-art jungle PlayPlace. While you're there, pull up a seat and enjoy a Big Mac with the inventor; race to sing the world famous tongue twisting recipe "jingle"; or just look at all the classic memorabilia on display.

OHIO PYLE STATE PARK

Ohiopyle - *PO Box 105 Rt. 381 North, Off Rt. 40 15470. Phone: (412) 329-8591. https://www.dcnr.pa.gov/StateParks/FindAPark/OhiopyleStatePark/Pages/default.aspx Admission: to PA State Parks is FREE however swimming, marina and camping/lodging fees apply. Note: Search Whitewater Raft Companies in the area.*

More than 14 miles of the Youghiogheny River Gorge churns through the heart of Ohiopyle. The famous Lower Yough, below the scenic Ohiopyle Falls, provides some of the best whitewater boating in the Eastern US. You can also hike or bike the 28-mile Youghiogheny River Trail. Ferncliff Peninsula Park - trails, flowers, trees, birds and wildlife abound. Sit in the creek bed and ride the water through two natural waterslides in Meadow Run. Parking is available adjacent to the SR 381 bridge. Visitor Center, Boat Rentals, Mountain Biking, Fishing, Trails, Winter Sports.

Pittsburgh

PITTSBURGH SPORTS

PITTSBURGH STEELERS FOOTBALL - www.
steelers.com. NFL Professional football team and
6-time Super Bowl Champs! Home games played at
Acrisure Field. Acrisure Field's horseshoe shape allows for a beautiful view
of the city's unique skyline and the Point while watching a University of Pitt
(Saturday) or Steelers (Sunday/Monday) home game. Using the guidelines
you download from the website, we found parking for cheap at a garage
across the street from the bridge to the North Shore. Once inside the park, the
bright yellow-gold seats were super comfy. We'd recommend any sports fan
going to a pro game get there at least two hours early. Pregames really set
the tone & build excitement.

PITTSBURGH PIRATES BASEBALL - (412) 321-BUCS or www.pirateball.
com. PNC Park. MLB Pittsburgh Pirates Baseball (April-September). On
game nights, the city closes the Roberto Clemente Bridge to vehicles and
street performers, vendors and pedestrians swarm the area - every other group
walking towards the stadium might very well be a family - even babies dressed in
their black and gold fan apparel. What a feeling to be part of on a nice summer's
eve. The concessions at the park are upscale fair food and many are grilled
upon ordering.

PITTSBURGH PENGUINS HOCKEY - Phone: (412) 642-PENS. http://
penguins.nhl.com/. PPG Paints Arena. National Hockey League (October-
early April). Official home of the Stanley Cup Champions. Look for Family
Programs where kids get discount admission with paid adult.

PRIMANTI BROTHERS

Pittsburgh - www.primantibros.com. Locations are throughout Pittsburgh -

*even Heinz Field & PNC Park (gamedays & special
events). Even the shortest visit to the Steel City will
teach you that Pittsburgh pride runs deep—starting
with the Steelers, and ending with the sandwich.
Every Primanti's sandwich begins with an inch-
plus foundation of soft Italian bread. Then, it's piled
with your meat and cheese of choice, layered with
hot fries, slapped with peppered slaw, tomato, and
crowned with the second slice that somehow balances on top.*

*Primanti Sandwiches - It's all wrapped in waxed paper and given to you with a smile and offering to add Heinz 57 Sauce and Heinz mustard (it is Heinz headquarters, after all). Fries ON your sandwich AND crunchy coleslaw – crazy good. Some like classic cheesesteak meat but others prefer pastromi. Start with the classic Pitts-burger and then see where that goes...*_____

The original location is: 46 18th Street in the Strip District (open 24 hours, 7 days a week)!

SAND CASTLE

Pittsburgh - *1000 Sandcastle Drive (I-376 exit 5, west Route 837) 15120. Phone: (412) 462-6666. www.sandcastlewaterpark.com. Hours: Daily (June-Labor Day); June 11:00am-6:00pm, July & August 11:00am-7:00pm. Admission: ~$36.00 general, Junior Whitewater Pass (46 inches and under) ~$26.00 and senior (65+). Under 3 yo FREE. Parking $6.00. Tidal Wave Café buffet can be added.*

15 water slides including "Cliffhangers" pond slide and Two shotgun slides (patron rides on her/his back to a surprise ending - it drops in a free fall to the water below), giant Lazy River, Wet Willie's waterplay, Japanese tidal wave, kiddie and adult pools, Boardwalk and the world's largest hot tub. Riverplex.

PITTSBURGH IRISH FESTIVAL

Pittsburgh - Riverplex. www.pghirishfest.org. Entertainment, food, marketplace, cultural, children's activities, bingo, Irish dogs. Admission. (second weekend of September)

PITTSBURGH ZOO & AQUARIUM

Pittsburgh - *7370 Baker St (In Highland Park, SR 28 North to exit 6, follow signs) 15206. Phone: (412) 665-3640. www.pittsburghzoo.com. Hours: Daily 9:30am-6:00pm (Summer), 9:00am-5:00pm (fall/spring). Reduced hours in winter. Zoo is open year-round except Thanksgiving, Christmas, and New Year's Days. Admission: ~$20-$25 (age 2+). Parking Free. Reduced fees winter. Zipline extra. Tours: The Zoo Tram provides a covered ride through the Zoo with stops at eight different locations. Simply purchase a Tram wristband and you can board or disembark as many times as you wish. You can explore at your own pace, then proceed on the tram to your next adventure. The Tram stops at each well-marked location approximately every 20 minutes. Note: Food available. Fun "incline" escalator takes you up the hill to the zoo. FREEBIES: the PPG Kids: games, quizzes and printables. www.pittsburghzoo.org/ppgkids*

Over 4000 creatures both great and small. Natural settings with themes like: Tropical Forest, African Savanna (elephants), Water's Edge and PPG

For updates & travel games visit: **www.KidsLoveTravel.com**

Aquarium - wonderful use of glass that allows you to feel you can almost "touch" the fish. Tunnels, too!

- <u>WATER'S EDGE</u> - Stories woven by Inuit natives who live side by side with these magnificent creatures provide the introduction to the bears and their environment. Paw prints lead to the polar bear den for a nose-to-snout encounter when the bears lounge in this temperature-controlled climate. Two large viewing windows intensify the excitement of seeing the young bears as they splash in their freshwater waterfall and play in their dig yard. 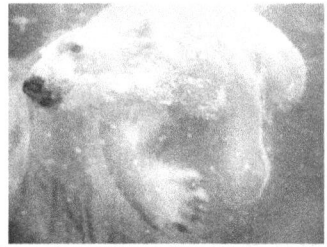 The paw prints continue down a nature trail to Pier Town, a replica of an Alaskan fishing village. The setup actually allows you to look above, beside and below the water in a cute seaside town motif. Wow!

- <u>KIDS KINGDOM</u> - Where kids can act like animals! This interactive facility is complete with playground equipment that replicates animal motions and behaviors so kids can play like the animals play. It's also full of hands-on animal experiences, like the walk-through Deer Yard & Kangaroo Yard. There's also a friendly Goat Yard, the meerkat exhibit through a see-through tunnel, beaver and otter exhibits and a fabulous sea lion pool featuring several of these playful marine mammals. Swing-like spiders, Turtle Race, Penguin Slide, or climb through Mole Tunnel (big hits with the kiddies!).

Another popular place to mark on your checklist of things to do: feeding time at the Bear habitat or with the Penguins!

THE FRICK ART & HISTORICAL CENTER

Pittsburgh - *7227 Reynolds Street (I-376, Exit # 9) 15208. Phone: (412) 371-0600. www.frickart.org. Hours: Tuesday-Sunday 10:00am-5:00pm. Reservations suggested holiday weekends. Admission: FREE. Clayton is $15.00. Reduced for Family Days tours. $8.00 students.*

Henry Clay Frick's (industrialist & art collector) mansion (Clayton) with original possessions, gardens, art museum and children's playhouse (now the Visitor's Center). Check out the floorboards that were once the bowling alley. Kids will love the pretend food displayed in the dining rooms and Helen's bedroom. Family Days (ages 6-12) teach about late 1800s life in Pittsburgh with a hands-on activity (dress up or craft) after the shortened tour with teen docents. The best theme tour for kids is: Growing Up at Clayton or something similar. Every room features a special "touchable" item, from a swatch of red velvet very like Mrs. Frick's chaise longue to stereoscopes and curious household tools. Got a question? They want your children to be actively engaged as you learn about growing up in Pittsburgh over 100 years ago.

CHRISTMAS OPEN HOUSE

Pittsburgh - The Frick Art & Historical Center. Tours of decorated, historical buildings. Refreshments and musical entertainment. Admission. Reservations suggested. (third Thursday in November - early January, Tuesday-Sunday)

DUQUESNE INCLINE

Pittsburgh - *1197 West Carson St (use either West Carson Street, or the Station Square access road which parallels the Monongahela and Ohio rivers) 15211. Phone: (412) 381-1665. www.duquesneincline.org Hours: Monday-Saturday 5:30am-12:30am. Sundays and Major Holidays 7:00am-12:30am. Admission: $1.25-$2.50 (age 6+) - Fares are each way. Seniors (age 65+) are FREE. Free parking at lower station.*

One of the few remaining cable cars still in use. Look for the red lights heading up the hill and the wood carved, paneled and trimmed cars. The cars climb

and descend 400 ft at a 30 degree angle. The Upper Station, on Grandview Avenue, includes a new platform for the public to view the Incline's historic hoisting equipment, as well as displays regarding the history of the Incline and the City of Pittsburgh, and pictures of other cable and rail cars from around the world. The observation platform outside has the best view of the city.

CARNEGIE SCIENCE CENTER

Pittsburgh - *One Allegheny Avenue (near Stadium - off I-279 or I-376) 15212. Phone: (412) 237-3400. www.carnegiesciencecenter.org. Hours: Wednesday-Sunday 10:00am-5:00pm. Admission: $25.00 adult, $20.00 senior (65+), $15.00 child (3-12). General admission includes exhibits, SportsWorks, Buhl Planetarium and USS Requin. Omnimax & Laser Fantasy Show extra. $5.00 parking. Note: XPlor Store. Restaurant café. Educators: fun, downloadable Educator Guides are found here: www.carnegiesciencecenter.org/educators/educator-web-resources/*

Bringing the world of science alive, the Carnegie Science Center is for visitors of all ages. This Science Center features more than 400 hands-on exhibits, three live demonstration theaters, a four-story IMAX Dome theater, an interactive planetarium, a 36,000 square foot science-of sport exhibition, a Cold War submarine moored on Pittsburgh's Ohio River, and a world-renowned model railroad display. Over 250 hands-on exhibits! Here's a menu of what you can expect at this fun-filled science center:

- BRICKSBURGH - Take on the roles of architect, artist, engineer, and builder at brick activity tables, stocked with thousands of bricks!
- PLANETARIUM - Keeps you on "an edge". Laser light shows.
- WW II SUBMARINE - Climb aboard the authentic USS Reguin. See demonstrations on dives, power generators, even touch a real torpedo!
- SCIENCE STAGE & WORKS THEATER - Push a button to create a 4 ft. tornado or learn cooking chemistry. Lots of waves and air here!
- Mars: The Next Giant Leap. Imagine a human settlement and consider how to solve the questions that face life on Earth when you create a new society on Mars.
- H2Oh! - Learn about river habitats and water play table.
- SPORTWORKS - Experience virtual reality basketball and pitching cage. Cruise down Olympic bobsleds, hang glide the Grand Canyon or mini-golf Math. 60 + interactives. Family-interactive.

- BODYWORKS - Rotate your brain, save a patient, look inside, or trick your senses.
- MINIATURE RAILROAD & VILLAGE - Huge re-created village connecting the culture of southwestern PA between late 1800s and the 1930s.

CHILDREN'S MUSEUM OF PITTSBURGH

Pittsburgh - 10 Children's Way - Allegheny Square (off I-279, follow signs - just blocks from the stadium) 15212. Phone: (412) 322-5058. www.pittsburghkids.org. Hours: Daily 10:00am-5:00pm. MuseumLab open Saturday & Sunday Noon-5:00pm. Admission: $16-$18.00 (ages 2+). Parking extra. Note: Café offers lunch. The Nursery Area for infants/toddlers. Changing Lower Level Gallery. Gift Shop.

Children learn more when their parents are interacting with them as opposed to standing back and watching. So, moms and dads, grandmas and grandpas, be prepared for family centered spaces. The expanded Museum offers exhibits based on the philosophy of "Play with Real Stuff." Many of the new exhibits are interactive art.

Here are some favorites:

- <u>GARAGE AND WORKSHOP</u> - Roll up your sleeves and get busy, because the Garage/Workshop is a place where you can build things and take things apart, see how machinery and engines run, and learn how to fix them when they don't. You can also climb a rope net to go high into the planetarium dome on a platform where you can launch parachutes and use a pulley to bring them back up (funny, we saw more dads "supervising" this than kids). A giant slide brings you back to the ground floor. Tinkering is the rule.

- <u>BACKYARD</u> - The Backyard (outdoors) has clever interactive sculpture where you become part of the sculpture's movement and maybe even make music by your actions. Bubbling Mud has clay you "boil" to fit your mood - a babbling brook or an explosion.

- <u>KINDNESS GALLERY</u> - Loved Mr. Rogers Neighborhood? Try different forms of communication to send messages of kindness, drawing from the work of beloved Fred Rogers, and lessons from Daniel Tiger's Neighborhood. And, favorites like the Gravity Room and Animateering are here too.

- <u>WATERPLAY</u> - The River is so unique as its the only one we've seen with walk in water play spaces. RainCoats and Boots are required because you might build a water fountain to the sky and then want to jump around in it.

© Albert VecerkaEsto

Make sure you interact with some art while you're here. You can have some psychedelic visual fun with Text Rain or Arc Tangent - playing with walls and floors is always fun!

ACRISURE FIELD TOURS

Pittsburgh - *100 Art Rooney Avenue 15212. Phone: Tour Hotline (412) 697-7150. https://acrisurestadium.com/stadium/tours/. Admission: $10 adult. Highlight Tour/Public Tours April-October. Public Tour must be made at least 24 hours prior to a scheduled tour time. Stadium Experiences are available Wednesday - Monday from 11:00am-4:00pm. Not available on Tuesdays and on University of Pittsburgh home game days. Meet under the Honor sign located on Art Rooney Ave by 15 min beforehand. Tours are not conducted holidays or event days.*

Heinz Field is not only the home of the Pittsburgh Steelers and the University of Pittsburgh Panthers football teams but a proud icon in downtown Pittsburgh. Tours of the Field consist of the Great Hall, club &suite levels, press box, players lockerroom, and exit with a good-luck touch on a large football plaque tacked with letters that spell "Men of Steel.", walk into/around the field, etc. The Hall of Honor is the biggest treat: From the Six Championship trophies to the Immaculate Reception by Franco Harris in 1972 to the personal artifacts in famous players lockers (ex. Bradshaw, Swann).

NATIONAL AVIARY

Pittsburgh - *Allegheny Commons West (off I-279 North Shore exit - follow signs) 15212. Phone: (412) 323-7235. www.aviary.org. Hours: Daily 10am-5pm. (everyday but Christmastime & Thanksgiving). Admission: $17.95 adult, $16.95 senior (60+) & $14.95 child (2-12). Note: Get up-close-and-personal with African Penguin "Stanley" or resident owls daily right before or after lunchtime.*

At the National Aviary on Pittsburgh's North Side, visitors can meet African penguins, flamingos, and many more colorful birds. See 220 species of birds living in natural habitats like rainforests, deserts, and marshes. The tropical areas have rare, exotic birds in free-flight atriums. Favorites to look for are the live Toucan (so animated, it appears mechanical!), a real cuckoo bird (that sings a loud, sweet sound), and the funny billed marsh birds (boat & spoon shaped). The Tropical Rainstorm at 12:30pm daily in the Wetlands of the Americas huge walk-through exhibit is so-o-o cool!

SOLDIERS & SAILORS MEMORIAL MUSEUM

Pittsburgh - *4141 Fifth Avenue 15213. www.soldiersandsailorshall.org. Phone: (412) 621-4254. Hours: Monday-Saturday 10:00am-4:00pm. Admission: $15.00 adult, $10.00 senior (55+), $5.00 child (5-17). Military, Veterans and family of those deployed and their guests are invited to visit the museum at no cost.*

Soldiers & Sailors National Military Museum & Memorial is one of the country's largest museums dedicated to honoring & remembering our Veterans. The museum houses exhibits that span from the Civil War to present day conflicts that tell the stories of ordinary citizens called upon to do extraordinary duties for the United States of America. Also African-American and Revolutionary War films. Their goal is not to idealize war but to honor and educate about the sacrifices during it. Interesting perspective.

ALLEGHENY OBSERVATORY

Pittsburgh - *159 Riverview Avenue (US19 in Riverview Park off Perrysville Avenue) 15214. Phone: (412) 321-2400. www.pitt.edu/~aobsvtry/. Hours: Thursday-Friday (by appointment - evenings - April - October). Admission: FREE. Tours: All tours begin at 8:00pm and last until approximately 10:00pm.*

One of the foremost observatories in the world. A short film presentation is shown followed by a walking tour of the building, ending up at the 13" Fitz-Clark refractor. If it's a clear night you will be shown whatever celestial objects are within range of the telescope that night. Dress for the temperature outside.

GATEWAY CLIPPER FLEET

Pittsburgh - *Station Square Dock - 350 W Station Square Drive (I-376 exit Smithfield Street) 15219. Phone: (412) 355-7980. www. gatewayclipper.com. Admission: Average $30.00 adult, $15.00 child (1-12) signtseeing. Add $10.00-$20.00 for lunch or dinner cruises. Tours: Sightseeing / Theme cruises usually depart between 11:00am-4:00pm (except Sunset at 7:00pm). Note: On board gift shop/snacks.*

The "Pittsburgh River Tradition" has sightseeing cruises sailing the three rivers. They are the largest and most successful sightseeing vessels in the America. There are several different boats in their fleet (all climate controlled) and many targeted toward ages 12 and under. These include Sunday Fun Cruises (w/ DJ Dance), Princess, Pirate or Pups Cruise (characters), Lock N Dam Adventure Cruises and 2 hour Sunset Cruises. Other mascots who frequent kids' cruises are Deckster Duck, and River Rover.

EASTER BUNNY BOAT RIDES

Pittsburgh - Gateway Clipper Fleet. Candy treats with the Easter Bunny riding along. Easter crafts, DJ Dance Party. Admission. (Easter Weekend)

SANTA FAMILY FUN CRUISES

Pittsburgh - Gateway Clipper Fleet. 2 hours of DJ Dance Party with costumed mascots, visit from Santa with treat, and make your own ornaments. Admission(Dec. weekends)

GRAND CONCOURSE RESTAURANT

Pittsburgh - 100 West Station Square Drive 15219. Kids Menu in the magnificent 1901 Victorian Train Station (kids like trying to find unique stained glass window themes) consists of items like pasta, chicken, fish, shrimp, burgers and grilled cheese. A great way to take in the "flavor" of old Pittsburgh at a real train station. Lunch/Dinner daily, Sunday brunch. www.muer.com/grand-concourse/ 🍽

MONONGAHELA INCLINE

Pittsburgh - *Carson Street at Station Square 15219. Phone: (412) 442-2000. https://monongahelaincline.com/   Hours: Monday-Saturday 5:30am-12:45am, Sunday & Holidays 8:45am to midnight. Admission: $2.50-$3.50 round trip.*

The first US incline...boasting a 35 degree climbing angle and 358 foot elevation, this incline transports tourists and commuters daily from downtown to Mt. Washington. A special note
to point out to the kids is that this
engineering feat was designed in
1870 - before electric streetcars and
the automobile! The trick is that one
car climbs while the other descends
- look for the green and yellow lights
highlighting the track.

FORT PITT MUSEUM & POINT STATE PARK

Pittsburgh - *101 Commonwealth Place (off I-376, I-279, SR8, or SR51 on the forks of downtown, Ohio River) 15222. Phone: (412) 281-9284. www.dcnr.state. pa.us/stateparks/findapark/point/ Hours: Daily 10:00am-5:00pm. Admission to Fort Museum: $8.00 adult, $7.00 senior (60+), $4.50 student/child (6-17). FREE admission to park. Fee parking lot. Note: Blockhouse welcome center and gift shop (free to visit). Living history re-enactments (Summer-Sunday afternoons).*

This was the site of the largest British post in North America until they were forced to leave during the American Revolution. The fort played a pivotal role in the French and Indian War. Exhibits re-create the story of war, trade, and the founding of Pittsburgh. Listen to a taped explanation of the fort while viewing a scale model of Fort Pitt. A large diorama on the first floor contains a model of the fort. There's also an 18th century trading post.

Located at the tip of Pittsburgh's Golden Triangle, POINT STATE PARK has a fabulous water fountain, paved promenades along the riverfront & overlooks with dramatic views of the city, busy waterways, and impressive hillside. The traceries of both Fort Duquesne and Fort Pitt are lit by LED lights for a spectacular view at night. The original location of the rivers edge during the mid-1700s is depicted by a granite tracery within the Great Lawn area. Wayside exhibits and interpretive programs are planned for the park and are listed within the Point State Park Interpretive Plan.

PITTSBURGH THREE RIVERS REGATTA

Pittsburgh - Fort Pitt Museum & Point State Park. http://yougottaregatta.org/ Downtown rivers and shores host the world's largest inland regatta. Air shows, powerboat races, hot air balloon races, fireworks and water-skiing demos. FREE. (first wkend in August).

HEINZ HISTORY CENTER

Pittsburgh - *1212 Smallman Street (in the Strip District, off I-376, Grant Street exit) 15222. Phone: (412) 454-6000. www.heinzhistorycenter.org. Hours: Daily 10:00am-5:00pm. Closed Easter, Thanksgiving, Christmas, New Years. Admission: $18 adult, $15 senior (62+), $9 student & child (6-17). Note: Museum shop, café. Educators: assorted links to curriculum: http://archives.dreamhosters.com/*

The initiative of this museum is to preserve Western Pennsylvania history through intriguing exhibits such as:

*   GREAT HALL - 1949 restored trolley with audio and a Conestoga wagon. ISALY's Dairy (Klondikes!) and a greeting from a robot that speaks fluent Pittsburghese.

*   PITTSBURGH: A TRADITION OF INNOVATION: Come face-to-face with a king of empire, Indians and inventors. Talk to George Washington, take a ride on America's First Superhighway or a sneak peak at innovations of the future.

*   SPECIAL COLLECTIONS - Emphasis is placed on Steelworkers who were immigrants. Meet Mary, the mother of 5 children and married to a steelworker. Or, an African American journey to Freedom. Neighborhood - Displays use ethnic costumes, toys, vehicles - even clothing - Mr. Roger's sweater and sneakers to be exact. From the invention of the airbrake and automobile shock absorbers to the development of railroad signaling and the modern day weekend are all part of Western Pennsylvania's 250 year history of innovation. Audio players featuring local Pittsburgh personalities help to tell the stories behind many of the items so kids will engage in the items vs. passing by.

*   WESTERN PENNSYLVANIA SPORTS MUSEUM - includes high school, collegiate, and professional sports in the Pittsburgh region (go Steelers!). A place where you can enjoy the great works of Maz and Mario. Art and Arnie. Roberto and Franco. Suzie and Swin. A place where you can relive the moments that made them great. The Immaculate Reception. The Home Run. Olympic gold. Super Bowls. Stanley Cups. The space promises to "get you in the game" with more than 70 hands-on interactive exhibits, a two-story video theatre and 20 audio-visual programs for visitors of all ages. The Interactive Football Exhibit, Make Your Own Medal, and Franco Harris' Immaculate Reception Shoes are the highlights for kids.

*   DISCOVERY PLACE – Design a piece of pop art, create a rocketship and watch it fly in the wind tunnel, and build bridges using massive foam blocks in the engineering playground!

- HEINZ - Three stations depict the lives of children who grew up in Western Pennsylvania, including a touch-screen, interactive trivia game called "Get to the Point" that challenges visitors to use their new found knowledge of Pittsburgh innovations. Kids can "go to work" and climb through a steel mill. Children even as young as 12-14 were laborers – learn how some of them did their jobs (ex. packing pickles for Heinz or ironing clothes for pennies).

- KIDSBURGH - Kidsburgh is an fun, interactive, two-tier playplace. Children will enjoy serving up Isaly's "ice cream" at their own play deli and milking a full-scale fiberglass "mooing" cow above Reymer's Old-Fashioned Deli. An interactive model of Pittsburgh allows kids to design their own city of Pittsburgh using models of buildings, boats, and sports stadiums. When they're done, kids can zoom down a 12-foot spiral slide, nicknamed the "Liberty Tube."

Pittsburgh should be very proud and touched by this emotional history center!

SOCIETY FOR CONTEMPORARY CRAFTS

Pittsburgh - *2100 Smallman Street (Strip District) 15222. Phone: (412) 261-7003. www.contemporarycraft.org. Hours: Monday-Saturday 10:00am-4:00pm. Admission: FREE.*

Visitors discover latest trends in the gallery, the store and the children's studio. Weekends for Families include demos, performances and workshops related to current exhibits. Because families are one of their primary audiences, they have developed the Drop In Studio, a free hands-on activity area for children and adults. The space, which is open during all public hours, allows visitors to participate in a hands-on art activity that has been developed by artists to tie-in to the special exhibitions.

STRIP DISTRICT DINING

Pittsburgh - *15222.*

The Strip District is several city blocks at the edge of downtown offering enticing food markets, coffee shops, restaurants and quirky shops (ex. a store that makes and sells handmade giant crayons that actually work).

Start your day with breakfast at PAMELA'S (60 21st Street, 412-281-6366, www.pamelasdiner.com).Serving Breakfast and Lunch everyday, most meals around $5. Try the crepe hotcakes or french toast w/ chocolate & bananas.

After shopping and lunch, bring your crew into KLAVON'S ORIGINAL ART DECO SODA FOUNTAIN (Penn Avenue & 28th Street, www.klavonsicecream.com). They serve old-fashioned ice cream treats and "penny" candy.

For lunch, choose <u>PRIMANTI BROTHERS</u>. Pitts-burger sandwich. We just love local flare on sandwiches and this one has fries ON the sandwich NOT on the side! (check it out under separate listing.www.primantibros.com).

And, if you get lost meandering Pittsburgh streets around construction zones, just stop a native and they'll be glad to help you find your way. Some even wrote a map on napkins, others volunteered to drive ahead with us following.

BICYCLE HEAVEN

Pittsburgh - *RJ Casey Industrial Park, 1800 Preble & Columbus Ave, Pittsburgh, PA 15233. Phone: (412) 734-4034. www.bicycleheaven.org Hours: Open 7 Days A Week 10am - 7pm. Admission: FREE.*

Bicycle Heaven Museum is the world's largest bicycle museum & shop. You can get your bike fixed, tuned up, or trade it in for a newer (or older) bicycle. They also rent out bikes. You can see their bikes in movies such as: A Beautiful Mind, Super 8, Fathers & Daughters, Fences and many others. On display in the museum is a bike from the movie Pee-wee's Big Adventure! They have the Bowden Spacelander, the first fiberglass bike made and one of the most sought after bicycles. Only 30 or so to be found, Bicycle Heaven has 17. We have close to 6,000 bicycles vintage to new under one roof.

BEECHWOOD FARM NATURE PRESERVE

Pittsburgh - *614 Dorseyville Road (SR8 & SR28) 15238. Phone: (412) 963-6100. www.aswp.org/pages/beechwood/ Hours: Tuesday-Saturday, 9:00am-5:00pm. Sunday, 1:00-5:00pm. Admission: FREE.*

Headquarters of the Audubon Society of Western Pennsylvania. Acres of fields, woodlands, ponds, and trails. Beechwood's 134 acres contain more than five miles of walking trails, which are open to the public from dawn to dusk everyday, year-round. The Bird observation room, Discovery Room & Outdoor Discovery field programs are favorites for kids.

INTERNATIONAL CHILDREN'S THEATER FESTIVAL

Pittsburgh - Allegheny Center, North Shore. https://pghkids.trustarts.org/ Indoor main stage performances by world class professional theater companies along with outdoor stages, strolling performers, workshops, and recreational, educational, & cultural activities. Admission. (second week of May)

PITTSBURGH VINTAGE GRAND PRIX

Pittsburgh - Schenley Park. www.pittsburghvintagegrandprix.com. Racing and car shows. Run by volunteers with proceeds benefiting mentally retarded and autistic children and adults. (starts third weekend in July thru fourth weekend race)

PITTSBURGH LIGHT UP NIGHTS

Pittsburgh - Downtown. www.downtownpittsburgh.com/holidays. Celebrate the holiday season in downtown Pittsburgh! Over 1,000 displays, performances, activities & events - many free! Boat rides (www.gatewayclipper.com). Wintergarden Santa Display & outdoor Ice Rink at PPG Center. Nativity Scene at US Steel. Holly Trolley; Polar Express and Mini RR & village (Science Center). Includes Parade, fireworks and carriage rides. Admission (every Saturday from 3rd week Nov - 1st week of Jan)

MEADOWCROFT ROCKSHELTER & VILLAGE

Pittsburgh (Avella) - *401 Meadowcroft Road (I-79 - Exit 11 Bridgeville to SR50 West) 15312. Phone: (724) 587-3412. https://www.heinzhistorycenter.org/visit/ meadowcroft/. Hours: Wednesday-Sunday 10:00am-4:00pm (Memorial Day-Labor Day). Weekends only (May, September, October). Open some weekends in November and December for special events. Admission: $15.00 adult, $14.00 senior (62+), $7.00 (6-17) Rural Life Museum, Village and Rockshelter. Note: Visitors Center and Café. Best during festivals for" hands on history".*

Re-live rugged rural life from 200 years ago as you walk the dirt and stone roads of this reconstructed village. By touring a settler log house, schoolhouse, country store, barn and blacksmith shop - you'll be introduced to inhabitants like the Native Americans, frontier settlers, farmers, lumbermen, coal miners, and conservationists who have worked the land. Get involved by taking a real school lesson (with slate and chalk) in a 1 room schoolhouse. Shear sheep and then spin and weave wool.

Meadowcroft Rockshelter has provided archaeologists with a rare glimpse into the lives of the first people to arrive in the New World. Visitors may go inside the open excavation and see evidence of tools and campfires made by these first Americans thousands of years ago. Discover how these ancient people survived - from what they ate to the weapons they relied on everyday - and, actually practice using a Native American "atlatl" (spear throwing).

JULY 4TH CELEBRATIONS

Pittsburgh (Avella) - Meadowcroft Rockshelter And Village. Parades, music, food, fireworks and contests. Historical patriotic activities. Admission.

RURAL HERITAGE DAYS

Pittsburgh (Avella) - Meadowcroft Village. Tractor pulls, antique steam engines, parades, food (made with steam), threshing, baling, cider and apple butter making, hayrides, petting zoo & fall crafts. Admission. (third weekend in October)

TAFFY PARTIES

Pittsburgh (Avella) - Meadowcroft Village. Taffy pulling party in log house, holiday programs in one-room schoolhouse. Make an ornament.(mid-Nov & early Dec wkend)

LITTLE LAKE THEATRE COMPANY

Pittsburgh (Canonsburg) - *500 Lakeside Drive, South 15317. Phone: (724) 745-6300. www.littlelake.org.*

Plays for the entire family for 50 years. Looking Glass Theatres, Fall Family Matinees. Youth plays run $15.00-$25.00 per person.

PITTSBURGH'S PA MOTOR SPEEDWAY

Pittsburgh (Carnegie) - *(US 22/30, Noblestown Exit) 15106. Phone: (724) 853-RACE. www.ppms.com.*

Auto Racing every Saturday Night, April through mid-September featuring the Super Late Models, Advance Auto Parts Crate Late Models, Pure Stocks, E-Mods, Amateur Stocks, Young Guns, and Demos on Dirt's Monster Half Mile. Visit their Sister Track Motordrome Speedway on Friday Evenings for exciting NASCAR Dodge Weekly Series Action. Tickets run $15.00. Their slogan: "We'll sell you the whole seat, but you'll only need the edge!"

PITTSBURGH HOLIDAY TRAIN SHOW

Pittsburgh (Gibsonia) - 5507 Lakeside Drive (I-79N exit Wexford to Rte. 910 east & Hardt Road). www.wpmrm.org. Holiday Miniature railroad displays the transportation systems in Pittsburgh during the 1950's. Accent on coal, steel, and steam production. Admission. (Fri evenings & weekends, mid-Nov- early Jan)

BOYCE PARK SKI AREA

Pittsburgh (Monroeville) - *675 Old Frankstown Road (near U.S. 22 and right off of I-76) 15639. www.alleghenycounty.us/parks/bpfac.aspx. Phone: (724) 733-4656. Snow Report: (724) 733-4665.*

This ski area may be tiny and run by a county park, but lift tickets are inexpensive ($9.00 weekdays and $13.00 weekends). The park offers nine runs including moguls, halfpipe, timing runs with gates, jumps and night skiing. Lodge with a roaring fireplace, hot food and drinks. There's also a fitness center, roller skating, swimming, outdoor hot tubs, snow tubing, sleigh rides and even bowling.

CARNEGIE MUSEUM OF ART

Pittsburgh (Oakland) - *4400 Forbes Avenue (connected to Natural History Museum) 15213. Phone: (412) 622-3131. www.cmoa.org Hours: Wednesday-Monday 10:00am-5:00pm. Open until 8:00pm on Thursdays. Admission: $25.00 adult, $20.00 senior (65+), $15.00 child (age 3-18). Admission includes Carnegie Museum of Natural History. Note: Café for lunch.*

Check out whatever new exhibit is on display at the art museum - we saw packing tape philosophical art. Very funky and fun. With every kid visit, be sure to pick up a gallery search scavenger hunt card. Complete them and stop back for a prize at the end of your visit. ARTventures pop up artmaking stations change often. Paintings, sculpture, film and video projections reflect ideas from cultures long ago and today. Hall of Sculpture. Hall of Architecture. Add this museum to your visit to the Museum of Natural History (included).

CARNEGIE MUSEUM OF NATURAL HISTORY

Pittsburgh (Oakland) - *4400 Forbes Avenue (I-579 to Oakland/Monroeville exit to Blvd. Of the Allies OR I-376E to Forbes Ave exit 2a) 15213. Phone: (412) 622-3131. www.carnegiemnh.org. Hours: Wednesday-Monday 10:00am-5:00pm. Thursdays open until 8:00pm. Admission: $25.00 adult, $20.00 senior (65+), $15.00 child (3-18). Admission includes same-day access to Carnegie Museum of Art. Note: Store, café. Earth Theater. Family Programs on weekends. Educators: www.carnegiemnh.org/exhibitions/extras/. Discovery Basecamp and Discover Carts & Exploration Stations are hands-on. BioTech Lab is often open for families.*

See a world famous dinosaur collection with a T-Rex and 9 other species plus a PaleoLab and Bonehunters Quarry (Dino Hall fossil digs). You won't want to miss the Natural History's "revamp" of their dinosaur collection - "Dinosaurs in their Time". Take a few moments observing the Paleo Lab where actual dino doctors work on real pieces. The exhibits showcase cast bones in natural settings with bright, contemporary lighting (not old dark hallways). Parts of the path allow guests to walk under the huge tails of several dinos.

...all aboard, the "Stratavator"

In the Stratavator, a simulated elevator ride takes you 16,000 feet down into the Earth below the museum. The stratavator stops at the museum's basement storage rooms, a coal mine, a limestone cave, and other geological features. As the cab vibrates, rock strata whiz by. American Indians Hall examines the beliefs, philosophies, and practical knowledge that guide Indian people. Polar World illustrates the Arctic environment and the Inuit way of life. Scenes depict kayak hunting, ice fishing, and a life-size recreation of an Inuit snowhouse. Additional sites include Egyptian mummies and a crawl-thru Egyptian tomb; a Discovery Room (hands-on); Hall of Botany; and the Hall of Minerals and Gems (fluorescent minerals, crystals). Watch, around every corner you may be greeted by a giant surprise!

PHIPPS CONSERVATORY

Pittsburgh (Oakland) - *One Schenley Park (I-376 East, take the Forbes Ave./ Oakland exit 2a). 15213. Phone: (412) 622-6914. www.phipps.conservatory.org. Hours: Daily 9:30am-5:00pm, Hours extended to 10:00pm on Friday. Admission: $13.95-$21.95 (age 2+). Tours: FREE docent-led tours occur daily right before or after lunchtime. Summer-Butterfly Forest. Christmas candlelight tours.*

A historic landmark 13 room Victorian glass house featuring tropical and desert motifs plus one of the nation's finest Bonsai collections. Feel the heat in the desert or smell the wafting fragrance in the Orchid Room. Explore the Amazon Rainforest or try to spy Chihuly glass. Discovery Garden - outdoor hands-on learning for children (boxwood maze, sensory garden). Visit a Discovery Table in the Conservatory for a hands-on, fun look at a specific subject.

PITTSBURGH PLAYHOUSE JR.

Pittsburgh (Oakland) - *222 Craft Avenue 15213. Phone: (412) 621-4445. https:// playhouse.pointpark.edu/about/our-companies/aboutPlayhouseJr $10 seats.*

Over 50 years of children's classics like Snow White or Winnie-the-Pooh (Nov - May). Playhouse Jr. brings children and young adults into the world of imagination through live theatre with fairy tales, modern and timeless stories adapted for young audiences and classics from children's literature. The productions are crafted to be family friendly for children of all ages.

RODEF SHALOM BIBLICAL GARDENS

Pittsburgh (Oakland) - *4905 Fifth Ave. 15213. www.rodefshalombiblicalgarden.org.*
Phone: (412) 621-6566. Hours: Sunday-Thursday 10:00am-2:00pm. (June - mid-
Sept) . FREE

The garden is the largest of its kind in North America (1/3 acre) and the only
one with an ongoing program of research. Visit the land of the Bible in a
setting of a waterfall, a desert, a stream, the Jordan, which meanders through
the garden from Lake Galilee to the Dead Sea. All plants are labeled with
biblical verses accompanying them. See wheat, barley, millet and many herbs
grown by the ancient Israelites along with olives, dates, pomegranates, figs.

CATHEDRAL OF LEARNING NATIONALITY ROOMS

Pittsburgh (Oakland) - *1209 Cathedral of Learning (I-376 west to exit 7A,*
University of Pittsburgh) 15260. Phone: (412) 624-6000. www.pitt.edu/~natrooms/.
Hours: Monday-Saturday 9:00am-4:00pm, Sunday 11:00am-4:00pm. Admission:
$10.00 adult, $6.00 child (6-18). Tours: 90 minute guided or tape recorded tours.
Please request a tour that is adapted to younger audiences. Their Christmas Open
House is wonderous. Note: While of campus, musically inclined may want to visit
the Stephen Foster Memorial Museum (ex. Foster's piano, musical instruments
and compositions. www.pitt.edu/~amerimus/museum.htm).

"Tour the World in 90 Minutes!" - Visit 24 classrooms depicting heritages of
different ethnic communities. Inspiration flows from such varied sources as
Athens in the time of Pericles, a palace hall in Beijing's Forbidden City, an
ancient monastic Indian university, flowers that grow in Czech and Slovak
valleys, a 6th-century oratory from Ireland's Golden Age, an Asante temple
courtyard in Ghana, London's House of Commons, and the intimate hearth-
centered life of America's early New Englanders.

See authentic examples of cultural architecture and décor from Africa, Asia,
Middle East, and Eastern and Western Europe including: Ukrainian Room –
wood carvings on beams and doors, hand painted pottery and tile. German
- stained glass fairy tales. African - Sankofa birds. University classes meet
in the classrooms from early morning to late at night, amidst surroundings
designed to enhance learning and engage the senses. A steady stream of
people -- often families of three generations -- come to see the world-famous
rooms, which evoke pride in their own heritage and warm appreciation of other
cultures. I don't think there's anything like it.

KENNYWOOD PARK

Pittsburgh (West Mifflin) - *4800 Kennywood Blvd. (I-376, Exit 9) 15122. Phone: (412) 461-0500. www.kennywood.com. Hours: Monday-Sunday 10:30am-after dark (Mid-May - Labor Day). Open some weekends in early May & early September. Admission: All day general passes available ~$60. Discounted ~ $20 or more (Junior and senior passes). Good online deals. Children 2 and under are FREE. Parking is free. After 5:00pm reduced Night Rider $27.00. Note: Shoes, shirts, pants or shorts are required in all parts of the park. If your family plans to ride the water rides, you may want to bring an extra set of clothes because the water rides WILL get you WET! Comfortable shoes and appropriate clothing to keep you warm/cool as temperatures change throughout the day are recommended. Lockers are available in the park for $1.00 per entrance.*

Known as "America's Finest Traditional Amusement Park," Kennywood was established in 1898 near Pittsburgh. Kennywood brings the old-fashioned amusement park feel into the 21st century with the towering "Steel Curtain" roller coaster. With a record-breaking 9 inversions, 197 foot-tall loop, and 220-foot maximum height, "Steel Curtain" is an adrenaline rush like no other, speeding across 4,000 feet of track at 75 miles per hour (adjoining it is a Steelers football training camp inspired play/train area). The park features thirty-one major rides, including three water rides, three classic wood coasters, the Phantom's Revenge steel coaster, and a one-of-a-kind indoor, dark coaster, the Exterminator. Kiddieland offers 14 "just for kids" rides. Home of the world's fastest coaster, live shows, arcades, mini-golf, paddle boats, and Lost Kennywood Lagoon area. Thomas Town is huge and features four family rides based on characters from the beloved program, and a life-sized Thomas the Tank Engine™ traveling on a redesigned Olde Kennywood Railroad. In addition, Kennywood still maintains two of its original 1898 buildings, housing the carousel pavilion and restaurant. Want to take a break? Sit around the Dancing Waters for a while.

LINN RUN STATE PARK

Rector - *Linn Run Road (US 30east & PA Rte. 81south) 15677. Phone: (412) 238-6623. https://www.dcnr.pa.gov/StateParks/FindAPark/LinnRunStatePark/Pages/default.aspx. Admission: FREE however swimming, marina rentals & camping/lodging fees apply.*

The varied topography and mixed hardwood and evergreen forest make this park a scenic place for picnicking, hiking and cabin rentals. Grove and Rock runs join to make Linn Run, an excellent trout stream which has a waterfall, Adams Falls. Several trails are short - Adams Falls Trail is a 1-mile loop that features a mountain waterfall tucked in among rhododendron and hemlock.

LAUREL RIDGE STATE PARK

Rockwood - *1117 Jim Mountain Road 15557. Phone: (724) 455-3744. https://www.facebook.com/laurelhighlandshikingtrail. Admission: to PA State Parks is FREE however swimming, marina and camping/lodging fees apply.*

Laurel Ridge State Park stretches along the Laurel Mountains from the Yougiogheny River at Ohiopyle to the Conemaugh Gorge near Johnstown. Most visitors come to hike the 70 miles of the Laurel Highland trails. The Laurel Highlands Hiking Trail is open year-round. Connector trails lead to and from parking and shelter areas. Mileage monuments are every mile. Pets are permitted. Snowmobiling and cross-country skiing on trails in winter.

WESTERWALD POTTERY

Scenery Hill - *40 Pottery Lane (US 40 - 7.5 miles east of I-79) 15360. Phone: (724) 945-6000. www.westerwaldpottery.com. Hours: Monday-Friday 8:30am-4:30pm. Saturday 10:00am-4:30pm, Sunday Noon-5:00pm. Admission: FREE. Tours: By appointment. Walk-ins, if you would like to watch craftsmen best to plan your visit Tuesday thru Thursday, before 3:00pm. Note: Gift shop.*

Potters making their signature country-style decorative wares are simply amazing to watch! See a pre-measured lump of clay get hand thrown on a wheel and shaped before your eyes. They make pots, plates, mugs, and cute apple bakers. The Westerwald signature is on every piece and they specialize in personalized gifts. You'll even get to see the drying (kilns bricked up for 3 days) and the artists who glaze and paint each piece by hand. The blue and gray stoneware is a reproduction quality of those made in Germany's Westerwald region as early as the 16th century. Look for a specialized name piece as a souvenir.

WEST OVERTON MUSEUMS

Scottdale - *Overholt Drive (West Overton Village - SR819) 15683. Phone: (724) 887-7910. www.westovertonvillage.org Hours: Thursday-Sunday 10:00am-4:00pm (mid-May - October). Admission: $10.00-$12.00 (age 7+).*

A 19th Century industrial village with a museum, barns, and a gristmill. Visitors to the Museum may view the film, Pillars of Fire, illustrating the process of turning coal into coke; visit the Overholt Homestead and Shop; tour two floors of the Overholt Mill/Distillery, containing a large collection of household, farm and industrial tools; see the birthplace of Henry Clay Frick (young millionaire with steel coke business); and tour the wash house and smokehouse.

FLIGHT 93 NATIONAL MEMORIAL

Shanksville (Stoystown) - *6424 Lincoln Highway (exit #110 of Turnpike), Stoystown, PA 15563 Phone: (814) 444-8339. https://www.nps.gov/flni/index.htm. Hours: Daily 9am-5pm or 7pm. FREE*

On September 11, 2001, nearly 3,000 people tragically lost their lives. Because of the actions of the 40 passengers and crew aboard one of the planes, Flight 93, the attack on the U.S. Capitol was thwarted. The site is dedicated as a memorial and tribute in honor of the heroes of Flight 93 and all others who perished that day. Everything about the design of the center is reminiscent of the story of Flight 93 and so the visual experience brings the visitor's thoughts back to that place and time. One mile away is the Plaza and crash site.

KOOSER STATE PARK

Somerset - *943 Glades Pike (PA Route 31) 15501. Phone: (814) 445-8673. https://www.dcnr.pa.gov/StateParks/FindAPark/KooserStatePark/Pages/default.aspx. Admission: to PA State Parks is FREE however swimming, marina and camping/lodging fees apply, with reservation or entrance.*

Kooser State Park is bound by Forbes State Forest on two sides and is an ideal spot to start an overnight backpacking trip on the 70-mile Laurel Highlands Hiking Trail. The early settlers told of an American Indian battle that was fought nearby and a number of war arrows and spearheads have been found in the area. A 350-foot swimming beach is open from late-May to mid-September, 8:00am to sunset. Campsites, Rustic Cabins, Fishing.

LAUREL HILL STATE PARK

Somerset - *1454 Laurel Hill Park Road (Pennsylvania Turnpike Exit 110 (Somerset), drive west on PA Rte. 31) 15501. Phone: (814) 445-7725. https://www.dcnr.pa.gov/StateParks/FindAPark/LaurelHillStatePark/Pages/default.aspx. Admission: to PA State Parks is FREE however swimming, marina and camping/lodging fees apply.*

The 63-acre Laurel Hill Lake is a focal point of the park. A beautiful stand of old growth hemlocks lies along the Hemlock Trail.

Remains of a logging railroad, like a wooden cross-tie or a rusty rail spike, can be seen along the Tramroad Trail. A 1,200-foot sandy beach is open from late-May to mid-September, 8:00am to sunset. Year-round Education & Interpretation Center, Boat Rentals, Campsites, Fishing, and Trails. Some feel this park is best in the winter with abundant snowfalls and winter sport recreation opportunities in abundance.

SOMERSET HISTORICAL CENTER

Somerset - *10649 Somerset Pike (SR601 and SR985) 15501. Phone: (814) 445-6077. www.somersethistoricalcenter.org Hours: Wednesday-Saturday 10:00am-4:00pm. Admission: $3.00-$6.00 (age 5+). Note: 12 minute film about the history of the mountain barrier area.*

This center interprets daily rural life in southwestern Pennsylvania from 1750 - 1950. Isolated because of the Allegheny Mountains, they had to produce necessities from home - maple sugar, ginseng, and furs were traded - food was produced on the farm. With the Industrial Revolution came advances in farming (hand labor to machines and commercial crops). The site includes a log house, a smokehouse, a log barn, a covered bridge, a maple sugar camp, a general store, and various machines (corn husker & shredder, reaper, buggy). Pioneer and agricultural demonstrations daily.

TOUR-ED MINE AND MUSEUM

Tarentum - *748 Bull Creek Road (SR28 north, exit 14 - Allegheny Valley Expressway) 15084. Phone: (724) 224-4720. www.tour-edmine.com. Hours: Wednesday-Sunday 10:00am - 4:00pm. (Memorial Day-Labor Day). Admission: $9.00-$9.50. Tours: approximately 1.5 hours leaving at 10am, Noon, and 2pm. Note: Cool temps- about 50 degrees F. - a jacket is suggested. Gift shop.*

Experience what it was like to be a coal miner in the 1850's and today. Your guides are experienced coal miners, who treat you to an amazing, educational tour 160 feet below the Earth's surface. Wearing required hard hats and ducking down a little, you'll board a modernized mining car as you travel 1/2 mile underground into an actual coal mine. Original mines began in 1800 when labor was all done by hand. See demos of this plus setting up a new mine area (roof supports to prevent cave-ins), and the most modern mining - a continuous miner (robotic). Above ground, you can take a stroll to the past as you view company stores, housing, strip mines, and a sawmill. They have lots of photo ops.

SEARIGHT TOLL HOUSE MUSEUM

Uniontown - *US40 west 15401. Phone: (724) 439-4422. www.hmdb.org/marker. asp?marker=257. Hours: Tuesday-Saturday 10:00am-4:00pm, Sunday 2:00-6:00pm (Mid-May - Mid-October). Admission is $1.00 for adults and children are free.*

In 1806, the National Road began construction connecting the East and West. Searight Tollhouse received its name from its location near the village of Searight, named for its most prominent citizen, William Searight.

Searight owned a prosperous tavern on the National Road, the ruins of which may still be seen today. The National Road tollhouse is kept as it once was, with a toll keeper's office, kitchen, and living room.

PENNSYLVANIA TROLLEY MUSEUM

Washington - One Museum Road (I-79 to Meadowlands, exit 8) 15301. Phone: (877) PA-TROLLEY. www.pa-trolley.org. Hours: Tuesday-Sunday 10:00am-4:00pm (Memorial Day-Labor Day), Long Weekends (Friday thru Sunday) & Holidays only (April, May, September-December). Admission: $13.00 adult, $12.00 senior(62+), $11.00 child (3-15). Admission includes the orientation video, car barn tour and trolley rides. Note: Museum store. In cooler weather, heated trolleys are running. Trolley theatre videos. Air conditioned museum.

Because the kids will be heavy with anticipation once they see the rail yard full of trolleys - plan on taking a ride right away! The trolleys are run on four miles of Pennsylvania rail and each ride takes approximately 30 minutes. Along the rail, you'll learn the history of the vehicle that you are riding on and why it's so special. As you complete your guided or self-guided tour, you'll get to meet CAR #832 - "The Streetcar Named Desire" used in the stage play.

EASTER BUNNY TRAIN RIDES

Washington - Pennsylvania Trolley Museum. Candy treats with the Easter Bunny riding along. Admission. (Easter Weekend & weekend before)

PUMPKIN PATCH TROLLEY

Washington - Pennsylvania Trolley Museum. Ride orange-colored trolleys and the kids get to pick a pumpkin, too! (second or third weekend in October)

TRAIN RIDES WITH SANTA

Washington - Pennsylvania Trolley Museum. Sing songs and eat treats as you ride the train with Santa aboard. Toy train lay-out. Admission. (Thanksgiving - Dec weekends)

WASHINGTON COUNTY MUSEUM

Washington - 49 East Maiden Street (Route 40 - downtown) 15301. Phone: (412) 225-6740. www.wchspa.org Hours: Tuesday - Friday 11:00am-4:00pm and reserved group tours on Saturdays (March-December). Admission: $3.00-$4.00.

The stately stone house, located in downtown Washington, Pennsylvania, was built in 1812 by John Julius LeMoyne, the father of Francis Julius LeMoyne. Both father and son were practicing physicians, but it was the courageous Francis Julius LeMoyne who, despite the strict Fugitive Slave Law of 1850, risked his personal freedom and fortune to do what he knew was morally right — take a stand against the institution of slavery. This successful 19th Century doctor, reformer and builder of the first crematory in the western hemisphere, opened his home and properties as stops along the Underground Railroad. Dr. LeMoyne was also a leader in herbal health remedies. See the beds under which runaway slaves hid and the beehive in the herb garden on the roof.

Waynesburg

GREENE COUNTY MUSEUM

Waynesburg - *918 Rolling Meadows Road (I-79, exit 3 to SR21) 15370. Phone: (724) 627-3204. www.greenecountyhistory.org Hours: Tuesday-Saturday 10:00am-3:00pm (May - October). Admission: $5.00-$10.00. Note: The Historical Society also maintains the Young Foundry and Machine Shop - Century old, belt driven machine shop and foundry with 25 fully operational machines.*

Colonial to Victorian... displays of local artifacts dating from the early native Monongahela culture to the early 20th Century. One of the rooms is devoted to an exhibit of early watches and clocks. The early watch and clockmaker was a talented craftsman, capable of very precise work. He was also the village jeweler. "Monongahela Culture" is the name for prehistoric Indians from the area. Look at the way they constructed their houses, the types of pottery they made and used, the stone materials they used for their tools, weapons, and cultivation of crops. Also on display are quilts, period clothing, early glassware & pottery, and an extraordinary birdhouse that stands over six feet tall and contains 104 rooms. The Early School and Early Children's Toys displays interest kids. A fun and informative worksheet is available for an interactive view of the exhibit.

FALL HARVEST FESTIVAL

Waynesburg - Greene County Museum. Tractor pulls, antique steam engines, parades, food (made with steam), threshing, baling, cider and apple butter making, hayrides, children's activities, petting zoo & fall crafts. Admission. (second weekend in October)

CHRISTMAS OPEN HOUSE

Waynesburg - Greene County Museum. Tours of decorated, historical buildings. Refreshments and musical entertainment. FREE. (December weekends)

BATTLE OF THE BULGE RE-ENACTMENT

Waynesburg - Fort Indiantown Gap. www.wwiiha.org. World's largest WW II re-enactment with battle demos, equipment displays and many veteran reunions. (last weekend in January)

RYERSON STATION STATE PARK

Wind Ridge - *361 Bristoria Road (both sides of Bristoria Road, just off of PA Route 21) 15380. www.dcnr.state.pa.us/stateparks/findapark/ryersonstation/. Phone: (724) 428-4254 or (888) PA-Parks. Admission: to PA State Parks is FREE however swimming, marina and camping/lodging fees apply.*

Pool, Visitor Center, Boat Rentals, Sledding, Campsites, Fishing, and Winter Sports. The trails invite you to explore the park on foot during spring, summer, fall and on cross-country skis in winter. The trails traverse many habitats, like forests, wet valley bottoms, evergreen plantations and fields. There are several opportunities to observe the beauty of Duke Lake.

AMUSEMENTS

ANIMALS & FARMS

HISTORY

For updates & travel games visit: **www.KidsLoveTravel.com**

MUSEUMS

Activity Index

OUTDOOR EXPLORING

For updates & travel games visit: **www.KidsLoveTravel.com**

SEASONAL & SPECIAL EVENTS

SCIENCE

Activity Index

SPORTS

SUGGESTED LODGING & DINING

THE ARTS

For updates & travel games visit: **www.KidsLoveTravel.com**

TOURS